Leaving Fundamen

Leaving
Fundamentalism

⊠ Personal Stories

Foreword by **Thomas Moore**
Edited by **G. Elijah Dann**

Wilfrid Laurier University Press
[WLU]

We acknowledge the support of the Canada Council for the Arts for our publishing program. We acknowledge the financial support of the Government of Canada through the Book Publishing Industry Development Program for our publishing activities.

Library and Archives Canada Cataloguing in Publication

Leaving fundamentalism : personal stories / G. Elijah Dann, editor ; foreword by Thomas Moore.

(Life writing series)
ISBN 978-1-55458-026-2

1. Fundamentalism. 2. Christian biography. 3. Ex-church members—Biography. I. Dann, G. Elijah II. Series.

BT82.2.L43 2008   277.3'082   C2008-900382-9

Cover design by Blakeley. Text design by Catharine Bonas-Taylor.

© 2008 Wilfrid Laurier University Press
Waterloo, Ontario N2L 3C5, Canada
www.wlupress.wlu.ca

This book is printed on Ancient Forest Friendly paper (100% post-consumer recycled).

Printed in Canada

Every reasonable effort has been made to acquire permission for copyright material used in this text, and to acknowledge all such indebtedness accurately. Any errors and omissions called to the publisher's attention will be corrected in future printings.

Contents

THOMAS MOORE

Foreword

 In the matter of religion and spirituality, I feel that I live on a small island between two continents: modernism and fundamentalism. I don't live in the modern world because I don't want science to have the last word on what is real and valuable, but neither do I want to whisk away all religious and spiritual ideas into the pastel realm of metaphor. On the other hand, I'm happy to live in a time when the many spiritual traditions of the world are easily accessible and I can shape my spiritual life with responsibility and creative pleasure. I have a poetic mind. I value insight over fact, and the deep resonance of a story or image over a factual claim of truth.

I wish this word "truth" could be expunged from the language overnight. It creates divisions and gives illusions. The spiritual life lies in a realm of mysteries, not facts. We live in a world that we don't fully understand. We don't know for a fact what the afterlife might be like or that it even exists. Here, the most sincere and intelligent spiritual people differ in their ideas and expectations. We are not certain about the origins of this universe, but we can relate to life itself as a source beyond comprehension.

The certainty with which fundamentalists speak of their truth is so aggressive and self-defined that it seems anxious and unsteady. Fundamentalism's display of certitude "protests too much" and looks more like doubt and uncertainty whistling in the dark. As it is used today, the word "truth" is not nearly subtle enough to convey the mystery that is God or how to live in a complex world.

The word used in the Gospels and translated as "truth" is *aletheia*, from *a-lethe*, "not forgetting." In earlier times the word was used of the great poets who "remembered" the profound origins of life and the immeasurably deep patterns that shape our destinies. These issues can and should be reflected on for a lifetime, shifting in nuance as you grow older and wiser.

I sit on my little island reading William Blake, the poet who railed against both religious and scientific fundamentalism. For Blake, religion is about the way we imagine human life to be and work. Like most soulful poets after the Renaissance, he continued the humanizing efforts of Marsilio Ficino and his friend Pico della Mirandola, who wrote an unfinished book called "Poetic Theology." That is my ideal, a theology and spirituality that takes the imagination seriously and that understands religion as the artful effort to remember the deepest realities that shape our world.

It is fitting to have a book of *stories* about the experience of fundamentalism. We are all fundamentalists at one time or another and in one sphere or another. We could all write stories about our leaving certain fundamentalisms behind. My own list of them is very long. The way to deal with them is to tell the stories of how they appeared, what they did, and how they departed. Storytelling is one of the chief instruments of the imagination, and if there is one ingredient that spirituality needs in this day of facticity, it is imagination.

It is also useful to have in this volume a remarkably intelligent and open-minded introduction to the stories, a historical story about the nature and progress of Christian fundamentalism. There, we can trace the back-and-forth movement between a tendency toward tradition and a prizing of the individual. If there is a solution to this tendency to split into factions, it would be to take the gist of fundamentalism and the core of modernist materialism into a tension where the outcome is neither extreme nor some centre of balance. There is something in our fundamentalisms worthy of our attention and much in our skepticism worth keeping.

In depth psychology we approach a neurotic or symptomatic pattern by going deeper in reflection *into the symptom*. We try not to compensate by turning in an opposite direction. In the same way, it is not wise to respond to fundamentalism by trying to banish it or out-reason it. Better to reflect on it with an open mind until something of its core value appears. To me, the obvious core value in fundamentalism is the open receiving of a spiritual idea without twisting it to fit any comfortable agenda. For example, rather than dismiss Jesus' miracles as an extravagance of hagiography, I would rather tone down the sensationalism and literalism of them and see whether there is indeed anything miraculous, awe-inspiring, and unexpectedly potent in his message. It would certainly be a miracle if everyone on earth became a peacemaker. As a psychotherapist I have seen people find "miraculous" healing—astonishingly unexpected and spontaneous but not against the laws of nature.

Another example: For many years I have written favourably about angels. I'm not talking about science fiction plasma beings that pass through doors and walls, nor about metaphors and symbols. I'm talking about inspiring presences like a muse or a sensation of warning. These angels are real, but they are not invisible bodies.

So I do not want to leave my fundamentalisms without taking their riches with me. I want to remain on my island of poetics, neither a materialist skeptic nor a naive believer. But I want to keep up a good trading relationship with my continental neighbours. They have much to offer me.

Acknowledgements

 I would like to express my appreciation to those who made this book a reality. First, I'm grateful to one of the contributors, Jacob Shelley, who, after one of our long discussions about Christian fundamentalism, suggested putting together a book of this nature. Later, as the volume editor, it was a pleasure to read the chapters in their various stages of gestation and through to their eventual birth. The contributors, in their own ways, showed faith in this project, and even helped to find the right publisher, Wilfrid Laurier University Press. On that note, I am indebted to the Press's former acquisitions editor, Jacqueline Larson (who has now moved on to the Monk Institute), for her enthusiasm for this project. I would also like to thank Lisa Quinn, who took Jacqueline's place as acquisitions editor, for her own enthusiasm—even excitement—for the initial proposal, and ensuring the book's timely publication. My thanks to Matthew Kudelka for his care as copy editor and to Lynnette Torok for her own careful copy editing. For his thoughtful preface, I would like to thank Thomas Moore, who took time out of his busy writing and speaking schedules.

G. Elijah Dann
Victoria, British Columbia

G. ELIJAH DANN

An Introduction to Christian Fundamentalism

 The title of this book will have some readers asking what kind of fundamentalism this book is about. Understanding our particular meaning of the word has been made all the more confusing because of the 9/11 terrorist attacks in the United States. Before that infamous date—though some nuances were already shifting among various Christian groups—fundamentalism referred almost exclusively to conservative Protestant churches in the United States and Canada. The events of 9/11 have changed many things. For example, the public's attention is now riveted on the notion of religious extremism, and the so-called "War on Terror" has become part of public parlance. U.S. government press releases and 24/7 cable news programs are focusing on Islamic extremism so that fundamentalism now means "Islamic fundamentalism" and includes the possibility of terrorism.

Definitions change with the times; even so, it's important to remember how words were coined. There is no better example than the word "fundamentalism." For the purposes of this book, it does not apply to Islam but rather to Christianity—in particular, to Christian fundamentalism as it developed in North America in the twentieth century. This is the etymology we're concerned with here, one that I'll explain in this introduction. It's a word whose origin and development provide fertile ground for the stories recorded in the following chapters.

Today's Christian fundamentalists prefer other descriptors, such as "conservative" or "evangelical." As I'll explain, this has come about because of trends in American and Canadian culture that were extant long before 9/11, though the bad press over Islamic extremism acceler-ated this shift. Nonetheless, and whichever terms Christian fundamen-talists now prefer, their theological views remain much the same, as do their practices. They continue to believe and behave as before.

What originally defined and continues to fuel Christian fundamen-talism (or conservatism, or evangelicalism) was and is its quest for the-ological purity—that is, its desire for scriptural Truth. Yet this quest hardly popped out of nowhere, without precedent or historical impulse. If we approach this matter as an archaeologist would, digging for artifacts—except in our case digging into the history of ideas—it can be argued that the actual beginning of this quest by Christians was made possible by the Roman emperor Constantine.

Constantine claimed that while fighting the Battle of Milvian Bridge, just outside Rome in AD 312, he had a vision. A bishop interpreted it for him. Constantine ended up believing that he owed his victory in that bat-tle to God. Whether he actually converted to Christianity is debated by historians, but the importance of what he did afterwards is undeniable. He declared that all persecution against Christians must stop and that Christianity was to be a legally recognized religion. Things moved quickly, and by the end of the fourth century, Christianity was the only form of public worship permitted throughout the Roman Empire. Chris-tians came out of hiding, theologians banded together, and church coun-cils met to establish church doctrine. Not surprisingly, during the first cen-turies of their newfound power, divisions developed and arguments ensued among church leaders, resulting in charges of heresy and apos-tasy. Yet this was only the beginning. Turmoil and divisions continued among Christian communities in the centuries after Constantine. One of the most significant splits—the Great Schism of AD 1054—shook the Christian church to its foundations and created the division between the Roman Catholic and Eastern Orthodox churches. This drawing of theological lines, however, did not end disputes over doctrine.

Events of great ecclesiastical and theological importance took place in the centuries following the Great Schism, all of which are worth inves-tigating. For our purposes here, though, the next significant event took place in the sixteenth century: the Protestant Reformation. The reform-ers emphasized Christian autonomy—that is, "self-governance"—a con-cept that had also been gaining importance in philosophy as well as in secular matters of politics and law. In theological terms, the doctrine of autonomy emphasized the "priesthood of all believers." It asserted that no human intermediary, whether priest, bishop, Pope, or the Virgin Mary, need play an interceding role between God and the believer. The proof text for Protestant theologians came from none other than the Apostle Paul, who proclaimed that "there is one intermediary between God and humanity, the man Jesus Christ" (I Timothy 2:5). This brazenly individualistic interpretation by the theologians amounted to a radical rethinking of how the Bible was to be read and understood. The best-known reformers, Martin Luther and John Calvin, declared that any humble Christian was as capable of understanding the Scripture as the parish priest or the Magisterium in Rome. However innocuous this pro-nouncement may sound to modern ears, Vatican officials responded to the Protestant reformers with the savage brutality of the Inquisition. Clearly, the ecclesiastical authorities in Rome were not about to tolerate reforms to doctrine and practice. Dissenters had no choice but to aban-don Catholicism and strike out on their own.

The Protestant Reformation further divided the Roman Catholic Church. Another schism soon followed, this one in England, driven in part by Henry VIII's intent to divorce his wife—an act the Catholic Church would not allow. The king wanted a male heir, and his wife, Catherine of Aragon, was unable to provide him with one. She had already given birth to a girl, Princess Mary, but Henry feared that his dynasty would not survive without a male successor. So he had per-sonal and pragmatic reasons for breaking with Rome; that said, the Reformation spirit with all its theological underpinnings had already been growing in England. These elements working together fractured the Catholic Church once again. The result was the establishment of the Church of England (known as the Anglican Church in Canada, and the Episcopalian Church in the United States).

With churches being transplanted through colonization, the New World provided fertile ground for unprecedented growth. The Ameri-can spirit of independence from the Old World—political, cultural, and otherwise—prepared the ground for further splintering. Despite the resulting divisions, the established churches in North America—Pres-byterian, Lutheran, Episcopalian, and so on—remained powerful.

It is difficult to sift through and summarize two thousand years of church history in these few pages. Nevertheless, one general observa-tion bears repeating: a sense of urgency drove the early church councils (the first of these in Nicaea in AD 325) to decide doctrinal matters and demand strict adherence to them, and the same sense of urgency later roused Orthodox and then Protestant churches to break with the Catholic church. To be sure, without a central ecclesiastical authority to rule with an iron hand, and with a high value placed on religious autonomy, there would be little to unite the emerging churches, be they Orthodox or Protestant. This came as a startling realization for Protestant congregations. The early theological divisions among the Lutherans, the Reformed church of John Calvin, and the Anabaptists evidenced a divisive spirit that has continued to this day to operate in the Protestant movement.

This brief overview of Christian history points to a characteristic that all Christian communities have shown throughout the centuries, be they Catholic, Orthodox, Protestant, or Anglican. Fracturing inevitably occurs as a result of the conviction that certain theological matters cannot be compromised. Thus a pure Christian community can be brought about only if its members are willing to strike out on their own. In good conscience and before God, churches divide and go their separate ways to worship and understand the Scripture as each believe it right. They are walking the same path taken by Moses and the people of the Old Testament, who sought their own liberation by fleeing Egypt in a quest for the Promised Land. Yet as Moses discovered with his own people, emancipation does not bring an end to life's complexities. In fact, liberation and autonomy more often than not bring people face to face with even greater questions, which they are left to answer for themselves.

For the churches of the Reformation, the freedom gained by leaving the Roman Catholic Church inspired fresh divisions. Thus when further disputes arose in the newly formed churches, there was no choice but to separate yet again. Congregations would divide along the most recent doctrinal lines and set out once more on their own respective paths, always with the hope that they would finally realize the true church. Like the people of Moses, they would forever wander in the hope of finding the Promised Land.

Always, this is a search for the true and faithful religious community, one where theological purity can be found and where all believers agree on matters of faith and practice. Believers hope optimistically that theological differences will be resolved quickly by a transparent reading of the Bible. Inevitably, though, fresh theological arguments develop among the ranks. The resulting schisms see groups of believers going off to start new assemblies, each with its own doctrinal imperatives and certainties. No church, established or new, is immune. As I write this, the Church of England is fracturing over the issues of same-sex marriage and the ordination of homosexual ministers. Meanwhile, the Russian Orthodox Church is encountering tensions with the Ukrainian Orthodox Church. And so the cycle continues.

This quick survey allows us to bring into focus Christian fundamentalism, which originated in late-nineteenth and early-twentieth-century North America. In more conservative Protestant congregations, some members yearned deeply to identify and reaffirm the true and original meaning of Christianity. This need was inspired by the alarming tendencies that conservatives thought they saw both in the church and in society at large. Thus among mainstream Presbyterian, Lutheran, and Episcopalian congregations there was growing interest in more critical approaches to biblical studies. These approaches, employing so-called 'higher criticism,' sharply questioned conventional views of biblical history, both chronological and geographical, as well as the miraculous element of the Scripture.

These new attitudes toward biblical studies were the fruit of growing intellectual trends that Darwinian theory had launched in the nineteenth century. Various offshoots of the theory of evolution strongly affected biblical studies. For example, *naturalism* posited that events in the natural realm should be interpreted scientifically rather than supernaturally; and *materialism* argued that the known world (at least the world that merits knowing, or that we are capable of knowing) consists of matter, not spirit. Conservative Protestant congregations contended that these emerging world views were attracting mainstream theologians and contributing to a watering down of Christian doctrine and orthodoxy. For them such world views were signs of a secular encroachment best described by a third term: *modernism*. They regarded modernist views as antithetical to the tried-and-true traditions of Christian faith and practice—a way of life that fathers and mothers taught their children to respect and revere, one that accepted the truths of the Scripture as they were passed down from generation to generation.

If liberalization of the Christian faith was to be countered, the tenets of that faith would need to be identified and vigorously defended. Those tenets were listed and described in popular form in a series of booklets published between 1910 and 1915 that collectively were titled *The Fundamentals: A Testimony to the Truth*. They were authored by various American conservative theologians and were broadly circulated among church leaders as well as the laity. The essential tenets those booklets offered were six:

1. Inerrancy of the Scriptures
2. The virgin birth of Jesus
3. The deity of Jesus
4. The doctrine of substitutionary atonement through God's grace and human faith
5. The bodily resurrection of Jesus
6. The miracles of Scripture

These doctrines were both indispensable and interdependent—simply put, remove one and the others would fall. The inerrancy of Scripture (1) assured Christians that the Bible was true in its entirety and that it recounted without error all the stories, historical or narrative. Thus if the Old Testament said that a certain king lived, then archeology would bear it out. If the Bible said that something happened, and specifically named people or places, then that is precisely what happened. To this day many North American Christians embrace a rather literal reading of the first few chapters of Genesis: the Bible says that God created the heavens and the earth in six twenty-four-hour days, so it's true. If "science" says otherwise, then science has it wrong. The virgin birth of Jesus (2) is also treated as a historical fact, which of course requires an acceptance of the miraculous (6), which is itself a fundamental truth that holds the Bible together. After all, without belief in miracles, little would be left of Christianity. The same can be said of the belief that Jesus Christ was more than just a beneficent do-gooder or an important prophet. He was the Son of God (3) and the Second Person of the Trinity. He was God made flesh and therefore must have been born of a virgin. The nature of Jesus, as the Son of God, is inherently linked to his atoning death on the cross (4). This means that salvation is only possible by accepting his death as payment for our sins. The deity of Christ assured that his sacrifice would be perfect, as he was without sin: he did no wrong during his time on earth, nor did he inherit Adam's sin by being conceived from natural sexual intercourse (thus another important component—the virgin birth, which Catholicism takes even further with belief in the Immaculate Conception of Mary). The bodily resurrection of Jesus (5) is final proof that his sacrifice was seen by God as providing perfect and complete payment for humanity's sins. These are the fundamentals of the faith—truths that cannot be compromised by Bible-believing Christians. The leaders of this movement, logically enough, quickly adopted the term *fundamentalism*. This title both announced and underscored their uncompromising commitment to theological integrity.

Christian fundamentalism in North America, viewed charitably and simply, amounts to a desire by well-intentioned people to affirm the fidelity of their religious faith. For the most part, this is what defined its beginnings. Unfortunately, like the turbulent religious history it was so much a part of, it couldn't last. Around the time that fundamentalists were staking out their ground, in terms both of doctrinal essentials and of establishing borders with an encroaching wider culture (already regarded as hostile), a test of nerve was presented to fundamentalists in the form of John Scopes, a Tennessee science teacher. Scopes was taken to court for teaching evolution in the classroom, which in 1925 was an illegal act. This famous court case, known as the Scopes Monkey Trial, transformed the spirit of Christian fundamentalism in North America. Just like today, with the ongoing battle over the teaching of evolution and Creationism (now called Intelligent Design), the issue forming the back-bone of this controversy wasn't so much about science. It was what we today would call a "culture war," one that pitted religious and social conservatives against religious and social liberals, along with atheists and skeptics. And just like today, in its own day the Scopes Monkey Trial was seen by both sides as a battle over the hearts and minds of the American public. As it turned out, the decision eventually came down against Scopes. But for the Christian fundamentalists, the trial was—to put it again in modern terms—a media disaster. The Christians who were most vocal in their criticism of Scopes were widely perceived as narrow-minded and antiscientific religious extremists. This description was largely a caricature (aided in part by the Hollywood film *Inherit the Wind*). Even so, it stuck.

In response, fundamentalists retreated sharply from mainstream society into cloistered churches and institutions. Their newfound dis-trust for science, and for higher education generally, led pastors to dis-courage young members of their congregations from attending public, secular universities. In the place of these, Bible colleges supported by fundamentalist congregations sprang up across the country, all with the intent of properly teaching their young people the unfiltered truths of the faith. Founded in conjunction with these were independent seminar-ies for training fundamentalist pastors. These seminaries were meant to supersede the established schools of theology, which by this time were viewed as bastions of Christian liberalism.

The fundamentalists were still licking their wounds from the bad press of the Scopes Monkey Trial and were convinced that the truth of Christianity could not be debated according to the rules of secular science and higher education. Furthermore, they now believed that the Christian lifestyle ought to be the definitive evidence for the existence of God, the truthfulness of Christianity, and the transforming power of Christ. So they formulated a list of "blue laws" to offer further guidance to Christians regarding the behaviour they should exhibit in an ungodly and unbelieving society. (The term "blue laws" goes back to the nineteenth century, when Sabbath laws were first enforced.) The "shall" and "shall not" rules were extended for modern days: Thou shall attend church at least once a week. Thou shall pray and read the Bible every day. Thou shall take every occasion to tell others about Jesus so that they might also be born again. Thou shall *not* go to bars, play cards, dance, go to the movies or the theatre, listen to secular music, smoke, drink alcohol, or swear. Perhaps most central to this new code: Thou certainly shall *not* have premarital sex. However, thou shall get married and *then* be fruitful and multiply.

The label "fundamentalism" is now pejorative, but remember that when originally coined, it was proudly accepted by those who embraced a conservative theology and way of life. This is not to suggest that all conservative-minded Christians were happy with the movement. While they insisted on certain doctrinal truths seen as foundational to Christianity, many considered it a mistake to retreat from society into insulated religious communities and institutions. And many rejected the idea that Christians should regard science as hostile to the faith; they saw this as a rejection of the intellect. Emnity toward intellectual thought was by now becoming increasingly common among fundamentalists, in stark contrast to the profound scholarship—theological, philosophical, and scientific—of historical Christianity. By the 1940s and 1950s another group of Protestants in the United States had decided that the fundamentalist movement had become too reactionary and that change was necessary. Though they remained theologically conservative, this new Protestant movement set out to counter the negative effects of Christian fundamentalism. This group described itself as "evangelical."

The evangelicals' choice of title makes sorting out this history somewhat more complicated. The term was already being used in Europe by the German Evangelicals in the Lutheran tradition, who used it to distinguish themselves from the Calvinist Reformed churches. The word evangelical derives from the Greek word for "good news" (translated in the Bible as "the Gospel"); it was also a preferred term among members of the Holiness Movements of the eighteenth and nineteenth centuries. In any case, this new movement by American theologians—sometimes also called the "neo-evangelicals"—agreed that the fundamentals of Christian doctrine should be defended. But they also thought it was a serious mistake for the church to withdraw from the broader culture, its universities and institutions, and from the public square more generally.

Not surprisingly, fundamentalists resisted the evangelical movement. In their view, the new evangelicals hadn't learned the lesson that secular intellectuals could not be battled on their own turf—in the humanities and the sciences, all of whose disciplines questioned traditional Christian beliefs. Philosophy wanted to question "truth"; sociology, the way humans organize themselves; and of course astronomy, biology, and anthropology all disputed the fundamentalists' scriptural interpretation of human origins. Fundamentalists considered this a terrible compromise, one that would chip away at the moral standards of Christian life and the doctrinal purity of Christianity.

This tension between Christian fundamentalism and evangelicalism simmered throughout the 1950s and 1960s and into the 1970s. Fundamentalists thought that evangelicals were in danger of liberalization; evangelicals thought that fundamentalists, though their intentions were good, had retreated too far from the rest of society. The evangelical movement, however, was gaining media and cultural attention. The most notable example was the election of a Baptist president, Jimmy Carter, followed by another openly Christian president, Ronald Reagan, also a friend of religious conservatives. In the late 1970s and into the 1980s, evangelicals became more visible on the cultural scene, whether politically as thinkers or in the universities as academics. Powerful fundamentalists such as Jerry Falwell, founder of Liberty Baptist University and the Moral Majority, were watching this trend closely and describing themselves more and more often as evangelicals, dropping fundamentalism as a descriptor.

Fundamentalists came to envy the growing cultural popularity of the evangelicals and began referring to themselves as evangelicals for the sake of the clear advantages it brought. When fundamentalists such as Jerry Falwell and Pat Robertson were on TV, they were often quick to call themselves evangelicals. This was a disingenuous move on their part. "Fundamentalist" had always been the movement's own term for itself, and its members had deliberately isolated themselves from secular society by steadfastly voicing their suspicion of it. They had done these things of their own accord. Yet now that American culture was looking with more favour on evangelicalism, they were piggybacking on its popularity.

In the present day the evangelical movement has become a victim of its own success. The conservative Christian church, now a blend of fundamentalist and evangelical members, is a powerful voice in matters of culture and public policy making, to the point that it played a key role in the two election wins of American president George W. Bush. Across this present political and media landscape, hardly a day goes by without some mention of Christian conservatism, whether in newspapers or on news networks such as FOX and CNN. Megapastor Rick Warren is interviewed on *Larry King Live* about "the purpose-driven life," and Christian celebrities such as Pat Boone talk about how Terri Schiavo was not in a permanent vegetative state. Viewers watching CNN, "the Most Trusted Name in News," can easily lose their bearings trying to distinguish medical facts from media chatter or to understand how a Christian, because he is a pastor or a singer, is qualified to debate medical and biomedical decisions. As a result of the high visibility of Christians in popular media, people outside the church are gathering the notion there is only one sort of Christian—namely, the type who is agitated by the mention of abortion, euthanasia, embryonic stem cell research, and same-sex marriage or who is invigorated by talk of prayer in schools, the Ten Commandments in the public square, and the mention of God in the Constitution. Yet with more than two billion Christians worldwide, there is more to Christianity than is represented by the fundamentalists—or for that matter by the evangelicals. The world's Christians and their respective denominations hold an incredibly broad range of beliefs on social, moral, and political issues. The fervour of church growth, coupled with ongoing divisions and mergers (including those between fundamentalists and evangelicals) has brought interesting developments in Christian doctrine and practice.

Two important Christian Protestant movements not to be overlooked in this developing history are the Pentecostal and Charismatic Movements. The Pentecostal churches arose from the so-called Holiness Movement, which started in England with the founders of Methodism, the brothers John and Charles Wesley. What set the Pentecostal churches apart from other Protestant and fundamentalist churches was their emphasis on the "gifts of the Holy Spirit." As they understood it, this was a reference to passages in the New Testament suggesting that certain "signs" and abilities would confirm one's identity as a true disciple of Christ—for example, the ability to heal, to give prophecies, to speak in tongues (from the Greek, *glossolalia*), and to perform miracles (I Corinthians 12:4–14, 27–30; Romans 12:6–8). The influence of Pentecostalism continued into the latter part of the twentieth century with the beginnings of the Charismatic Movement. The Charismatic churches, though they shared Pentecostalism's emphasis on the work of the Holy Spirit, thought that Pentecostals were too fixated on legalism. Also, the Charismatics thought that their Pentecostal brethren overemphasized the ability to speak in tongues at the expense of all the other gifts of the Spirit. The power of the Charismatic Movement was evident in its ability to cross denominational lines, which allowed it to become a real influence in various Protestant churches. Yet what was most unique about the Charismatic Movement was its capacity to reach beyond Protestant churches and arouse Roman Catholics and even members of Eastern Orthodox churches.

Because the Charismatic Movement was able to transcend not only Protestant denominations but also Protestant/Catholic/Orthodox divisions, it is somewhat difficult to discuss it in the same breath as fundamentalism. At a certain point, the similarities and distinctions begin to blur. For example, both Pentecostals and Charismatics emphasize a Christian lifestyle close to that of the fundamentalists, insofar as the fleshly pleasures of the world are concerned (drinking alcohol, smoking tobacco, dancing, and, of course, premarital sex). They also share socially conservative views, in that they oppose abortion, euthanasia, same-sex marriage, and embryonic stem cell research. And they are all theologically conservative, at least insofar as their view of the historical and miraculous elements of the Scripture are concerned. Despite these similarities, keep in mind that both Pentecostals and Charismatics came out of historical circumstances quite different from those of the Protestant fundamentalist movement. For example, Pentecostals and Charismatics differ from traditional fundamentalists regarding the gifts of the Spirit—speaking in tongues, healing, and so on—and Pentecostals and Charismatics are much more exuberant in church. The fact of the matter is, that while Pentecostals and many fundamentalists hold similar conservative views when it comes to moral bounds and foundational doctrines (such as the Trinity, and the deity of Christ), they generally would feel quite uncomfortable if forced to worship in each other's churches on a regular basis, though even here, strict divisions are not absolute. Perhaps some imagery will help illustrate this idea: Many of you are familiar with the scene in *The Blues Brothers* where Jake (James Belushi) and Elwood (Dan Ackroyd) visit a Baptist, albeit Charismatic, church where the Reverend Cleophus James (James Brown) happens to be pastor. Imagine someone like the late Jerry Falwell or Pat Robertson in the congregation, even though the church portrayed is supposed to be Baptist! Both Falwell and Roberston would be squeamish there, just as they would be in a Roman Catholic service celebrating the Eucharist.

I have not kept to the strict definition of fundamentalism while selecting the accounts for this book. If we were to abide to the history of Christian fundamentalism, the title of this book would be inaccurate. Many of the contributors do indeed come from Protestant fundamentalist churches, but there are also stories from people with conservative Roman Catholic and Pentecostal backgrounds, some with a Charismatic influence. As I outlined earlier, these churches were not originally part of the fundamentalist movement; thus I am using the book's title in a more encompassing sense. Broadly included are those who have left conservative Christian movements—that is, churches that insist on radical transformation from their members, a transformation reflected in lifestyle as well as theology.

There is perhaps a greater oddity that bears notice, given the contributors' varied religious backgrounds. As I've mentioned, the original fundamentalists were deeply troubled by the liberalizing tendencies of traditional churches and by the encroachment of secular culture. Some of these concerns were held in common by the Vatican as well as by Pentecostal assemblies. But there was a double edge to the fundamentalist sword: the other side cut against theologically *conservative* churches— theologically conservative with a different bent to be sure, but conservative nevertheless. Owing to their strong Protestant traditions, for example, fundamentalists were highly suspicious and even openly antagonistic toward Catholicism. Fundamentalist pastors commonly interpreted the "Whore of Babylon" mentioned in the Revelation as the Catholic Church, with the Pope somehow in allegiance with the Antichrist if not the Antichrist himself. Many Protestant theologians and laypeople continue to think this way. Similar suspicions were directed toward the Pentecostal and Charismatic churches, which the fundamentalists generally perceived as dangerously exuberant. From speaking in tongues to the emphasis on the Baptism of the Spirit, fundamentalists feared an overexaggerated, unbridled emotionalism at the expense of a true moving of God's spirit. And the suspicion wasn't one sided. All of these groups viewed one another at best askance, at worst with open derision and accusations of heresy.

This brings us full circle. Socially conservative Christian churches are presently willing to set aside their theological differences, all in the effort to combine their forces in the frontal battle over what they perceive to be the failings of traditional values in our society. I have already noted that the central issues for these churches are well known: abortion, euthanasia, embryonic stem cell research, and same-sex marriage. On these particular issues the conservative churches are united. Yet one can only wonder how they would sort through other matters if, their collective views having won the day on these topics, they were left to decide their more idiosyncratic differences. For instance, would the distinctly Roman Catholic view that birth control is a mortal sin be a value that conservative Protestant churches would agree should be turned into public policy? Would Protestants think that governments should pay for state visits from the Pope? Many of the deep theological battles that have divided these Christians over the centuries have ostensibly been put on hold while they focus their combined attention on the greater threat of "secular humanism."

I was curious about this phenomenon while studying at the University of Notre Dame on a post-doctoral fellowship. My fellowship was in a centre of research headed by a well-known and respected Christian philosopher who also happens to be a Calvinist. Back home, my colleagues would ask me how he, as a devout Protestant, got along in a university that was strongly Catholic. The fact of the matter is, they got along famously, because both he and many of his staunch Catholic colleagues at the university, whether philosophers or theologians, had a common enemy: "secular society." Of course, if they ever found victory (whatever that would entail), it wouldn't take long for them to take notice of their theological differences and once again revive old Calvinist and Catholic battles over matters of faith and practice.

I'll leave these matters for others to sort through. I only wish to point out that I am using the designator "fundamentalist" in a broad sense, one that doesn't cover just those whose theological roots are within the Protestant tradition that speaks of a conservative Christian mindset and religious environment. This dynamic will become more clearly defined and nuanced as you read the accounts collected in this book.

One other matter should be dealt with before we proceed to the stories themselves: the language of Christian fundamentalism. Just as in any other movement be it religious, political, or otherwise, a particular terminology goes along with it—a way of speaking that outsiders won't at first understand, engendering a feeling, perhaps, akin to that of a disoriented foreigner in a country where a strange language is spoken. I won't try to explain all of the idiosyncrasies of fundamentalists' language, but I should mention a few of its terms, especially as they pertain to Protestant theology.

Christian fundamentalism closely embraces the very Protestant emphasis on the need for a *personal* Christian faith. This is in contrast to what they view as the empty formalism of religious practice that has Catholics and traditional Protestants going to church, observing all the rituals, but seemingly showing little in the way of a spiritual life or a vibrant relationship with Jesus. An important contention of the fundamentalists is that being a Christian is not a decision that parents can make for their children (via infant baptism), or that priests can make for those going through catechism. Moreover, for fundamentalists, we certainly are not Christians merely because we attend church services on Christmas and Easter and are married with the blessings of a minister or priest. One can only be a Christian through a thoughtful and deliberate decision. This notion is what has led fundamentalists to emphasize the "born again" experience. This term became popular in the 1970s. But what exactly does it mean?

According to those who are born again, listening to blasé hymns in long-established churches and to all the sermons on social issues is not enough to get a person into the Kingdom of Heaven. For fundamentalists, salvation is found only in the Bible, and the formula is expressed in the Gospel of John 3, which I paraphrase as follows:

A fellow named Nicodemus, convinced that Jesus was a great teacher, came to talk to Jesus at night.

Jesus said unto him, "Unless you are born again, you cannot enter the Kingdom of Heaven."

Nicodemus was confused, as anyone would be. He asked:

"How can I be reborn out of my mother at my age?"

"No, no," Jesus replied. "Just as you are born once physically, to enter the Kingdom of Heaven you must be born spiritually."

For fundamentalists, this passage is a plain and simple reading of how to become a Christian. It demands clear and determined action— namely, we have to be born again. That is the brief explanation, but there is more to the Gospel story, which doesn't begin with the New Testament. Rather, it can be traced back to Genesis, the first book of the Old Testament, and to the Revelation, the last book of the New Testament. It can be condensed as follows: Because of Adam and Eve's act of disobedience against God, by taking the fruit of the Tree of Knowledge offered by the serpent in the Garden of Eden, all of us are sinners before a most holy and righteous God. Adam and Eve being our representative Father and Mother, their sin (the "Original Sin") has been passed down to all of humanity by this event ("the Fall"). Every human collectively participated in the Fall; not only that, but this wilful disobedience affected all of Creation. This is why Nature is so brutal, evidenced by animals killing other animals, and why humans do evil, as in wars and violence, and why there are natural evils such as earthquakes and hurricanes. The corrective, as recounted in the New Testament, is that Jesus the Son of God was sent to earth, where he lived a perfect life before his Father, which culminated in his death on the cross for all of humanity's sins. The Resurrection was evidence that Jesus' sacrifice was satisfactory to God, thus offering perfect redemption. So, Jesus died in our stead; salvation, though, isn't something we inherit at birth merely by virtue of being human. Fundamentalists insist that to become true Christians, in order to be saved and born again, each of us must acknowledge our estrangement from God because of our own sinfulness and wilful disobedience. The Gospel says that Jesus died for you and me and that each of us must pray for repentance, confess every sin, and "accept Jesus Christ as our Lord and Personal Saviour." If we do, Jesus will "come into our hearts" and we will be born again. Note the emphasis on the Personal Saviour— in other words, salvation is only possible through a personal relationship granted by being born again. Note also the familiarity reflected in fundamentalists speaking of "Jesus" rather than the more formal, "Our Lord" or "Christ."

As mentioned, an important characteristic of Protestant fundamentalist churches, at least insofar as their historical development is concerned, is their hostility not only toward mainstream Protestant churches but also toward Roman Catholic churches. There are a number of reasons for this disdain, but one of the more significant ones relates to the fundamentalists' suspicion of ritual, which they see as an empty form of worship. Whether in the shape of formalized prayers, the use of incense, or standardized formulas of incantation, rituals usurp what ought to be the focus of the service: the telling of the Gospel and the individual need to be born again. Of course, Christian fundamentalists don't dispense altogether with ritual. They merely replace one form with another of their own, such as the all-powerful "testimonies" given during their church services. Testimonies are the stories Christians recite to unbelievers and doubters to explain how Christians have come to "know the Lord" (another synonym for being born again). Testimonies are the sine qua non for setting up an audience to hear the Gospel—a powerful tool of fundamentalist (and now evangelical) churches. The testimonies considered best are those that provide the most dramatic comparison of pre-conversion with post-conversion life. Speakers with especially sensational pre–born again stories are often brought into churches and youth group gatherings to deliver their messages.

Two approaches are possible. The first is negative: ex-somethings, be they Satanists, gang members, drug users, or criminals (even better, all of the above) are just the sorts of people necessary for impressing kids on how their own lives can be changed. The alternative is the positive approach: the testimonies of Christians who are now pro athletes, movie stars, musicians, or others in the mainstream cultural spotlight. In either case, it's hoped that the reasoning will go like this for the typical teenager in the audience: with the negative approach, "If God can touch the lives of the thoroughly decrepit, Hell-bound, Hell-raising sinners, surely he can do the same with me"; with the positive approach, "If these incredibly popular (and very rich) people have found the Answer, the Truth, shouldn't I also join the Team?"

In a day when religious conservatives have placed their faith and practice at the forefront of our culture wars, we believe this book is extremely timely. It provides a very personal, intimate, and truthful look behind the sermons, church services, and church life of the individuals who make up this movement. These are views from the inside—within the congregations and homes of the religious conservatives, the exact places where, with all its complexities and problems, the professed, highly idealized faith meets the reality of life. The stories included in this book provide transparent access to this complex and often confusing world of religious conservatism.

This book provides outsiders with a sense of what it's like for many people who've been involved in Christian fundamentalism. Yet we also see this book as of interest to those presently involved in conservative congregations, those Christians who may be having their own doubts about whether their church is the best expression of who they are, both as religious people and as individuals living in a global community. In short, this book asks what the Christian faith is all about and how can it be practised. The contributors aim to give the reader vivid pictures, or snapshots, of their experiences, thoughts, feelings, passions, and pains, all of which are still raw in memory. These stories are autobiographical, not theological—the contributors aren't interested in getting into deep theological matters, though some include doctrinal considerations insofar as they played a role in their disenchantment from their faith. Nevertheless, these stories aren't meant to be read as theological treatises—they're meant to be highly accessible and engaging, in the hope that they'll reach as wide an audience as possible. Moreover, for many of the contributors, writing about their experiences has been therapeutic. But like so much therapy, it is also painful.

This book brings together authors who span a grand continuum of backgrounds, experiences, ages, and education levels, though all share three particular traits. First, at one time they were involved in Christian fundamentalism, broadly construed. Second, they have all at some point left fundamentalism behind. Their respective stories describe what it was like to be part of this Christian movement, what it can be like once the decision is made to leave, and how things may continue, sometimes years afterwards. But it's the third trait that I believe to be the truly defining characteristic of all these stories, and of this book: each writer provides a unique glimpse into the world of Christian fundamentalism. Lined up in this book, one after another like a grand interview, the spotlight moving from one author to the next, the result is a multidimensional and multiperspectival account of a way of life that is nothing less than dizzying.

Joseph Simons's story, "Rapture, Community, and Individualist Hope," is the first in this collection. In many respects his story is typical. He describes how, as a Catholic, the message of Protestant fundamentalism challenged his religious beliefs. That is, how being a Christian—albeit a Catholic—wasn't sufficient for salvation, and how he then converted and became born again. Perhaps most important, his story describes what is central to the spirit of this book: once his conversion was made, the difficulties, contradictions, and even hypocrisies that made life in fundamentalism so difficult become apparent. The challenge isn't to live a godly and upstanding life. Rather, it's to resolve the inconsistency between what is preached by the church and how the lives of fundamentalists are actually lived.

"From There to Here" is L.A. Livingston's contribution. Lori's account echoes a theme common among religious believers, and certainly among Christian fundamentalists: how personal crisis brings us either into or out of our spiritual frameworks. That is, when life-changing events happen to us, we can either be drawn into deep devotional spiritual engagement or be repelled by it. The most obvious example of this dilemma is demonstrated by Holocaust survivors. How does one reconcile one's faith in the goodness of God, having experienced unspeakable acts of evil? Lori's trial isn't as dramatic, but for anyone facing an accident where you suddenly see your life flashing before your eyes, the outcome of your religious beliefs is anyone's guess. Lori gives us an account of her own transitions, one that reminds me of watching a film whose introduction presents a chilling scene, only we have to wait until the end of the film to see the thread of thought in its completion.

Following this is David L. Rattigan's "Fantastic Voyage: Surviving Charismatic Fundamentalism." David's experience is a vivid example of how the lines separating fundamentalism, the Pentecostal churches, and the Charismatic Movement can be blurred and blended. His story is fascinating for its intimate look into the lives of Pentecostals. It contrasts with some of the other stories, especially the ones where we read about the experiences of those coming from the more staid fundamentalist churches, and of course, those who write about their lives in the Catholic Church. His story illustrates for us both the broadness and the complexities of Protestant fundamentalist churches.

"My Mother, My Church" by Margaret Steel Farrell is written, like Joseph Simons's story, from the perspective of someone who grew up in the Catholic Church. As the title suggests, the uniqueness of her story illustrates another feature of the lives of many former fundamentalists—that is, the role played by parents and family in our exposure to the church. (After all, we all grow up in a family of some sort, even if we were adopted, or orphaned and moved to a group home.) And those family influences, powerful enough in themselves, once coupled with religion, become imbued with even more power. Margaret's story describes her relationship with her mother and how it intertwined with her devotion to the so-called Mother Church, the Roman Catholic Church. As Margaret powerfully explains, this is not simply a witty play on words. It is deeply rooted in a religious upbringing, one that cannot easily be escaped. Now that Margaret is herself a mother, she sees how things have come full circle.

Keith Dixon's "The Ministry Revisited" is one of the more extensive accounts in this book, from his childhood exposure to a deeply devotional expression of Christianity, to his decision as a young man at university to become a pastor. This alone would provide enough for a significant contribution to this study of Christian fundamentalism, especially in light of his eventual decision to leave the ministry and the reaction by the church leadership. But Keith provides us with a richness beyond this set of events by describing how his journey for spiritual enlightenment continued for years afterwards. Keith is telling us his story with all the benefit of hindsight gained over many decades of a life well lived. And with this advantage of age, he adds a special portion to his story: he explains how, after leaving his pastorate, he continued on his spiritual journey, from Transcendental Meditation and Buddhism to meeting a Western mystic. He ends his story with his current perspectives, which I think are worthy of careful consideration for anyone searching for the Truth.

I've remarked in this introduction how these stories are diverse and multilayered. Julie Rak's, "Looking Back at Sodom: My Evangelical and Lesbian Testimonies," is no exception. Her title is an obvious indication of the focus of her narrative, one of those "hot button" values that have been heavily played in the media. It would be strange not to have stories from such perspectives in a book about Christian fundamentalism. But Julie's story is about more than her experience of coming to terms with being a lesbian in the midst of the fundamentalist church. Another

part concerns her relationship with her husband. In many ways it's typical for heterosexual couples within the church who are experiencing
marital problems to keep up airs among fellow church members. Because
they are born again and living the victorious Christian life, any difficulties, complexities, and heartbreaks occurring in the marriage have to be
hidden. In this environment of denial, all sorts of problems develop and
fester. In this regard Julie's story, besides many other things, is one of
courage. I trust it will provide inspiration for others in similar situations,
heterosexual or homosexual.

All the writers who contributed to this book have been part of Christian fundamentalism, broadly defined. Yet as we see, they are all talking
about it from different perspectives: some are lay people, some academics, others professionals, one is now retired. On the flip side, some have
abandoned religious belief altogether, with one clearly now an atheist,
and one or two just "regular folk" without any clear religious inclinations. Jeffrey W. Robbins in "The Slippery Slope of Theology" tells his
story quite clearly through the eyes of a now established theologian. Of
course we all, one way or another, recall events in our lives by filtering
them, consciously or not, through our current perspective. This filtering
adds value to Jeffrey's account, as theologians can offer special insights
into the world of fundamentalism. Christian fundamentalism, after all,
is part of the family of Christianity, whether they (or we) like it or not.
Jeffrey talks about his experiences in fundamentalism like a family member talking about a close relative. He has the advantage, like the other
writers in this book, of having lived inside the borders of Christian fundamentalism. Now, as a theologian of the Lutheran persuasion, he can
provide the additional advantage of technical analysis.

Jacob Shelley's "Life Stages" provides another story from within the
Pentecostal church. His vivid description of his own experiences, neatly
presented as five stages, shows quite clearly the affinity that Pentecostalism has with fundamentalism. Notwithstanding the more exuberant
behaviour of Pentecostals, Jacob's struggles are typical. But at the same
time, there are elements to his story that make it especially important
for this collection: his age, his disposition to the brand of fundamentalism he encountered, and how recently he has left fundamentalism.
Jacob is one of the youngest contributors to this book, being in his twen-
ties (with the oldest writer in his seventies). The particular struggles of
the older writers are similar in some ways, quite different in others.
Jacob's story may resonate with younger readers especially. Another

tension will perhaps also resonate: Jacob is by nature skeptical and philosophical, so from the outset he was somewhat suspicious of the practices of his church. This is quite different from some of the other writers (like myself), who drank deep at the well of fundamentalism. Yet, with a heart open to spiritual matters, he also could not escape the defining characteristic of fundamentalism: a pietism and well-intentioned devotional disposition to spiritual matters. His perspective remains fresh, and his journey is only just beginning.

Andrea Lorenzo Molinari's "'More Catholic Than Thou': One Man's Journey Through Roman Catholic Fundamentalism" reaffirms the connections among Christian fundamentalism, Pentecostalism, and the Charismatic Movement. But there is a clincher: Andrea experienced it all without abandoning Catholicism. The importance of Andrea's story lies in his vivid description of how people belonging to conventional churches, such as the Catholic Church, may feel when they come into contact with Protestant fundamentalists. The latter have a stern message to deliver not only to non-Christians but also to those perceived "nominal" Christians who go through the motions of Christian worship yet lack religious zeal. Andrea describes how he saw his father negotiate an encounter with those particular Pentecostals who preach the "Prosperity Gospel," which declares that if one is living the Christian life God wants, all the while giving generously to the church, material wealth will come as a blessing. Andrea's description is very timely, as this movement is swiftly gaining prominence in the United States and some parts of Canada. Andrea, close to his father, followed along, observing and participating, all the while feeling a strong pull from his Catholic foundations. He then saw how the Charismatic Movement had influenced his own church. Andrea, like some others in this book, has remained in the church, albeit in a parish that better expresses his present Catholic sentiments.

When I brought these authors together in my role as editor, I wasn't searching for a specific demographic balance except for that of gender. The stories largely jelled quite on their own. In a day when homosexuality is a prominent concern for fundamentalist and conservative churches, Beverly Bryant's "Inching Along" could not be more timely. In light of the recent news that a prominent fundamentalist pastor had homosexual relations, but was then "cured" after only a few weeks of therapy, Beverly's narrative is powerfully instructive. In fact, her story is one that thousands of people belonging to fundamentalist churches are familiar with: these same people feel they must overcome their homosexuality in order to be "right with God." In Christian fundamentalism, homosexuality is viewed as a sin that may very well doom a person to eternal damnation. It's a rather strong view, even allowing that there may be different levels of punishment in Hell. Nevertheless, someone who is good and gentle—but otherwise homosexual—will suffer in the same place as Pol Pot, Adolf Hitler, Josef Stalin, and Idi Amin. The force of Beverly's story and others like it shows there are other ways of interpreting Scripture, God's love, and being gay and a full-fledged Christian.

Glenn A. Robitaille's "From Fear to Faith: My Journey into Evangelical Humanism" tells another story of a Roman Catholic who was "saved" by Protestant fundamentalists. But in Glenn's case, he hadn't been practising his religious life as a nominal Catholic, then been swept off his spiritual feet into the life of an active Christian believer. Even as a child he took the teachings of Catholicism very seriously. Nevertheless, the Protestant fundamentalist message, in the form of the Jesus Movement, resonated with him for reasons that are important for us to reflect on—and for reasons not exclusive to his own story. Because of Glenn's very serious spiritual nature, he continued his journey through Protestantism, becoming a pastor. The mechanisms by which people leave fundamentalism—those triggers that start them reconsidering the viability of their practices and beliefs—will by now be familiar. Glenn's story points to another important way that the transitions can occur. In his case it led to, as he puts it, an "evangelical humanism." As with many other contributors to this book, his religious experience hasn't become compartmentalized. Glenn now combines his training in counselling with a chaplaincy assignment and has found that his experiences in Christian fundamentalism enable him to help others.

To be sure, James Feiser's "The Jesus Lizard" has one of the most intriguing titles. I won't spoil it here by saying what such a thing is and why it makes for a great title. James, now a professor of philosophy, also finds himself an atheist. The goal of this book is not to say what one must do after leaving fundamentalism: certainly atheism, agnosticism, and skepticism are all options. James's narrative exhibits the breadth of possible lives one can have as a fundamentalist *and* as a former fundamentalist. Like James, many of us as fundamentalists found ourselves strongly influenced by charismatic and outgoing personalities. But just as we can be drawn toward any movement by such people, so too we can be repelled once we eventually see all too human tendencies on their part, or our own. James's story begins with a very powerful medium for the fundamentalist, the Christian rock band. He journeys along but finds himself gravitating toward intellectual matters through religious colleges, meeting old acquaintances from the church who have since left, and coming to terms with what philosophers describe as the problem of evil. In short, why, if God is all good and all powerful, does he allow terrible things to happen? For many, the answer is clear: God does not exist. Meaning in life is possible without religion or God. James's story reminds us of how we all come to have views—strongly philosophical or not—based on our life experiences and on significant encounters with others.

Leia Minaker, another young contributor and one of the more recent to leave the fold of fundamentalism, shares her story, "Are You a 'Real' Christian?" There is a certain freshness to her story, which she composed as a twofold account. The first is a negative version, akin to a newly opened wound resulting from disagreement between her and members of her family. Our immediate family usually cares for us most, and if they see us in danger of losing our salvation, and possibly headed toward eternal punishment in Hell, their concern is understandable. The positive component of Leia's story functions, it seems, as an antidote to the negative, with the openness and straightforward honesty she shows in her steadfast need for answers to matters of faith. In certain respects, both sides are equally zealous, as Leia's family ardently wishes to see her faith remain as it always has been, and Leia fervently believing that her faith demands evaluation. Leia's story demonstrates this determination *not* because she is being lured away from the path of truth, but because she indeed seeks the truth. This is a quality of doubt that fundamentalists cannot accept. Everyone in this book, no matter where they are now, has travelled this same road.

I've known the author of "The Naked Empress, Queen of Fundamentalism," for some years now, and I respect his request for anonymity. Some people, still live close to fundamentalism and must have consideration for family, friends, or colleagues. As illustrated in many if not all of these stories, we still have relationships that are bound to our experiences as former fundamentalists. Leaving fundamentalism can often be a complicated matter, and for practical, personal, or professional reasons the severance of all bonds is not always as simple as it might appear to outsiders. In any case, the actual identity of our writer isn't really important. What he *describes* is important. The form of fundamentalism our writer tells us about has a captivating "thickness" to it—in his story, its harshness and seemingly incomprehensible mysteries are seen through the eyes of a child, a teenager, and then an adult. And through the unstoppable torrent of questions and experiences, an unravelling of conviction is set in motion.

My own story, "Confessions of an Ex-Fundamentalist," like some of the others, is still in the making. But I think you've read enough of my thoughts now. It's time we move to the most important part of this book—the stories themselves.

JOSEPH SIMOŃS

Rapture, Community, and Individualist Hope

 I "came to the Lord" at the age of twenty-one. By means of this now common phrase, I understood that although I would remain a sinner till death I would escape the Lake of Fire. I'd live with God for eternity.

A baby boomer to the core, my conversion happened on the phone. While not exactly a snap decision, it was the surprising outcome of considerable dialogue with good friends who had explained to me the basics of salvation. Simplified, the fundamentals of the evangelical creed, now my creed, contained four indispensable points:

1. I am a sinner and damned, for two reasons:
   a) My heredity as a human includes me in the general "fall from grace."
   b) My own evil choices are enough to consign me to Hell.
2. God loves me and wishes to live in harmony with me, but because he is perfect he cannot tolerate the presence of my sinfulness.
3. God created a way to reconcile himself to me, and me to him, via the sacrificial death and atonement of his Son Jesus.
4. God's gift of salvation is not applied to individual sinners like me unless a conscious choice is made to accept his gift.

Once I had accepted Jesus according to the evangelical formula, I immediately experienced a lightening of heart. A freed prisoner, I was given a reprieve from the burden of responsibility for a world that was daily changing too quickly for mortals to comprehend. Would there be a nuclear war? Was pollution on earth a stoppable force? Was it time to get out of Dodge, find some hole in the back country, and live a hand-to-mouth existence, as many survivalists in the 1970s were doing? "No," I was told, "someone is in charge." Or better, "Someone."

To this fresh convert the world might look like it was rushing toward nuclear meltdown, but the turmoil was part of a great plan. One day, I was assured, God would reveal His glory to a fallen mankind. At any moment the heavenly trumpeter could sound the Messiah's arrival and heaven's armies would charge down on cloudy chariots, drawn by flaming horses. We waited for a Messiah who'd make sense of everything. We waited for nothing less than perfection: soon every blemished action and evil thought throughout time would be dealt with, settled forever. My concerns about our crowded planet evaporated overnight. A transformation was coming whereby every particle of nature would be remade and pronounced holy, fit for God's presence. Who needed the old particles that were now so tainted by that ultimate power of the universe, human activity?

I found myself in the theatre of God. There might be staging problems, but at the "End of Days" there'd be no surprises. The Playwright had scripted a plot that, while murky at the moment, must emerge as eminently logical and necessary. Faith was my assurance of a front seat. This awesome future event, also known as the Apocalypse, was the end-of-time event foreseen since the dawn of prophecy. It included fireworks, judgment, retribution, and even magic. On that day mute stones would render glory to God. All of which I was somehow no longer a part. Being "redeemed" turned me into a spectator. The plagues of The Revelation would be experienced by others, the pitiable yet blind "unredeemed" mass of humanity. Having missed their chance for salvation, the masses had only misery to look forward to, an eternity of screams, singed nostrils, and sulphurous demons. For me, however, eternity would bring the spiritual equivalents of scented flowers and ice cream. Benevolent angels waited at my side even now, eager to usher me, a humble believer, into a chamber of heavenly delights that would at the very least afford a superb view of all time.

It felt good to be part of a long tradition. My faith evoked the faith of the Giants of the Faith, whose deeds were recorded in the Bible. In itself my faith was tiny as a mustard seed, but somehow my faith was heroic too, as was every believer's faith. As for those Biblical forefathers, I'd get to meet them someday. I'd swap stories of faithfulness with Noah, get his take on the Great Flood. I'd corner Adam, ask how come it all went so wrong. If I asked nicely, maybe Eve would clarify her role in the "Fall," which had blighted every Adam, animal, and atom in a universe suddenly old before its time. The millennium of God's rule was rolling toward us all, lost and saved, vegetable, mineral, or animal, inevitable as Bob Dylan's "Slow Train." Pretty soon now all creatures would lead upstanding lives. No more "nature, red in tooth and claw." According to our reading of the Old Testament, lions would shortly prefer salad, lamb having been stroked off the king of beast's grocery list. During this time, death must disappear along with any infirmity and unpleasantness. The Millennial Reign of Christ on Earth would be a time of cleanliness, concord, prosperity, and universal handshaking for all creatures and nations.

I experienced an immediate welcome into a group of like-minded individuals, each one "called," and each having many things to talk about. There was Camp David, a fresh yet forlorn hope of Israel living in peace with her neighbours. At least "Israel was in the land." This was, for the evangelical community, the single historical development to support any serious eschatological musings. Punk rock, just invented, was an affront to sacred music, itself in the process of abandoning the traditional hymn book for plastic three-ring binders filled with insipid choruses intended to make churches "relevant to youth." Two *Voyager* spacecraft had been launched. Would they find life out there in the vast realms of space? It was scary to think they might, but comforting to know they couldn't. If so, God would have told us.

Since the big stuff had already been hammered out to the satisfaction of everyone in my church, conversation often swung back to the subject of The Rapture. The term comes from the Medieval Latin, *raptura*, "seizure." In the language of our evangelical eschatologists, "Is The Rapture premillennial or postmillennial?" Put another way, would Jesus collect the redeemed before or after the thousand years of peace and prosperity? Although this was a small point of procedure when compared to other events of "that day" (for instance, tombs everywhere would burst upward as those "asleep in the Lord" awoke and sprang straight into new business under new rules in a "new dispensation"), this topic provided a lot of diversion. When that ancient trumpet sounded we'd all be seized and whisked up to Heaven "in the twinkling of an eye." Although the summons included the dead, there was a tangible benefit to living at "the end of the age of grace." Namely, some of us would see God without the bother of dying. How fortunate we were to live in this worst and best of times. It has been awaited by saints of every age, but in actuality only talked about for the last century as evangelicalism has spread and prospered. Christians of any previous era have been far less literal-minded. Perhaps our predecessors were too humble to force God into timetables of their own devising, timetables that time must find wanting. They did not mind investigating the obscure, fiercely handing down opinions on any minutiae. Remember that tough nut, the legendary debate on how many angels could dance on the head of a pin? That one kept the coffee shops full for centuries. Is it then a feature of evangelicalism or merely a feature of our age to decode all the secret symbols we can find (whether these can be pried out of theological treatises, financial prognostications, treasure maps to King Solomon's Mines, or Little Orphan Annie secret decoder rings)? A symbol decoded gives the savant the inside scoop. Knowledge is power; advance or secret knowledge places us at the front of the queue of privileged individuals who do stuff and go places and see things. What's happening? Look no further: it is me. *I* am happening. And I know for sure when the Lord will return. I must be worth listening to.

Or perhaps this recent expectation that God would step palpably into human history a second time was merely due to a second turn of millenniums (CE). Over a thousand years ago there was a flurry of anticipation around the turn of the first millennium. If this is the case, the passage of time will reveal The Rapture as less and less of a future event and more of a historical curiosity, not to mention as possessed of a cyclical nature.

And what would we discover among the rewards of heaven? Would we pray all day in the company of six-winged angels? Could these rickety knees take the strain? Would we traverse the universe using a Star Trek transporter beam, or would we travel through it à la Descartes: "I think, therefore I am [there]?" Surely we'd do neat things like bring good news to cone-headed beings in unknown worlds a million light years away. And what if humankind's sin had not yet reached so far? Well, in that case maybe these beings had fallen from grace all on their own and would still need a saviour. Come weekends, feet up and gates closed to the business of The Kingdom, would we dwell in suburbs of heavenly mansions? What honours would accrue to us for our impeccable timing?

Meanwhile, we were still on earth. And I was still in my home village of Beachville, Ontario. Abruptly, people I'd known for years were not "saved." It didn't matter what faith they espoused, I saw them as doomed. They couldn't articulate the Four Spiritual Laws (detailed above). Statistically speaking, how could it be otherwise? "Strive to enter in the narrow gate," said Jesus, "for few there be that enter by it" (Matthew 7:13–14). Surely Jesus referred to eternal salvation. The masses were storming the wide gate leading to destruction. And since only the "elect" had been foreordained to be with God, the chances of people exchanging their belief systems for the evangelical "Truth" was a thousand to one at best—even though I had done so. Whatever they believed was "religion, not faith" and involved "dead rites, not a living Saviour." I was surrounded by outright heathens! My duty was clear: I had to tell everyone about Jesus' death and resurrection and how each sin was paid for. I remember a receptive teller working at her bank wicket during my presentation of the gospel; the words "Credit Union" ring across the decades with new meaning.

The doomed kept plodding heedlessly toward their annihilation. But my disappointments in converting them were tempered by the success of gaining new Christian friends, especially the family who had helped me convert. Like the blue sky awaiting its Lord, my respect for them was mile-high. Their evangelical approach to life, their outgoing friendliness, and their confident beliefs had a dizzying effect on me, a doubtful Roman Catholic. As early as grade five I had turned my head away when the priest offered me some of his mumbo-jumbo, smoky incense, and holy water. That priest was too different, too weird to have anything to do with my main concerns of horses and hockey. He wore a black dress, too. What boy with two good legs would bow to the "mysteries" when the sun was shining outside? After all, every question in Catechism class boiled down to mysteries that took forever to explicate. Ten years later that shaky Catholic adherence deserted me altogether. I had "seen the light."

Nonetheless, my conversion did not enlighten my family. Much tension was created as I worked my new values into every conversation. I kept up my "biblical" assertions as if no one before me had ever read the Bible. For her part, my mother just wanted us all to get along. My views, she thought, weren't in conflict with her way of seeing God. She only wanted me to believe in the intercession of Jesus. For her, even though the Virgin Mary and numerous saints were major players throne side, we all prayed to the same God. My father would brook no change of tradition. Catholicism had flourished for millennia, and after one lousy little experience was I going to change the whole system? I was obviously a know-it-all. For my father, our task as believers was minuscule—we had to accept without protest the forms of piety constructed for us by our forbears. My two brothers and five sisters were simply intimidated by the new me. I was too different, too weird to have anything to do with a kid's main concern—staying clear of conflict. And I wore that happy insidious grin, treacherous as a TV preacher working the crowd.

Our Catholicism was a gentler faith, neither talked about nor "a personal relationship with the Lord"; it was not a faith afflicted with the pioneer spirit of self-improvement at all costs. Moreover, Dutch immigrant Catholicism was concerned with being Canadian, peaceful, a good citizen; it was not wound up with visions of solidifying one's own niche in a distant empire. This community's accepting attitude was almost antithetical to evangelicalism, for which "Kingdom"—God's expanding reign over all humanity—lay at the very core of its mandate. From the world's vast selection of religions I could hardly have found one more offensive to everyone I knew.

But I had found "faith, not religion." I had found people defined by a faith they could talk about, and so found a new way of seeing the world and operating within it. Putting both feet to the ground, I began to identify with evangelicals and their creed(s). I guessed I might as well go live with them, too, since no one at home understood me. Like a Bible prophet, I was persecuted. No one wanted to debate me on "what it says in the Bible." They'd just turn their faces from me, as Pilate turned his from Jesus. Isn't that where persecution starts? Six months after my conversion, in a bitter exchange with my father, I was ordered never to come home again. For ten years, I would obey.

Full of sorrow mingled with a strange joy, I moved away. *Sorrow* because no sheep likes being cut from the flock. *Joy* because it was an adventure to move in with a new family who entirely understood me. I went to their church, a friendly place led by a cheerful and learned pastor from the very conservative, Texas-based, Dallas Theological Seminary. I continued to read the Bible voraciously, soaking up every sermon on how to understand its archaic text. Having a good job driving trucks, I gave oodles of money. I bought a new car with cash. A girl caught my eye. I believed. I belonged.

Then I went on vacation with a friend, the youngest son of my adoptive family. We each had just bought brand-new motorcycles. By the second day of riding we'd reached the Florida Keys. Returning to our motel room, I was hit by a car. Full of turtle soup and ruminating on the waitress, I had turned my bike in front of some poor guy on a three-day leave from the army. I nearly lost my leg that night, and in subsequent complications I nearly lost my life. During a night of incredible loneliness I was visited by a messenger. A nurse came into the room and talked to me for hours. Next morning, when I asked about her, nobody knew who she was. So I assumed she must have been an angel sent by a merciful God. After four months in bed and countless operations I emerged from hospital emaciated but determined to use the recovery time, projected at two years, in "busying myself for the Kingdom."

I meant to learn more about my faith, and that meant study at Briercrest Bible College, one of a few Protestant bible colleges sprinkled across Canada's Bible Belt—the prairies. There were closer schools, but my academic record was abysmal. If I lived close to home and friends, I reasoned, I'd never get through any course of study. I had to go far away. In September I drove west with my right leg, which could not bend anymore, resting on the passenger seat. The flat prairies filled me with joy. The blue skies arched overtop an impossibly flat earth, now dry and yellow with wheat stubble. The college was situated in the centre of the Palliser Triangle, the main dustbowl of the Great Depression in Canada. This windy, rolling land, this romantic sky, my new life, all seemed limitless. It is no wonder that three great religions began in the desert. Limitless also was the potential of one thousand young people who had come there to "heed the call."

Some deemed the region a wasteland, but I saw talented people, beautiful, sincere, and zealous people, each plucked from the embers of a dying world. And each was possessed of a similar "Christ centred mindset." Building the kingdom seemed not only possible but inevitable. Unlike high school, I didn't want to shirk my learning. I worked as never before, taking subjects like Greek, Ancient History, and Pastoral Studies. Preaching I dreaded, melting in fear before any crowd. But I had to conquer fear, take control of my life. The ascetic in me flourished. I hobbled around on crutches through the seasons, regularly slipping and falling on the ice at thirty below zero, happy as a spring lark. Ongoing surgeries ensured I would miss a semester here and there, so I couldn't graduate with my original cohort. I did meet Karen, the woman who was to become my wife. We often sat at the roadside coffee shop, which was part of the Bible College campus, watching grain trucks roll along the

Trans-Canada Highway. Distant trains seemed to inch along the wide valley.

Before long, I hated school. I wanted action. I didn't hate learning facts, changeable as facts can be, but I had come to loathe overhead presentations, any list, and lecturers' lifeless opinions. Likewise the managerial lingo around church planning, ministry, goals, outcomes, leadership, and so on. The college and even little rural churches were swinging to boardroom language. It seemed hip, on the edge. But that lingo processes ideas into jargon, just a small step from double-talk and plain bunk. Was all this jargon used to make the ideas more palatable?

Not surprisingly, I didn't complete the Bachelor of Religious Education degree offered by the college. I fled from the posturing and pastoring courses only to find a job with a non-Christian farmer. Working long, dusty, and happy hours, we brought in his harvest. He bought a grain dryer just so I could dry his grain and custom-dry his neighbours' grain. When all the harvest-related activities were over I had to find a job with a new farmer, this time a Christian. The first farmer came back with an offer: he'd buy another business to keep me busy, if I'd return. But having given my word to number two, I felt duty bound to decline the offer. I'd be milking cows.

Farmer number one, being as selfless an employer as I'd ever known, had got me scheming about agricultural missionary activities and all the material good a knowledgeable person could do. Since he was a non-Christian man, my developing missionary propensities could not have been further from his mind. A family man, he lived in a real world of grease and grain dust, operating the large farm passed down from his father. And when he saw real-world needs, he was there to help, whether that meant finding me a job or helping a neighbour with mechanical problems or just spending time talking out problems. His help was always practical and immediate. And free. He wasn't much of a theory guy. He'd be surprised to learn he was a source of inspiration for these emerging ideas of mine. That said, I'm sure he wouldn't have been pleased to learn that my ideas were tied to the gospel message. Binding my help to the gospel would take it out of the realm of philanthropy and into the realm of coercion.

So I planned to bulk up on first-hand experience, then go overseas and help "them in the Third World" deal with crop or water problems. That would meet real needs. That wasn't just wrangling with words. Unbeknownst to me at the time, seeing a good source of cheap labour, farmer number two, my "brother in the Lord," had other plans. His idea was to milk me along with his cows. I worked from dawn till dusk and also paid exorbitant rent and utilities on his mobile home. I found out later that because of low wages, a place to stay (plus milk and meat) usually comes free to farm labourers. He'd also promised times of light workload to balance out the normal work weeks. But I saw only heavy work, with every second weekend off. When I could hardly walk anymore, I asked if we could return to the original agreement. He told me he'd been planning to lay me off anyway. The fall was slower for him.

Funny enough, this experience did not shake my faith much. I'd seen plenty of self-centred Christians already, and heard of worse. Yet who wouldn't compare the two farmers, how they lived in the world, their priorities?

My new scheme in tatters, due to physical limitations, but my nose still on the trail of a worthwhile task, I found a job with a Salvation Army social service office. It was heartbreaking to see the "clients" trapped in their difficult lives. After two years their number had doubled. I decided to complete my bachelor's degree back at Briercrest. It had bothered me to leave that unfinished. I was probably burned out, too. The office had to hire two people to do my job after I left. But in the course of doing this job I had gained a lot of confidence. I could remember the names, social workers and in-house trustees of 750 clients, including many details of their personal situations.

Back at Briercrest, my new confidence, so hard won, came in handy. I was after theological and biblical courses, getting my head as near as possible to an academic culture. I concentrated my scholastic efforts on a few scholarly professors. And my marks soared to the top of the school. The strategy was to treat every school day like work, with regular hours and breaks. Weekends off. Learning about the Lord was a job I could do passably well.

In the mid-1980s we left Saskatchewan and went to Ontario so that Karen could attend university. We were active in church, preaching, teaching, and singing together. We kept up with Christian friends. We rented an apartment from a "Christian." I began to notice that it wasn't just my deadbeat farmer out west—a lot of Christians didn't seem very … uh, Christian.

I had to ask: Why, Sermon on the Mount notwithstanding, were evangelicals as likely as anyone else to collect too many possessions? As likely to be racist? As likely to be vain, proud, narrow minded, unforgiving, and wasteful of the world's resources? As likely to be vulnerable to get-rich-quick schemes and to run off with the church organist? The term "evangelical" is from the New Testament Greek: *euangelion*, "good news." But many of us were bad news. Struggling for success, we manipulated situations for our own good, at others' cost. A friend's father had an employer who kept a Bible on his desk. His father was exploited so thoroughly by this man that my friend decided that a Bible on the desk ought to be a sane man's first warning of personal danger.

Moreover, when Christians did bad things, like rip off the vulnerable or beat up wives, why did we rally around protectively? Is it a herd instinct that keeps the status quo going? By now, thanks to Farmer Rip-Off and other lesser lights in the depraved brotherhood, I was clueing in. By now, I had divined that human society consists of numerous idiosyncratic groups. Our community was part of a larger system, and was (is) governed by the laws of subcultures. Catholic versus Protestant, Salvation Army, the College, the Dutch, English versus French, any "believing church." Each one of us belongs to any number of interest groups that use common group dynamics to achieve ends that aren't as diverse as we imagine. Despite all my musings and realizations I wasn't ready to give up on the compelling figure of Jesus. But finally, after all these years, I'd begun to look around and think for myself.

Perhaps, I thought, we believers are just not up to our beliefs. That wouldn't necessarily make the beliefs wrong. But as time went on, familiar assertions grew less persuasive to me and then plainly wrong headed. Hearing "the fundamentals" pop out of friends' mouths trivialized them: Fundamentalism, the Religious Right, Zionism, Creationism, the Pro-Life movement. Our faith was bearing arms (not fruit) against its enemies of Secularism, Humanism, Communism, Feminism, and Evolutionism. And it seemed that much of our enemies' firepower lay in their heartfelt reactions to the abuses of the old religious guard.

Then there were the honest non-believers out there, perceptive people who advocated on every side of every "ism," achieving degrees of good in a complex society. So could our world really be a theatre of conflict between good and evil, as we "true believers" maintained? I began to see it rather as groups of people getting along as well as they could with limited resources. I also began to see the certainties of our systems as distancing me from a real world where real people and real creatures live and die. Systems appear to arise out of local concerns, so that their "answers" would not take into account the whole. Evangelicals want more people saved. Who can argue against that? But why is there only one kind of being saved? Out in the world are many forces, most of them beyond human control. It's scary to be alone. I felt the essential insecurity of this subculture. It is set up to direct attention away from fearful lives.

And me, I was feeling responsible again, and anxious in my gut.

I wasn't alone. Many of us were concerned about this world. God lived here, after all, right? Why ponder the vastness of space and time when we hardly know what it means to live upright and joyful lives in the here and now? Every day we witness a stampede for wealth in the West, homelessness in the global East and South. This happens in our very midst. Our humanness tells us (if our theology does not) that the earth and every particle that rides her around the sun are somehow not replaceable. That was the theme of the Prophets and is, I think, the essence of sacred experience. Smitten, believers of every sect, ours included, send out missionaries to help build and rebuild, feed and grow. And proselytize. We foot the bill and in return we expect "commitments." How many heathens have jettisoned beliefs and cultures? Enough to justify the effort to societies looking for quick results. Graphs and pie charts illustrate the transformation of the indigene. They now build square houses, shop, drive, eat fast food. It's clear that the "lost" want to be like us, but in what way? Would these peoples really have "accepted" our modern Western industrial ways, with all the attendant problems, if they could have developed their own cultures on their own timelines and according to their own values? Have we (and has "salvation") pulled the rug out from under them, removing other, more sustainable options?

How had we gotten to this point anyway? Who was this Lord? Is God someone to fear? With eyes six feet off the ground, we humans see a couple of miles out of the earth's circumference of twenty-four thousand. Can we tiny beings, with no perspective, really know God as anything but a very big, very invisible parent? Why was this big God we "knew" so interested in keeping score? Was there any reason to believe that sin had to be paid for?

During this time of doubt I wondered about my original evangelical liberators. What were they really like? I went back to visit. Although aggressive to "testify about the Lord's mercies and blessings," there were few signs of the social status markers found in most corporate evangelical churches: biggest house, new car(s), best clothes. Evangelicalism appeals to have-nots who are working up to being haves. What better place to find a submissive wife or to hook up to power connections than in your local church? Yet my friends had kept to their old way of living. They didn't seem to care for earthly treasures. In fact, they seemed immune to that corrosive "healthy, wealthy, wise" way of life that is decimating our earth and is practically a hallmark of evangelical aspiration. Reformers within the church have advocated the modest life for years, as have thinkers of every age and religious persuasion, but some people are simply satisfied with less because they don't care to collect more. I was relieved to see my friends in this group. And I saw that temperament rather than religious dictum had made them content.

Another decisive change came about when we moved to Vancouver for Karen to pursue graduate studies. Namely, I began to write fiction. I was struck by how good a story the Bible told, how carefully all the motives, actions, and effects are maintained. Lies, incest, murders, and political intrigues worthy of Shakespeare form the details of that long "history." As in Second World War Holland, which my mom keeps telling me about, it is difficult at times to tell the good guys from the bad guys. This is especially so in the Old Testament, which seldom takes the "do good to your enemies" line. Holy Scripture began to read like a ripping good yarn. Far from an unassailable foundation for a world view, none of it seemed real. Not literal, I thought, but literary. For appreciating raw life, this unique text can't be beat. It engages with its world, explores critical moments in society, and still finds beauty and hope. On that level the Bible is no less than luminous. It is brilliantly crafted, a record not of history but of our story, an intergenerational witness of the important things in human life.

I did not doubt that something happened back in Bible times, but who can say what it was? As in a newspaper article, where the same few ideas are stated and restated but seldom clarified, the Bible struggles to explain life that is bigger than the individual. Faith itself seems a group act. That ultimate individualist act, being "born again," appears a strange abnormality. Why should rebirth be on your own terms? Where is the mother, the father? Throughout our history humans have found themselves at the mercy of forces that have wiped out past success, security, hope for the future. But what makes the narrative force of a community moving through time greater than any individual deed and more compelling than the supposed history being recorded?

Truth versus falsehood? I like to stretch the truth, and the themes of beauty, mercy, and community—strongly Biblical themes—do well in fiction. Story gives life and life is history. Whether the events are "factual" or "made up" doesn't matter. A narrative puts desire, fear, and hope into a perspective that can be evaluated and shared. As a telescope reveals stars, story locates meaning in our lives, preferably with an intended beginning, a guided past, a numinous present, and a good end in sight. The uncertainties in our mysterious world can be focused, brought into balance. That's better than denying them, which is the job of institutions like the church. Where the interpretation of story becomes strictly literal, we trade life and diversity for certainty and death.

Although the certainty of my evangelical liberators seems to be what attracted me to evangelicals, and thus to their beliefs, I see now that I was also desperate to get some distance from my father. That's what kids do, or at least what this kid did. I wanted as little as possible to do with my father's inarticulate yet restrictive customs. His actual beliefs must have been only a tiny part of my antagonism, since I hardly knew what he believed. I did know that many young people were pushing outward, delving into deeply felt (and often equally inarticulate) countercultural values. And weren't The Beatles leading the way? *Imagine. Come Together. Revolution.* "We all want to change the world." By joining a different church tradition, I could march against "the man" in my own way. Unfortunately, identifying with a new group to escape the old familiar group is also not a good foundation for belief.

It must be time for confession. What *do* I believe, then? I believe very little in the way of "Truth"—statements about things we can't see and about someone we can't ask. God may be "there," but probably not in the way many of us imagine. Pronouncements about "the Lord's Will" are surely fraught with difficulties. I do concede that a part of us may apprehend God, leaving us with a sense of the divine. I may have seen that angel, after all! Creationism? The world is old, not young. Otherwise the dinosaur bones would be an awful trick. I'm confident that our ideas about God misrepresent reality because we have so little reality to go on, only lived notions of the way a few things seem to work. The universe is awfully big. Is it reasonable for a God who "holds the whole world in his hands" to bother about our petty decisions? The idea of a "final reckoning" seems foolish to me, especially when you consider how intellectually stunted and physically limited we humans are. And where did the idea that "sins must be paid for" come from, when simple forgiveness would do the trick? But simple forgiveness is not dignified; it requires only humility, perhaps a small act of inner contrition, but no grand acts of emancipation.

While we do make stunningly bad choices, I think our "sinful" actions often stem from chemical imbalances in the brain rather than temptations from the Devil. Our motives, those of the redeemed included, are murky, as any government rally or church social can demonstrate. As for the teeming masses of unredeemed, why would we judge adherents of different traditions by standards and methods that have failed us so often? I am not interested in hanging out with people who decry the sins of the world. Such people can turn on a dime. Give me someone I can trust in my daily dealings.

Can you trust Jesus? Although he may have been a real man once, I believe he has long since been fashioned into an ideal by those seeking ideological tools. One thing about Jesus does stick with me, though: his parables about faith were an affront to his hearers. Maybe it's time we thought of faith differently. What if we considered *communities* as saved or lost, and not individuals? We do not have to give up the hard-won freedom of individual conscience. We need no theology of salvation to include some and exclude others (and lead to more war). But if we must measure, let's do so in terms of "our group," how well we tolerate differences of opinion, how well we look after every last soul in the world society. The "state of grace" could become a state of mind and eventually a political entity. What if we made decisions with distant groups or later generations uppermost in our minds? Given our present headspace, this seems difficult to achieve. Yet in fact, indigenous groups have lived simple, far-seeing lives for millennia.

Isn't this fine, you say? In a few pages he's dismissed theology and institutional religion, and turfed personal experience. Where can he get meaning in life? I know people who have left evangelicalism but are still preoccupied with this question, which to a large extent is inseparable from a fundamentalist world view. The assumption seems to be that a life must have "purpose" to be of any value. But who is able judge what a worthwhile life looks like? I no longer look for designations of meaning or purpose, but we can, I think, find meaning and purpose in the relationships we have with our families, friends and neighbours.

I do look for joy, and find oodles of it: in working on my house and garden; in listening to the wind, or the pipe organ at church; in playing my ancient trombone, which was rescued from the dump; in telling a story; in my dog's joy; in watching neighbourhood birds, or hanging out with the kids at the school where I work; in my wife, friends, our families; in others' successes. In reality, there is no end to joy. True, there is a river of pain to wade through. But joy and pain together lead us to beauty. Don't we all ache inside when we notice it? If there is meaning in the world, beauty will be its throbbing heart.

In the end, beauty is a direction as well as a destination. And beauty does not leave anyone behind. What we need now are beautiful, vital ideas about how individuals fit into groups that can make their way peacefully through this uncertain world. Progress is always a suspect term, but why can't we try for a progress of culture, where everyone has enough of the basics to live well? Beyond the basics, how about all us groups co-creating a worldwide hope?

I have no regrets about my religious travels. I really am thankful to have "come to the Lord." But I am also thankful to have found my distance from any fixed ideas about who or what the Lord might be. For me, the Age of Grace will always be right now. It is acceptance and joy. It is stillness and running. I ran as a youngster, then I learned to stand, and then I tripped. All things considered, I'm glad an evangelical was quick enough to catch me, but now I'm up and running again. Thanks to you all!

L.A. LIVINGSTON

From There to Here

 I woke up, frantic, panicking. All I could see was the bleak, blurry, grey sky above me. A face appeared, a knitted toque perched on top.

"What's your name?" the face asked me. I recognized neither the voice nor the features.

"I can't move. I need to get out," I gasped, feeling claustrophobic.

"You've been in an accident," the woman replied. "What's your name?"

Other voices, the paramedics, told me not to move, even as they strapped me onto the stretcher, confining me past the point of moving even a muscle.

"Your name?" she asked again.

"Lori-Ann. Lori-Ann Livingston."

I passed out.

A single second, or series of seconds, can change a life. Those few ticks on the clock, as my car slid out of control at a T-junction and collided with a Ford Bronco that day in the tail end of 1996, changed mine. In the year that followed, I aged a decade. The days and months brought physical recovery, but the emotional and spiritual effects lasted beyond what the eye could see.

It was late November when the accident happened. The 23rd of November, 1996, to be exact. Moments before, I had hopped in my little maroon-coloured Mercury Tracer and pulled out onto the gravel side road. I wasn't familiar with the area; I was visiting a friend's parents on the day of their auction sale. I had met my sister and her husband at the St. Jacobs Market that morning. They had chided me about not putting snow tires on my car. I couldn't afford to. I was between jobs and had just registered to enter college for a post-degree diploma in print journalism.

The roads were slippery, but nothing that front-wheel-drive Ferdinand, so named because the car ploughed through snowdrifts like a bull, couldn't handle. I shifted into third and carefully navigated the road. I was headed for my parents' farm, but on roads I didn't know. With the map at my side, I set out. Cresting a hill, I saw a yield sign at a T-junction ahead of me. Unsure of which way to turn, I pressed the brakes only to fishtail sideways. Pumping the brakes didn't help, and I panicked. Just before I lost control, I spied a Ford Bronco on the other road. The next thing I remember is seeing its grill in my side window and thinking, "He's going to hit me." The grill ornament was the last thing I remember before impact. It was found later inside my crushed car.

I woke in the hospital in Mount Forest. My oldest sister, who lived in Cambridge, had been notified of the accident, and she had called my parents. They had just arrived home from watching my hometown's Santa Claus parade. This is what I'm told.

Those next few hours in the hospital were, frankly, hazy, except for a few moments that stand out in my memory. Like the young fellow driving the Bronco coming to see me in the hours after the accident, upset at my condition and the reaction of his father. Like the police-woman who insisted on charging me for failing to yield, even though the roads were icy. "We found your car in third gear," she told me, as if that was all the evidence of my carelessness that she needed.

Like Mom and Dad, and my brother and sister-in-law, a nurse, visiting me, and my listing all the things that needed to be done in the next few hours—people who needed to be notified, gifts for a shower to be distributed. "It was like your life was flashing before you," Mom told me later. Like my sister-in-law saying to Mom after I'd been given morphine, "She'll throw up just about … now." And I did.

The image of that Ford ornament imprinted itself on more than my memory. Part of the truck's grill had pierced the retina of my left eye, and the impact had pushed my driver's seat almost over to the passenger side of the car. If I'd been any bigger, I was told, I would have died. The tibia and fibula on my left leg were both broken. Aside from the emotional trauma, those were all my injuries. I was lucky.

That's about all I really care to remember about the event. But I can't forget it. And it would be telling only a fraction of the story. I spent time in Mount Forest, two hospitals in Guelph, and one in London, and was released from hospital care on December 9. Five weeks later, I started my journalism course. But that car accident changed my life, my perceptions, my spiritual connections, and my view of life and the rest of the world. All changed with that one event. The car accident is the beginning of the story of how my spiritual journey took a sharp turn to the left and how I left my conservative Christian beliefs behind.

I was aided and abetted on that journey by my husband, though he would never claim it. Then, he was my fiancé. We had become engaged in September 1996, a decision complicated by the fact that he lived in London, England, and I lived in Waterloo, Ontario. Our wedding was scheduled for May 16, 1998. We saw each other every three months or so in the time in between. An Irishman who grew up in the Church of the Nazarene in County Antrim, Northern Ireland, and who has a theology degree from Nazarene Theological College in Manchester, England, Mark became "post-evangelical" after a five-month journey through India and through his experiences as a social worker in London and Devon. He would now say he's not even post-evangelical, but that's his story to tell. My point is that he's a big part of my story and of my recovery from the accident.

That November day was a trigger point. It launched me from a safe, secure spiritual life onto a journey that led me around corners and down paths I had never considered, indeed had never been open to. To understand the shift in perspective and practice—where I am now—I must first go back. Back to where I grew up, to where I learned my first Bible verses and sang my first hymns.

I grew up in the Church of the Nazarene, a rather small denomination in Protestant evangelical circles, though moderately popular in North America and Britain. It was founded in the late 1800s in the United States, out of the Holiness Movement and is still known as a holiness church. It seems to me now to be an old-fashioned denomination, and in some ways I like that. It's a microcosm of Victorian principles, a faith community that could never be considered progressive but that looks after its own. Like many denominations, it is full of people who mean well but who stumble in their good intentions. And it continues to be led almost solely led by men.

Most of the people in my home church, my family included, were farmers. They came to church, scrubbed clean and dressed in their Sunday best, in clothes that were fashionable twenty years before. They had dirt under their nails, sunburn on their necks, hat lines on their weather-worn faces. They were, and are still, honest and hardworking people, stalwart and quiet in their trials, generous in someone else's. They value honesty, hard work, simplicity, and the status quo.

The pews of the church were bare and hard, the floors also bare except for a rust-coloured carpet down the aisles framing the centre section of pews. The music was picked out key by key on the piano. The hymn book held page after page of old standards like "Beulah Land," "When the Roll Is Called Up Yonder," and "Onward Christian Soldiers."

There was a large stained-glass window at the back of the church, which faced the street. Apart from that, there were no other decorations except a broad wall hanging above the choir loft that said "Holiness unto the Lord." It hangs there to this day. The church basement, where we held our Sunday School, was panelled. The walls were thin, the carpets threadbare, the small windows sported homemade curtains.

It was in this sparse environment that I was raised. My own family members reflected the same simple values of the church at the time, and to varying degrees they still do. I am the seventh in a family of eight. I have four sisters and three brothers, with a full twenty years between the oldest and youngest. We were raised on a farm, where my parents eked out a living selling cream from our small dairy herd and raising our own chickens and pigs and, later on, angora goats, as well as crops to support the animals. We grew our own vegetables and fruit, made jams, pickles, and pies from scratch, and drank milk straight from the cow. Again, progressive isn't a word that could be applied to the technology used on our farm, so the work was hard, the days long, and the money scarce.

My parents began their family in the 1950s and finished having children in the early 1970s. Parenting styles changed over those twenty years, but no one told Mom and Dad. We were raised on hard work, honesty, simplicity, and religion. We were taught to respect our elders, not to question authority, and to do what we were told. If we didn't, discipline sometimes came in the form of a spanking or a reckoning with "the strap," literally a portion of a heavy black-canvas strap that was used to run the threshing machine. It was about a foot-and-a-half long and six inches wide, and it hung on a nail behind the wood stove in the kitchen. It was used only in extreme situations. No one got special treatment in our family, the theory being that if Mom and Dad did some-thing unique for one, they'd have to do it for all of us. Better not to start in the first place than to be pestered with children crying, "But So-and-so got to go. Why can't I?" That said, I wanted a pony so badly that I bar-gained with God about it, and on my ninth birthday I got an arthritic pony that was older than I was. She came to me as Brylcreem, but I named her Dusty.

Mom and Dad themselves came from traditional farming families. Raised in the Depression and shaped by the rationing of the Second World War, they saved everything and recycled the rest. Women worked in the house and carried the babies and did their share in the barns and fields, too. Men looked after the land, the barns, the animals, and the equipment, but not the house. The house, its work and maintenance, belonged to the women. Men ate and slept there, but that was about it. My mother's background was conservative Baptist, and she holds dear many of the practicalities that stereotype the denomination—no drink-ing alcohol, no dancing, no playing cards, no going to bars or listening to unbecoming music, always wear a dress to church, and a hat, too. We always had to have a nap on Sunday afternoon because it was the Day of Rest. Dad was raised in the United Church and seemed to be much more laid back about some things than Mom. Though to my knowledge he never lets alcohol pass his lips, I do know he likes a good game of cards on his yearly moose-hunting trips.

I've always been a journaller. When I was a young girl, I wrote in those small five-year diaries: "Sunny today. Did chores. Maryanne told me I was too skinny. I hate her." When I was eleven, I wanted to be a writer. I wanted to be a jockey, too, because I was horse crazy and slightly built—scrawny, actually, weighing less than 100 pounds even as a teenager. I think I wanted to be a writer because one of my friends, someone who also bullied me, liked writing. I was a sensitive child who cried easily if someone shouted "Boo!" or made a face at me, and I desperately wanted to fit in. I was an easy target, really. This particular friend identified that weakness in me and preyed on it. She goaded others into it, too. So the writing, in the end, became an escape. I could lay out on the page just what I thought and felt without ever having to say it out loud. Pen and paper, like books, became my best and most constant friends when I was younger. I have hundreds of pages of journals I've been writing since those early years, when weather and obnoxious friends loomed largest in my world.

It wasn't just my everyday thoughts and notions I put into my journals. I expressed my faith in writing, too. I also have a number of notebooks dedicated to prayers I've written to God, each one a step on my journey of faith. I read them now and I think, "How naive I was," or "I don't even recognize that person." I see the transition—from single-minded faithful "servant of God" to guilt-ridden, depressed person struggling with post-traumatic stress, to who I am now—taking place on those pages. I see how faithful I was in those pages: how every relationship, every conversation, every struggle had a purpose or was conducted by the greater hand of God. I felt guilty because I no longer saw purpose in the struggle. I no longer felt I would be a better person after the struggle was over. I no longer felt the strength in the relationships I had with my fellow Christians, no longer heard subtle messages from the Spirit of God in conversation. I thought something was wrong with me. Somehow I had fallen. Somehow I had become a stranger to the faith I had known all my life.

Today I truly do not resemble the person I was then. That's what I think when I read those letters to the Creator. Others might say, "Well, you're still this, and you're still that, like you were then," but those qualities then were so much enveloped by an almost childlike faith that they must not really be the ones I exhibit now. Even the evangelical friends I had have all, almost without exception, dropped away, and I often wonder if they could not reconcile the person I became with the person they once knew. That, too, has been part of my faith story, the fickleness of some who once mentored me in the evangelical circles but dropped me like a baked potato out of a campfire when I began to question my faith. That burned me, to the degree that I left the church altogether for a couple of years. When I made my way back, it was to pulpits that were more liberal, more welcoming, more respecting of differences.

There was a time, during recovery in the very difficult year or two that followed my accident, when I could not reconcile my present situation and self with the self I knew I had been. Perhaps if I had not been such a dedicated writer of prayers and conversations to God I would have had an easier time of it. During my recovery I often looked back on those pages and thought how much I wanted to regain what I once had.

Those words set the standard by which I measured my life in 1997. It took some time for me to learn that I was developing new standards by which to measure myself and that it was an okay thing to do.

Oddly, my eventual complaints about the evangelical church had less to do with theological issues than with its culture. I have never studied theology and I have only a passing interest in it. My questions and doubts, then, were more to do with the relational aspects of that culture than with the academics of it. Perhaps it again goes back to my former deep-seated need to be accepted and loved. I still struggle with that need, but I am much more likely to recognize that sometimes you just need to move on, sometimes quickly. Relationships come and go, and even the friends who swore they were forever have slipped away. While I still grieve the passing of each friendship, I recognize the wealth of friends—new ones—I have around me now.

I plugged my nose, took a deep breath, and leaned back, trusting the person holding me not to let go. The dark, cold water closed over me briefly before I was lifted again to stand in the soft mud, drenched, in the cold late-September air. The sky was overcast and threatening, not at all suitable for a day celebrating the baptism of a number of people, including me and two of my four sisters, from a small church in a farming community in southwestern Ontario. The water was in a pond in someone's field, a murky human-made swimming hole used on hot days for cooling off and for corn roasts and campfires.

If I remember correctly, I was about twelve, and I had worn the best thing I could—navy-blue polyester pants with an elasticized waist, pants that I felt were dressy enough for the occasion but that I didn't mind getting dirty in the mud and water. Because elastics and water don't go together very well, I remember such details. I spent the rest of the afternoon, until we got home, holding my pants up so that they wouldn't fall to my knees. I also remember promptly getting into a fight with my sisters, though why escapes me now; we didn't seem to need much reason for a good scrap.

Baptism is an important occasion in the more fundamentalist Protestant churches, but it is a decision made when you are an adult, or close to it. Baptizing babies, as practised by other denominations, is frowned on. Mr. Gilroy, our minister at the time, asked my sisters and me why we wanted to be baptized. I distinctly remember saying, "I want to get along with my sisters better." There were other reasons, but I don't remember them. I knew it was expected, but I also know that my reasons were less spiritual than practical.

My grasp of my faith as I matured as a teenager led to an active involvement as a youth leader in the Nazarene Church. A core group of us in our youth group planned events for Friday nights. Sometimes we joined the closest Nazarene youth groups from churches that were about 30 kilometres away. Hayrides, corn roasts, toboggan parties, gym nights at the local primary school, campfires, and camp meetings at the Nazarene Church's camp in Clarksburg, trips to the beach and Canada's Wonderland amusement park—all were part of our youth group's planned fun events. Nevertheless, a devotional was assigned to keep our spiritual focus.

Our youth group also carried on the tradition started twenty years earlier by some of my older siblings when they were in the youth group—a canoe trip on the Civic Holiday weekend in August. I started going on the trips when I was fifteen and eventually began planning the yearly trip, choosing the area where we'd canoe and camp, arranging for tents and canoes and transportation, and planning the menus. These trips became reference points for me, an event I looked forward to every year. Some of my favourite memories were forged by the waters of lakes around Dorset, Parry Sound, Peterborough, and Temagami, all in Ontario.

Even now I feel wistful as I recall the intensity of the sunsets, sleeping under the stars, the quiet ripple of a paddle in the water, listening to music documentaries on a transistor radio that got poor reception so far north. I remember with fondness singing around campfires, eating food that tasted divine after a day's worth of paddling and portages that could break the most spirited body, and just breathing in the beauty of the landscape.

My years in the Church of the Nazarene laid a foundation for me. Once I moved away to attend university, I gravitated toward the culture with which I was most familiar. I began attending a church in the Evangelical Missionary Church of Canada denomination, a large church that one of my sisters also attended. I got involved first with the choir, then with the drama team, eventually becoming assistant drama director. By then (the early 1990s) the church leadership was leaning strongly toward the Willow Creek model, which Bill Hybels had founded in Chicago. Its vision—to bring unbelievers to Christ by making church more accessible using secular music, drama, and visual presentations—ultimately led the church to split, with half the congregation staying behind and continuing with the traditional service, the others leaving to start up another church, a community church, that ran "seeker services."

The seeker service was a concept made popular by Willow Creek. It was designed for people who had no experience of the evangelical Christian church and its message. Thus the service incorporated popular secular music, drama, audiovisual presentations, photography, and film—anything to make the "seeker" more comfortable, to make the strange more familiar. We met in funeral homes, restaurants, community centres, empty stores, and a Korean church. During those first couple of years we needed to define our vision and figure out what the new church would look like. We studied Steven Covey's self-help book, *Seven Habits of Highly Effective People*. We made trips to Willow Creek to reassure ourselves we were doing it right. We emphasized relationships and "loving people to Christ." Our main goal was to see people "come to know the Lord." We formed a tightly knit leadership group, to which I belonged for a while, and cell groups, urging the strictest regime of honesty and accountability.

We were very much a church of the 1990s. The decade of downsizing, contracting out, and closing up had led to an explosion of self-help advice, professionalism in arenas where it had never been before, a striving for perfection, and an emphasis on relationships. In industry and business, people's working lives were fracturing; in church, we aimed to reassemble those lives. We created certainty. We put broken things back together. We made sense out of confusion by applying black-and-white principles to murky situations. We were entertainment and message, fact and fiction, sound bite and analysis. It worked if you asked the right questions or you were happy enough to hear the ready-made answers. I was, until the accident. And so was Mark.

For about a month after my release from hospital after the accident, I was grateful I had survived. I prayed enthusiastically and journalled as if my life counted on it. But by starting school so soon afterwards, I had placed myself under a great deal of strain, physically and emotionally. While recovering from the accident I became depressed: I felt hopeless, abandoned by my friends and by God. Emotionally, I found it difficult to cope with day-to-day tasks and with a long-distance engagement to my greatest advocate. I sought counselling, and for a time I managed to overcome the worst, but I still experienced depression off and on for the next eighteen months.

During the year following the accident I became interested in the debates over the nature of Christ, the feminization of God, and the controversial theories of the moderator of the United Church of Canada. I read *The Post Evangelical* by Dave Tomlinson, a book that Mark had recommended, which spoke of Christianity in terms that were not absolute. Tomlinson wrote of paradigm shifts, of the absolute truth of evangelicalism versus the perception of truth of post-evangelicalism, of ambiguities and situational judgments. I was curious about some of the theories in Christianity at the time—that Jesus was gay, or that he wasn't really resurrected, or that God is a woman. I tried to discuss some of the issues about which I was reading, but I found only deaf ears and closed hearts. The wheels of separation had already started to turn, and I was leaving the station on a one-seat train.

I was so deeply embedded in the evangelical culture that when circumstances—my marriage and relocation to London, England—dictated my leaving, I felt bereft. Of friends, mentors, spiritual guidance. The move was not made easier by those I left behind. In effect, they dropped me. They had seen my relationship with Mark draw me away from all the answers they held, the truths they knew. All but two of the leadership team, the ones who had mentored me, declined to attend my wedding. My pastor told me that the Holy Spirit had told him that my fiancé wasn't the right man for me. I wondered why the Holy Spirit hadn't told me the same thing, if it was indeed true.

I guess in retrospect I felt like a project that would never be complete. There was always some flaw, some character trait, some relationship that needed work. The focus of the evangelical church is on the state of our inner soul, not the condition of the world around us. We didn't think outwardly about the world around us, except in terms of "bringing them to Christ." We strove to be alike, to be "perfect in Christ," but we never seemed to celebrate our differences. The emphasis was on "just as I am," but not really.

So when I married and moved to Britain, I felt isolated. My expectation that the relationships I had fostered and cultivated so carefully over a number of years at the community church would continue at some level was clearly misplaced. Short of a letter or two from others at the church, inadequately addressing my confessed isolation, I heard from no one. The clincher came about a year-and-a-half later, when we went back to the church while on holiday in Canada. Few people greeted us, and one friend who had been close couldn't even remember my husband's name. The leaders avoided eye contact and busied themselves with their tasks without saying hello. It all seems so silly now, but at the time it was very hurtful. I knew I would never go back, not there.

While living in London we attended a Church of England in our parish sporadically, eventually joining a cell group—very reluctantly on my part. Though I missed connecting with faith-rooted friends, I felt most comfortable keeping it all at arm's length. I came to understand that while the evangelical culture is introspective, so is Canadian culture. Living in Britain for three years exposed me to so much more of the wider world than all my years in Canada. On the whole, the average Briton seemed much more informed about environmental issues, social inequalities, global migration, and political wheeling and dealing. I met and worked with people of other faiths and cultures, who were every bit as sincere and faithful as I had been to my brand of Christianity. I met different kinds of people at work and in shops and pubs. I lived in areas where I, as an English-speaking Anglo-Saxon, was a minority. I became interested in social justice in the context of religion. I questioned how the Church was relating to the rest of the world. I found that traditional churches were doing more to address poverty, social issues, and injustice than the evangelical ones. When U2's Bono tells evangelicals there are 2,300 verses of Scripture about the poor, that it's the central message outside of personal redemption, it resonates with me. When only six percent of evangelicals want to do something about AIDS, what does that say about them? Why didn't I, as an evangelical, ever feel compelled to act on injustice and inequality? I'm still a long way from being an activist—I recognize that in myself—but these are questions I ask myself now. The evangelical church has a powerful voice, as the last American election revealed, but what is it using it for?

Although we attended the Church of England once in a while, Mark and I found other arenas in which to practise our faith. The main one was the Greenbelt Christian Arts Festival in Britain, which provided a forum for the Christian Aid campaign, Jubilee 2000, to lobby the G8 leaders to forgive the debts of the developing world. Greenbelt actively seeks debate on issues facing the Church—politics, environment, race, gender, and homosexuality, as well as theology—and offers no answers. Through music, visual and performance arts, workshops and discussions, and worship and meditation, Greenbelt offers a non-denominational, liberal challenge to traditional religion. The festival is a marker on my journey of faith.

By the time we moved back to Canada, in 2001, I had no interest in attending an evangelical church and neither did Mark. We turned instead to the United Church of Canada, which provided us with the openness, the tradition, and the equality we sought. The United Church is a leader, not a follower. It embraces debate, as well as other religions and cultures, and its policies speak out on divisive issues. The UCC accepts that sometimes there is a lot of grey on issues that evangelical churches would see as black-and-white.

In the downtown core of the city in which we finally settled we found our church next to a women's shelter and YWCA. We began attending in autumn 2002. Our church houses the homeless one night a week through the winter as part of the Out of the Cold program. It runs programs for refugees and supports the local multicultural centre. It shares its chapel with Romanian Orthodox congregations. Its ministers are a young woman and a former lay priest from the Catholic Church. Its hymns are inclusive and sometimes written in another languages. To ensure sustainability as congregations and buildings grow older, our church is involved in a partnership with three other downtown churches. These are all things I like about the church. My husband and I became members in 2005, and our son was baptized there in 2004 as an infant.

There are things I miss about the conservative branch of the evangelical church. Things like the strong sense of purpose and direction that drives a community church. I miss the certainty, though I would be uncomfortable now with feeling sure about what God wants and doesn't want, and even with the notion that God speaks so clearly, or speaks at all. Understandably, there is safety in being assured of the direction that one's life is taking, or that it is being directed at all by a greater power. I do believe things happen for a reason and that the desires of our hearts will also be realized. But I'm less likely now to credit God with manipulating events to make it happen.

I also miss the emotion-filled camp meetings of the Church of the Nazarene, which always had a passionate American preacher as guest speaker, and husband-and-wife singing groups, usually also from the States, along with altar calls and cries of "Amen" and "Bless you" rolling over the congregation during each sermon. I miss the comradeship, the moments of pure silliness, and the depths of emotion by which I measured the condition of my spirit.

I appreciate different things now. I miss the sense of all burdens being lifted when I enter the bare sanctuary of the Church of the Nazarene, but I also now feel a sense of awe when I enter the sanctuary in the grand hundred-year-old United Church I now attend. The organ pipes, the sleek balcony, the ornate stained-glass windows, the beautifully carved pulpit and communion table, the fresco painting above the pipes, the heavy leather-clad doors—I am grateful for the traditions and the worship these furnishings convey. Where informality once infused the practice of my faith, now formality, in the liturgy and architecture, brings me humbled into the presence of the Creator. My spiritual journey once emphasized freedom of the soul; now it emphasizes freedom for my fellow humans—freedom of belief, of lifestyle, of choice, freedom from injustice and inequality. Where it once was all about me, now it is all about the other, and that has changed me.

So it is in this environment that I feel I have found a home. I have made friends and have sat on several committees. I am planning a multicultural storytelling festival with the support of the church. My husband teaches church school. We feel accepted—just as we are, no more and no less.

Sitting with my in-laws in Northern Ireland on our last vacation—both my husband's parents attend the Church of the Nazarene and are recently "born again"—the topic of fundamentalism comes up. My husband will be preaching at their Church of the Nazarene next Sunday. The sermon is about doubt. It is a chore for him, now, to preach, something he once did willingly and often. He will carry through with the sermon, but he knows most people who hear him want to believe he is still the studious blue-eyed boy who went away to theological college with the thought of becoming a pastor. He knows he's not.

They will slap him on the back and say, "That was good," or "I enjoyed your sermon," and nothing more. There will be no discussion on the finer points of what he's said, no one picking up a thread and saying, "About what you said, what did you mean by ...?"

The words left unsaid are the same ones that will make him feel that there's hope in the wider world, in the twenty-first century, for the fundamentalist church. That the evangelical church will finally welcome questions and doubts without feeling that it always has an answer or that the answer is "Keep it simple, stupid" (K.I.S.S.) or "Let go and let God." Those responses deny legitimacy to generations of doubters, as far back as Thomas, whose doubt defined him in the end. Indeed, it was doubt that started the Protestant Reformation.

Somewhere along the line, doubt became seen as a spiritual weakness, not a sound point of view. It was silenced, and still is, by the strident voice of fundamentalist fervour. The new awakening in the United States of the evangelical church and the far right is perhaps the most obvious example. Reclaiming America for God—a specifically white, male, Christian God, in whom I also grew up believing. That God placed men above women. He wreaked havoc and bestowed peace on a whim. That God made guilt an inherent part of faith, all of which was coupled to a long list of do's and don'ts. That God placed the Christian religion as supreme over all others, which were then seen as targets to convert and evangelize. The "unsaved" were the people of other faiths, even those who went to the United Church or the Catholic Church. They were the backslidden, the sinners, the subjects.

I don't see the world that way anymore. The world is a much more inclusive place for me now. I no longer see things in black and white. I make and keep friends much more cautiously. God is an integral part of my life and the way I live it, but I don't feel that I have to be seen to be in the world, but separate from it. My faith is the skin I'm born in, not the clothes I wear. It is with me all the time, and like skin, it ages and wrinkles and stretches. And there is no shame in the way it changes over time.

DAVID L. RATTIGAN

Fantastic Voyage
Surviving Charismatic Fundamentalism

Everyone has stories to live by. To a Native American, the over-arching narrative of her life might be the story of how the white man invaded her country and subjugated her people. On the flipside of that coin, the patriotic Republican's narrative is the story of a glorious nation, a tale of how heroic men championed freedom and built a country founded on God. These are stories that underpin every-thing we do and think; they are lenses through which we view and interpret the world.

For more than ten years I was part of a particular story, and it was one that shaped my entire way of relating to the world. It was the story of fundamentalist Christianity, and it went something like this: God created the world; man was created good; Adam and Eve sinned; man was cor-rupted, and came under God's condemnation, specifically the judgment of eternal punishment; God sent Jesus to take the punishment for us; if we become Christians, we will go to Heaven and be saved from Hell. It was a story about good versus evil, God versus Satan, and the world was the battleground between the two. When you become a fundamen-talist Christian, typically by being "born again," you become a part of that story. A distant and alien story about God and a group of people thou-sands of years ago becomes the story of how you yourself, two millen-nia after the Crucifixion, crossed over onto the right path and became destined for heaven.

You will join a community where the big story will be told over and over again, explicitly or implicitly, in the songs you sing, the sermons you hear, the conversations you have, the language you use, and the rituals in which you participate. Present-day fundamentalists may well see themselves as part of a story about how society is getting worse and worse as standards decline and the ungodly have their wicked way, a story about how people have overcome by resisting this decline, and how you, too, can overcome. Within the big story are smaller stories, whether hypothetical or attached to actual events, about how accepting this, that, or the other is the beginning of the slippery slope into heresy and apostasy.

As in all good stories, there are heroes and villains. In the Christian fundamentalist story, the world is divided up unambiguously into Believers and Unbelievers, the Saved and the Unsaved. The Believers are faithful, Bible-believing, valiant defenders of eternal truth, heavenbound. Unbelievers are godless, blinded, hellbound. There are the Liberals, pretend Christians, attackers of the truth, rebellious against God, unbelievers masquerading as true believers. Everyone falls into one category or another. Fundamentalism presents a very black-and-white world. And if all this looks like a caricature of fundamentalism, perhaps that's because the fundamentalist worldview is a caricature of the world itself?

My own induction into the story was through my entrance into the heady world of Charismatic Christianity. I had been brought up Christian, first in the United Church of Canada and then in the Methodist Church when our family moved to Britain. Mom's brand of Christianity had always been fairly mainstream, but that had changed noticeably by the time I was ten. She had visited a well-known Charismatic Anglican church in York and had returned believing herself to have become a truly born-again Christian. The implication was that her past faith had been at best inadequate, at worst no faith at all. This was the beginning of a lot of tension with the other people at our church, whom Mom now saw as less spiritual, perhaps even non-Christian. It was an attitude I imbibed, for by now I, too, had been born again and was committed to an evangelical, Bible-believing faith, even at such a young age.

At the age of fourteen, I was rapidly growing dissatisfied with the Christianity my Methodist church represented. Few shared my evangelistic zeal and fundamentalist view of the Bible, and I was ripe to move on to a more "spiritual" type of Christianity. The opportunity came one day when I talked to the local Pentecostal pastor. Rather ashamed to admit I attended the Methodists, I confessed to the pastor it was a "dead church," knowing that such an epithet was guaranteed to arouse immediate sympathy, and confided that I probably ought to leave to seek better pastures. He was quick to challenge me: "Why don't you, then?" And so soon afterwards I attended my first service at the Pentecostal fellowship that was to become my church home for the rest of my teenage years. I discovered there a warmth and vibrancy in worship that I had never experienced before.

I was immediately thrust into a new realm of teachings and experience. At my new church God appeared to be taken a lot more seriously, as were Satan and his demons. I had already been introduced to the latter through the pastor's regular visits to my school, all done to warn students of the dangers of occultism and rock 'n' roll. The preaching seemed relevant—indeed, much of it I had never heard before, though it proved indispensable in guiding the course of my Christian walk. The worship was jubilant and stimulating, and the congregation seemed willing to be a part of each other's lives seven days a week, not just on Sunday evenings.

It was during my first year there that I learned the basics of what it was to be Christian and Pentecostal. I learned to use the right terminology to talk about spiritual things, and I quickly began to filter all my experiences through the lens of my newfound Charismatic world view. Midway through that first year the Gospel came alive to me for the first time: at the Bible camp I had been dragooned into attending, I had an intense emotional experience that left me convinced about the Lordship of Jesus and the truth of his death and resurrection. It was a seminal point in my journey, a point when I felt clearly that God was calling me to be a full-time minister. I had other plans—to be a film director, in fact, an ambition I had cherished for years—but I needed no coercion. From that time on all I wanted to do was serve God.

I returned home "on fire," to use the accepted Charismatic term. I busied myself in all kinds of church activities and evangelistic endeavours. "Witnessing" to my classmates became a priority. For a while, science class became no more than an opportunity to open my Bible and have a study right there with my friends. They would ask questions, usually on the more complex and intriguing points of the "End Times," and I would answer as best I could with recourse to Scripture. It was my final year in high school, and I was determined to make the most of it, convinced it was my duty to exploit every opportunity to make the maximum impact for Jesus.

The year 1994 was a crucial one for Charismatics and evangelicals worldwide. That was the year the "Toronto Blessing" emerged, a global revival characterized by bizarre manifestations believed to come from the Holy Spirit. I remember clearly the morning we first heard about the phenomenon. One Sunday in spring that year, it was coming to the close of our morning service. The pastor drew our attention to a newspaper article he had read about a church in Loughborough, England, where at the conclusion of a Sunday meeting an unprecedented wave of supernatural activity had apparently occurred on a scale comparable to the Day of Pentecost. Congregants had been overcome with the power of the Holy Spirit, some falling prostrate to the ground, others laughing and crying uncontrollably. When the service eventually ended, it was some hours past its usual finishing time.

Over the next few weeks we heard more reports of the Blessing breaking out in churches around the world. Hotspots of the current revival began to spring up in churches known for their abundance of peculiar manifestations and late-night meetings, often on most nights of the week. People everywhere were advocating the revival's life-changing effects: speakers and preachers were travelling from church to church to impart the blessing. "Ministry" teams from were sent out from revived churches to pass on the Blessing to others. Pastors and prophets from the Toronto Airport Vineyard Church, where the Blessing had first erupted, were travelling worldwide to explain and spread the revival, connecting it with various prophecies and predictions, some of which were said to go back several decades. By the end of that year the Toronto Blessing—whether for or against—had become a defining issue for evangelicals. Some could not understand how anyone could reject what was so clearly a "movement of God," bringing new spiritual life to dry believers; others thought the bizarre behaviours were just another manifestation of Charismatic lunacy; some labelled the whole phenomenon psychological manipulation, if not outright demonic deception.

Our small church was no exception to the generally warm acceptance of the Blessing among Charismatics. We had visiting preachers and prophets from all over Britain and beyond, including the minister whose church we had first read about in a newspaper article. His sermon was replete with anecdotes about the strange but fruitful happenings in Loughborough, and he offered something of a primer on what we should expect when the Holy Spirit arrived. It was merely a preamble to what we were all eagerly anticipating: the outpouring of the Spirit itself. In general, the people were not disappointed. The preacher personally laid hands on most of the congregation, and they duly fell to the ground, as we had hoped. But when he reached me, I simply did not respond as I was expected to. He pleaded earnestly with God to touch me, but when it became clear nothing was going to happen, he left me with an anecdote about a man who mined for days before he found the treasure he was looking for. In part it was an apologetic defence designed to assure me that something would happen in the end, even if nothing dramatic seemed to be happening there and then. I couldn't escape the uneasy feeling that the preacher himself was rather embarrassed, though he went to great lengths to assure me otherwise.

Nevertheless, I was soon to enter the revival full swing. That summer we arranged a bus trip to a church in Leicester, one of the hotspots of the Blessing. We arrived a few minutes late, though a friend informed me what I had missed: the pastor had announced he would hand a Bible over to another man on the platform, and that on receiving the Bible the other man would fall to the ground under the power of the Spirit. It had happened as he predicted. We were there just in time for the music, which consisted of several slow, intimate choruses. Those who wanted to be blessed were asked to walk to the front of the sanctuary to receive prayer. I did not want to refuse, and I stood at the front and watched as one by one the congregation succumbed to a seemingly irresistible power. I wondered how I would explain myself when I did not succumb in the same way, but I need not have fretted. The leader's hand had barely touched my forehead when my legs felt as if they had been kicked out from under me, and there I was lying on the carpet in a state of euphoria. I finally knew what it was to be "slain in the Spirit." I swore to myself I never intended to fall, but it was as if my body had lost all strength without my consent.

The day's schedule ran from about ten in the morning till four in the afternoon. There was little speaking or preaching, but much singing and repeated "altar calls" where people were urged to come to the front to receive "ministry." I was prayed over four or five times, and each time I did "carpet time," as it became jocularly known. On one occasion the leader simply blew on my forehead with the words, "Receive it," an echo of Jesus' words in the upper room (John 20:22)—a familiar technique with healing evangelists such as Benny Hinn.

The day provided a much-needed boost to my now waning spiritual life. My zeal and passion were restored, and I had a new experience of

God that I longed to repeat. And it certainly was, time and again over the next several years. Any opportunity I had to receive "more" (a watchword of the movement, often repeated like a mantra over people during prayer) was welcomed. Sometimes I would fall backwards, sometimes forwards, sometimes straight down; sometimes I would have to have someone there to catch me, occasionally not; sometimes it happened as the result of receiving prayer and the laying on of hands, sometimes before they even got to me or during ordinary worship. A pattern began to emerge: I would get blessed, run off on a path of spiritual euphoria, then sooner or later begin to lose the momentum, at which point I would feel I was becoming spiritually stagnant, backsliding even. But in time I would have another experience and be set in motion again. The "dry" times were periods of guilt when I was convinced I was at fault. The refillings were occasions to thank the Lord and promise not to let the fire grow cold this time. It always did eventually, leaving me once again wallowing in feelings of guilt and inadequacy.

Throughout that year our church continued to receive visits from leaders and speakers associated with the Blessing. On one occasion a "prophet" came and delivered words of prediction to various members of the church (some of which later appeared to be stunningly accurate), before going on to dispense the Blessing. I will never forget the sight of one of the elders reeling around supposedly "drunk in the Spirit." Clinging to a pillar to support himself, and giggling away childishly, he was watched by an amused and entertained congregation. The same prophet later tried to provoke the elder's daughter to the same reaction, even forcibly pushing her down in an attempt to make her either stagger or drop, I am not sure which. Her stifled laughter only reflected an obvious embarrassment, which I shared. I never expressed these reservations, however, and continued to pursue more of these experiences. A large Pentecostal church in the town next to us had enthusiastically greeted the Blessing and had become something of a hive of Charismatic activity. It hosted a number of conferences featuring many of the prominent names in the revival, such as Marc Dupont (the Toronto church's resident prophet at the time, who laid claim to having predicted this strange outpouring) and R.T. Kendall, one of the Blessing's most vigorous advocates on the British side of the Atlantic. I attended as many of these conferences and seminars as I could, hungry for God, desperate to keep the spiritual momentum alive.

The format of most of these gatherings was predictable but exciting: A session of testimony, preaching, and prophecy would be followed by ministry. Chairs would be cleared from the front of the auditorium, and people would be invited to step forward to receive prayer. As the band led people in a time of worship (in popular Charismatic parlance, "praise" is fast and lively, whereas "worship" is slow and intimate), the ministry team would make their way around the crowd, usually two to a person. The laying on of hands would swiftly be followed by the person falling to the floor, "slain in the Spirit," or being overcome with hysterical laughter, tears, or a state of spiritual intoxication. Certain catchphrases became part of the routine: "Touch her, Lord, from the top of her head to the tips of her toes," was one such stock phrase; "More, Lord, more," was another.

In my case, such "slayings" were becoming less frequent, and this absence of dramatic phenomena was becoming an anxiety for me. Often someone would pray for five minutes or so before subtly gesturing for another member to come and join. The clear implication, though always unspoken, was "I need help here: This one's not budging!" When it became evident that nothing was happening, I would be entreated: "Don't resist ... Don't resist ... Just let it come." This, of course, only ever had the effect of making me even more embarrassed and anxious for something to happen. Soon would come the assurances not to worry if there were no visible manifestations, but the ever lengthening and increasingly intense petitions for the Holy Spirit to do something seemed to contradict the notion that "the manifestations aren't what's important." A change of technique was often called for on the part of the person doing the praying. The *pray-er*, after a prolonged silence, would suddenly bellow out, "Touch!" (another buzzword), which would naturally tend to arouse some startled reaction! Or the hands would switch from the top of the head to the back or the side, occasionally the belly (the source of the anticipated laughter) or the forehead, which had the effect of causing one to lose one's balance, especially if the eyes were shut. Eventually, if all else failed, I would receive the customary promise that the inner work was the really important thing, regardless of any impressive outward signs. Such a blithe assurance seemed at odds with the frantic attempts to make something significant happen, and I would return to my seat trying unconvincingly to talk myself into believing the Spirit was at work in me despite how things looked on the outside. I would try to be happy for everyone else being blessed, but it was a disappointment to be constantly on the fringes.

> "Just let it flow. Don't think about what you're saying. Just let it come. Don't resist. Ohhh! Soh-rah-bah-bah-kee-ray!"
>
> His hands placed firmly on my head, the pastor laughed joyously as he continued in his prayer-language: "Ohhh! Soh-rah-bah-bah-kee-ray!"

It was not the first time I had received this special treatment in order to receive the much coveted "gift of tongues." There was a lot of pressure for folk in my church to speak in tongues, and there was something defective about you if it wasn't an ordinary part of your life. I lost count of how many times the pastor would lay his hands on me during the evening service, babble away in his tongue—always the same "Soh-rah-bah-bah-kee-ray!"—and urge me not to resist but simply to "let it come out." I would lay awake on my bed at night trying earnestly to speak in tongues, but every time I was never able to bring myself to do it. It felt phony, and the pastor's "Soh-rah-bah-bah-kee-ray" felt every bit as fake. I eventually did start to speak in tongues, and it was a load off my mind: I was normal now, having passed one of the main hurdles to being a properly Spirit-filled Christian.

It was at Bible College where I began to question the Charismatic world I had taken for granted. Bible College was a melting pot for every brand of Charismatic: There were "classical" Pentecostals for whom the gift of tongues was paramount; there were "health and wealth" proponents who followed and preached that faith in God was the route to financial prosperity; there were would-be evangelists sold on the latest wave of blessing. By now the Blessing had ceased to be identified with Toronto and was spawning a new kind of Charismatic ecumenism in which all kinds of teachings—including the most extreme prosperity teachings—were gradually filtering their way into the mainstream Charismatic Movement.

That first year of Bible College was a challenging time for me, for many of the doctrines I was starting to call into serious question were rapidly increasing in popularity in the wake of Toronto. In particular, I had grave reservations about the triumphalistic nature of most Charismatics' world view of the Christian life and the End Times. The notion that we were to expect a "Last Days" revival was rarely challenged, and the events of the previous few years only seemed to have confirmed the

Spirit was about to launch a massive revival without precedent in history. This expectation was becoming increasingly bound up with more detailed predictions of a Christian takeover of the world. It was a combination of Dominion theology, which claimed that God's rule on earth would come through the church prior to Christ's return, and the Faith teaching that the world's wealth would be transferred into the hands of the righteous in the last days.

My second year in college was a watershed. During that year I became fatally disillusioned with Charismatic Christianity and the seeds were sown for my eventual decision to give up altogether calling myself a Charismatic. A fellow student had graduated the previous year and had appointed me his successor in leading and organizing the monthly student renewal meetings. He was sold on the new wave of the Charismatic Movement, having come straight to college from Kensington Temple, a London megachurch at the forefront of the current renewal. The meetings he began and organized followed the routine Charismatic format: a time of worship, preaching from a guest speaker, and finally a time of "ministry." Some of the gatherings from the past year had stuck in my memory. On one occasion a travelling evangelist from Finland, already known to both of us, came and offered the students a severe reprimand for the lack of signs and wonders in our daily lives and ministries. The thrust of his message was that Christians ought to see miracles and healings every day, and the blame was placed squarely on our shoulders if they simply weren't materializing. There followed the usual pattern of people crumpling to the floor, shouting and wailing, crying and laughing. A few students left, later confessing they had found it all an embarrassing spectacle, a scene of utter chaos.

I had a lot to live up to when I took on the sole responsibility of coordinating the meetings. For me, a renewal meeting was precisely that— an opportunity for renewal. I had little interest in the kinds of manifestations that had previously characterized the meetings. This put me at odds, however, with some other members of the leadership team. Though it was never directly stated, the implicit assumption was that we should always aim for an outpouring of the Spirit along the accustomed lines. I was burdened by the expectation placed on me. I would, nevertheless (and to put it rather crudely), do my best to ensure that conditions were ripe for an intense outburst of emotion, a visible, tangible outbreak of signs and wonders, and all the anticipated Charismatic phenomena. Regardless of claims to the contrary, I was by now convinced that much, perhaps most, of what we had seen over the past few years was indeed the result of precisely this kind of attempt on the part of leaders to generate a hyped-up atmosphere conducive to such outbreaks. I had no desire to follow suit.

Charismatic worship was beginning to grate against me. I was increasingly aware that many of the most popular worship songs were manufactured to create feelings for their own sake. It wasn't far removed from the kind of emotional and psychological manipulation that was the standard in Charismatic worship. Worship leaders, of which I was one, knew just the right harmonies to provoke an emotional response, when to crescendo and decrescendo to create a sensational effect, and how to stir the congregation into a euphoric state accompanied by tongues, shouting, and "spontaneous" praise. Post-Toronto Charismatic worship was noticeably rowdier!

The self-centred legalism of Charismatic worship—the entire Charismatic world view, in fact—was beginning to wear me down. We sang, "These are the days of Elijah," but it expressed a sentiment that was part and parcel of a world view I was beginning to reject, a story bound up in the expectation that the world was on the verge of a mighty spiritual revival. "All the weaknesses I see in me will be stripped away," we would sing, but I always knew that perhaps some of those weaknesses might never be removed. The world I was singing and talking about was far from reality. There was little room for weakness and suffering, much less honesty and acknowledgment of our humanity. Our quasi-mystical songs exhorted us to climb to higher heights and plumb deeper depths, but I was starting seriously to wonder whether I wanted to keep carrying the relentless burden always to be trying to progress toward God, to improve spiritually—to become somehow *more acceptable* to God.

The seal on my departure from the Charismatic life of the college was a visit from an American "prophetess." She had visited a number of churches and conferences within our denomination, and I had heard impressive testimonies about her. She was said to pick people out of the audience at random and prophesy about them on the spot, relaying many fantastic and apparently accurate details about them and making predictions about their future ministry. When she was booked to come and host a conference for the students, she was greeted rapturously.

I was so disillusioned with college life that I did not attend her first meeting, an evening workshop designed to coach students in how to prophesy. When it was over, however, my roommate returned to the apartment feeling elated. "Prophesying is so easy, you know," he told me. "I think I could go up to anyone I didn't know on a bus and just start prophesying to them." Naturally, I was a little taken aback by such a bold declaration from a student who had never before made such claims. He gave me an account of how that evening's session had gone. The prophetess announced they would be dividing into groups of, say, five people. Four of them would surround the remaining person in a circle, with the person in the middle to be prophesied over. Three of the four would speak out whatever images or pictures came into their head, no matter how strange. The last remaining person would put all the pictures together and deliver an interpretation for the person in the middle. The prophetess pre-empted the question of how the participants could be certain it was really God speaking by referring to Matthew 7:11: "Which of you, if his son asks him for bread, will give him a stone?… How much more will your Father in Heaven give good gifts to those who ask him!" Thus, if they prayed and asked God for a prophecy, they were guaranteed that whatever they received had its source in God. This way of doing "prophecy" was not a new concept to me. A few years earlier I had waited in line by a platform at Bible camp ready to take the microphone and announce to an audience of five hundred young people what I had seen when I closed my eyes (in reality the back of my eyelids, a very hazy mixture of light and shadow I decided looked like a ribcage!). Back then, I had been given exactly the same advice: No matter how silly it sounds, say it. Luckily the meeting had ended before it came to my turn.

I was incensed that my friend had been duped into taking his own imagination for the voice of God, and that as a result of this seminar he had the confidence to want to go out immediately and dupe the rest of the unsuspecting world. I could not think of a better way of leading people into self-deception than encouraging them to elevate their own imaginations to the level of God. I decided to check out the prophetess for myself the next morning, when she was scheduled to speak at chapel. She gave a few prophetic words about various countries of the world and then related a series of visions and revelations she and her daughter had had on the subject of the wealth of the wicked. Just as I had heard John Avanzini, Creflo Dollar, and Benny Hinn tell me a few years earlier during my passing infatuation with the health-and-wealth movement, this lady told us that the world's wealth was ready to be passed into the hands of believers. Very soon, she predicted, all the businesses, financial institutions, and governments would be dominated by Christians. Every bank manager would be a born-again believer. The biggest companies would be owned and controlled by Christians. In other words, the world economy would be in the hands of the Church. At one time this notion was merely a "teaching" that could be refuted by a quick examination of the Scriptures being cited in its support. Now it was "End Times prophecy," and God's prophets all over the world were apparently getting the same message.

It was more than I could stomach. Mainly on the basis of her accurate "words of knowledge," most of the students and faculty were swept up in enthusiasm for the prophetess. Everyone was talking about it. She was booked for further seminars and meetings, and plans were being made for her to return the following year to teach an entire module on prophecy. My time in the Charismatic movement was up. Over time I had become convinced that most of the "supernatural" events I had witnessed and participated in—prophecies, being slain in the Spirit—were more the result of human manipulation than of genuine spiritual power.

At the end of that final college year I moved back to my native Canada and became associate pastor of a small-town Pentecostal church in the B.C. Interior. At that point I was a moderate evangelical in a fairly fundamentalist environment. The icing had fallen off the Charismatic cake, and remaining in a Charismatic world was a source of intense frustration and loneliness for me. After all, most of the congregation was living in a completely different story to mine. It was not a simple disagreement on a few minor points; the structure of my world was entirely different from theirs. I was now an alien in their world.

My discomfort reached its peak when a few others and I were ministering to a young man who, though professing faith, was constantly battling with drugs and alcohol. The senior pastor's wife had concluded that the answer was to meet daily in order to lay hands on the young man and pray for his deliverance from demons. The search was on for "generational spirits," supposedly demons passed on from one generation to the next. Some of these were (unconvincingly) identified, and the appropriate prayers and commands were offered. Then it was decided that the young man needed to speak in tongues, so he was surrounded by three of us, one of whom would pray in tongues herself. For about ten straight minutes she encouraged the obviously embarrassed young man to open his mouth and speak in tongues. He was not the only embarrassed one.

By now, my doubts were extending beyond the Charismatic world. They were about conservative Christianity as a whole, a religion oriented toward the belief that the Bible was the inerrant Word of God. I was questioning the entire story. A few years earlier I had been part of a spectacular drama *cum* outreach called "Heaven's Gates, Hell's Flames" in which I had warned spectators to accept Christ or burn in Hell. Now I doubted the justice of such a God. I had condemned others for not submitting to supposedly biblical morality, yet it was becoming clear to me that this kind of religion was a smokescreen for prejudice, intolerance, and hatred. Against what Jesus had said, the fundamentalist religion I had bought into seemed always to be "shutting the Kingdom of God in people's faces." Within the narrow confines of the Charismatic world, it was those who didn't speak in tongues or who "resisted" the Holy Spirit who were excluded, whether deliberately or not. In the wider fundamentalist world the outsiders who didn't meet the standards were the gays, the cohabiters, the drinkers, the smokers. I was rapidly becoming one of the excluded myself by moving outside the bounds of what was considered acceptable—Bible-believing, Spirit-filled, conservative.

I left that church, eventually leaving British Columbia to return to England. Though I immediately joined a non-fundamentalist Anglican church, I had not entirely left fundamentalism behind in my mind. Leaving fundamentalism is a lengthy process full of pain and frustration. The fundamentalist world was oriented around a particular story, and within that story were smaller stories, and those old stories died hard. In *Blankets*, Craig Thompson recounts convincingly his adolescent departure from the strictures of his fundamentalist upbringing. Paraphrasing Plato, he writes:

> [Since] childhood, humans have been prisoners ... bound at their neck and feet, facing a wall, and unable to turn their heads. Behind them is a walled path, traversed by people carrying statues of animals and humans ... and beyond that is a fire illuminating the cave. From the prisoners' perspective, all that can be seen are the shadows of these statues projected upon the wall by the fire; sort of like a shadow puppet show, only the prisoners aren't aware that what they see are shadows or puppets ... [They] think they're studying reality. Now if a prisoner was released from his binds, allowed to turn about and examine his surroundings; it'd be a shock to his entire system. In fact, he'd probably believe that what he'd previously known was the truth, and that this was a sort of heresy ... What an even greater shock it would be to bring the prisoner out of the cave and into the sunlight. The initial effect would be blinding ... The final step would be the ability to study the sky in the day ... to look directly into the light of the sun.

I cannot think of a better way of expressing the journey out of fundamentalism and why it hurts so much. It very much comes down to this:

> In fact, he'd probably believe that what he'd previously known was the truth, and that this was a sort of heresy.

We cannot simply trade in the old story for a new one in one quick, tidy exchange. Like the child told all his life he was useless, shaking off the nagging guilt that he is useless is a process lasting far longer than the one moment at which he realizes he was lied to by an abusive parent. The old stories are so deeply ingrained, so much a part of our version of reality for so long, that thinking in terms of those stories is a habit of mind we still have to shake off. It was our reality for so long that thinking outside its conventions is not something we can all of a sudden just decide to do. It's a process.

When you pick up the Bible and question whether such-and-such is really true, there's that story going round and round in the back of your mind. The story is called "The Christian Who Let Doubts Creep in One Day and Began Sliding down the Slippery Slope of Heresy." When you walk into a store, pick up a book that claims something is amiss with fundamentalism, and consider that there might actually be some truth in its pages, you're haunted by the story called "The Once-Faithful Believer Who Listened to the Devil and Lost Her Salvation." When you start to question traditional "morality," the story of "The Christian Who Bought into the Lie of Liberalism" is a weight in the pit of your stomach. Is it any wonder the pilgrimage out of fundamentalism is full of pain and heartache and fear and hurt and shame and guilt?

Today I inhabit a different story. It is a story that often changes as new things and experiences come to light. It is a story that is not afraid to engage with those whose stories are different from mine. My world now has room for ambiguity, doubt, and uncertainty without fear. I am a liberal Anglican, and after three years outside fundamentalist circles I have found the courage to be an openly and unashamedly gay man.

MARGARET STEEL FARRELL

My Mother, My Church

 When Pope Benedict XVI was elected the 265th pope in April 2005, I was talking about the announcement to a Catholic friend of mine. She said, "So we have a new pope." I said, "No, *you* have a new pope."

A feeling raced through me—as if I was stepping out. I had never before said anything like that out loud, which so clearly divided me from my former Catholic self. I felt like I was staking my claim: "Hello, my name is Margaret and I'm an ex-Catholic."

I felt a little scared, too, like I was going to be struck down and rejected. Or worse—perhaps the next day it would be revealed once and for all that Catholicism really *was* "the one true faith" but now it would be too late for me because I had actually, finally denounced it out loud ("No take-backs!"). But it also felt deliciously affirming. I had finally declared who I was and I was standing by it. I wondered a little if this was the religious equivalent of what it felt like to finally "come out of the closet." After all, in some ways, I was a closet ex-Catholic.

Twenty-seven years earlier, when John Paul II had been elected pope, I was thirteen years old, attending a Catholic school. He *was* my pope. So what had happened in the course of those years? What had changed? What had caused the shift?

There is no easy answer. There was no dramatic event, no sudden inappropriate situation that scarred me and left me hating the Church or priests. It's horrible that such things happen to people. But that is not my story. Leaving the Catholic Church for me was more the result of an innate ultimatum that led to a slow erosion of allegiance. Simply because of *how* I was raised in the faith, leaving it became an inevitable necessity.

Growing up Catholic was a very strict experience in my family. There were many rules to follow and none were to be questioned. In many cases it was difficult to distinguish between the rules of the house and the rules of the Church: living made them one and the same. For example, we were not allowed to talk back to our parents. This was a family rule. But it was also related to one of the Ten Commandments, to "honour your father and mother." So if we broke that rule (yeah, right!), we had broken not just a family rule but a commandment. This meant we had sinned big time. It was not tolerated.

I am currently working with my mother's eighty-four-year-old sister to compile her memoirs of growing up in the 1930s. In many ways her stories of life at that time are similar to how I was raised. For her, it was always difficult to distinguish between the home, the school, and the Church—they were so closely tied in how they governed one's behaviour and thinking. Children did not question the authority of their parents, teachers, or priests. You did what they dictated without question. Strict obedience was demanded. In turn, my mother raised her own children that way, with the same iron will and exacting standards. Though I was born in 1965, I was raised with the same values and rules that my mother and her sisters were raised with a generation earlier.

For me, the Church is inextricably tied to my mother and my mother to the Church. They are so connected in my experience that I cannot talk about one without the other. Attending mass and following the rules and the teachings of the Church was my mother's life. She devoted herself to God and worshiped Him by following the dictates of the Roman Catholic Church. It guided all her decisions. The Church dictated that her husband was the head of the family and she lived by that. She was bound to welcome all children that came out of the marriage and so gave birth to eighteen. She gave her life to her husband and her children, in accordance with the Church's teachings.

My mother was the spiritual and religious cornerstone of our family and organized our lives around her beliefs. We were raised to see the Church through her eyes and to believe in it the way she did. As a result, my relationship with the Church, at least while I was a child, was modelled on my mother's. I was obedient, I did not question authority, and I believed the Church was infallible. It's what was expected of me.

My mother was a loving woman who taught her children to work hard, to think of others first, and to appreciate the little things in life. A woman of simple means, she took her responsibility as a religious role model seriously, to the point of individual alienation and annihilation, which eventually became the undoing with nearly all my siblings.

My mother tolerated absolutely no fooling around in church. We were to sit still, our hands in our laps, our heads facing forward and our mouths shut. Dad was an usher so we always sat alone with Mom, in a pew five to seven rows from the front, on the left-hand side of the church. Sitting in the back was out of the question because we needed to be close enough to pay attention to the mass. And sitting any closer to the front would have been showy, not humble. Our pew selection was strategic—close but not too close, and left of centre.

My sister and I often argued while we were growing up. Sometimes we'd be in the middle of a dispute when it was time to go to church so we'd argue quietly in the car on the way there. If the issue was unresolved by the time we got to church, we would continue it through stares, dirty looks, elbow nudges, and pushing with our arms and legs. We weren't allowed to speak in church except to pray and sing.

If our mother caught wind of what was going on, she would give us a look that threatened certain death if we didn't cease and desist. We'd stop, for a while. Then the pushing and shoving would start up again and she would reach over and cover the nearest offending child's hand and whisper "Stop it!" as fiercely as she could without letting anyone else around us hear. That was usually enough to make us stop. We knew we did not want to get in trouble for acting up in church. If we did that, Mom would tell Dad and then we'd *really* get in trouble at home.

One day my sister and I pushed it too far. My mother told us to stop a couple of times but to no avail. We were entrenched in our disagreement, and against our better judgment neither of us would relent. We thought we were doing it subtly but our mother wasn't fooled. When the mass ended, we went to the back of the church to meet Dad, as usual. He was talking with some of his buddies when my mother announced that she was walking home and left. We froze with terror. Our mother had never done this before—it mattered deeply to her how we, as a family, looked in public. To make such a display of emotion was unprecedented. We knew we were dead.

When Dad eventually came over, he asked where Mom was. We told him she was walking home, and he was understandably flabbergasted.

But he knew his wife and that for her to do that we must have really made her angry. "Get in the car!" he barked, and we set off down the road to find her.

Mother was a quick, purposeful walker: my whole childhood I was warned not to "dilly-dally" or "dawdle" but to walk quickly when I had somewhere to go. When we finally caught up with her she had walked more than half the mile-long journey home. Dad tried to call her into the car but she refused and told him to go on. After a couple of attempts, she gave him "the look" and he heeded her wishes, not without a few choice words for us. When she eventually got home and told Dad who the culprits were, my sister and I received my father's wrath. I don't remember what our punishment was, but I do remember this—we *never* fought in church again.

Church meant so much to our mother. I think it was likely her sanctuary, her one hour per week of peace and reconnection with what she held dear to her heart. If she had her way, she would have attended mass daily. My aunt, her sister, tells me she did just that as a young war bride and mother in Wales during the Second World War. She eventually returned to this ritual once we were all grown and out of the house, some forty years later.

Now, as a busy working mother myself, I can understand why it upset her so much that we disrupted that precious time with our self-involved bickering. I will never forget her walking home that day. The image in my mind makes me smile in spite of myself. She was *so* angry with us.

Prayer was integral to our daily lives. We prayed to bless each meal, we prayed to ask God to watch over us while we slept, we even prayed to keep ourselves from arguing with one another. After supper each night, the youngest children were put to bed by the oldest while the middle crew did the dishes. Dishwashing wasn't a favourite chore as there were so many of us. Because we washed them by hand, it often took the better part of an hour. Often it was later in the evening and we would be edgy because we still had homework to complete before going to bed, so bickering was not uncommon. If our mother heard us arguing in the kitchen, she would make us say Hail Marys out loud while we washed and dried. She said that if we were going to be using our voices, then she could think of a better way to use them—better to be praying than arguing. Of course, the argument continued on silently with nasty looks and small pushes and shoves.

Every now and again, our mother would suggest we say a family rosary after supper. Well, you never saw so many people offer to do the dishes as they did on that night! The kids washing and drying still had to pray out loud from the kitchen (inevitably making silly faces to one another while they recited the prayers), but they didn't have to kneel on the hardwood floor in the living room for half an hour. The rest of us, from the youngest through to the teenagers, knelt on the floor with our mother. Father sat on a couch beside us.

It was a mysterious time, saying the rosary as a family. It took some time before I knew all the prayers. I remember, when I was very young, thinking how much there was to know and noting how quickly everyone spoke. One person would "lead" by saying the first half of each of the prayers, then the family would reply in unison with the second half. There was a lyrical rhythm about it that I liked. But it was also very sombre, and there was a protocol to it. You didn't dare sit back on your heels. You kneeled straight up with your head bowed, not making eye contact with the others, keen not to miss your cues. And when it was done, I would have the strange feeling that somehow we had accomplished something. It felt good.

So many aspects of my life were dictated by the edicts of the Catholic Church—my home life, my relationships, my schooling. I was raised to believe that the Church was infallible and that you were to follow all of its rules. You didn't pick and choose which ones you wanted to follow and which ones you didn't. You either accepted them all or you accepted none. You obeyed without question or you were not a good Catholic. And if you were not a good Catholic, you would go to Hell. So there was no real choice. You were baptized Catholic as a baby and you followed the rules or you were going to Hell. It was pretty straightforward.

A couple of my siblings were not married in the Catholic Church so my parents did not attend their weddings. My understanding is that my parents spoke to their priest beforehand about the situation and that he told them they could not attend. They *did* attend the weddings of those who married non-Catholics as long as they received the proper instruction and blessing from our priest. And the wedding had to be in a Catholic church accompanied by a mass. I think the non-Catholic spouse also had to agree that any children born into the marriage would be raised Catholic.

Years later, when I got married, Mother did attend my wedding even though it was not a Catholic service (Father had died three years earlier).

She had checked with her priest and he had told her it would be okay. I really don't know what had changed except that it was a different priest. That a factor so minor could make such an impact on a family baffles me to this day.

I was taught that if I did not follow the rules of the Church, I was sinning. And if I sinned, I needed to be contrite and confess my sins to a priest. My mother insisted that confession was not to be taken lightly. I couldn't knowingly sin and then go to confession and expect it all to be okay—it didn't work that way. I was to try to avoid sinning, but if I failed I could confess and I would be forgiven if I was truly repentant. But I never quite knew my status with God because I never knew if I was repentant enough for Him. So I never knew if I was forgiven and had a chance of going to Heaven or not. I always had this fear that when I died, I'd get to Heaven and God would say, "Ah-ha! Remember that time you did such and such! Well, you thought you were forgiven but you weren't! You're going to Hell!" I've never really quite resolved that one.

Mother had no tolerance for people who could not accept all the teachings and practices of the Church. She said you accepted it all or nothing. So I accepted it all. As a young child, my mother's strong beliefs were a beacon for me. They're what guided my actions and words. As an adolescent, though, I began to feel that approval was tied to my relationship with the Church. The better my relationship, the more approval I received. Of course, the opposite was true. This was a struggle for me because every girl wants approval from her mother. This was especially true in my case, because approval played a powerful role in our relationship. At the same time, I began to resent being judged according to my mother's strict and narrow belief system. I still enjoyed going to church as a teenager, but I wanted to like it simply because I liked it, not because of how it would please her.

When I stopped attending mass at twenty, I knew my mother would be disappointed and perhaps even think less of me. I never asked what she thought about it. Perhaps she only feared for me. After all, I was no longer following the rules of the Church. Hell was on the horizon. If this is what a mother firmly believes, how it must grieve her heart to think that some of her children will meet that final destination. I only hope she expressed this to a compassionate priest who comforted her with hope for her children's souls, however he might express it.

I miss a couple of the priests of my youth, Father Murray and Father Jim, because they were gifted speakers and thinkers. I was very fortunate to have been part of St. Aloysius parish in those years. Each gave wonderful sermons. I loved listening to them talk about the Scripture they had just read to us and how they interpreted it and related it to our everyday lives. They were spiritual and understanding, funny and realistic. They related Scripture to the psychology of living and the difficulties we all face. They were compassionate in their speaking. It made all the difference to me. They were speaking to my mind and to my heart, and I loved it. Both had a sense of humour, but Father Jim was hilarious. He was so buoyant and happy—I can still see his smiling face. He worked with the youth in the Catholic Youth Organization (CYO). He encouraged us in our spiritual development without denying that we were teenagers who had our own personal struggles and questions. He recognized that we needed to challenge our world in order to grow.

CYO was a lot of fun because we not only participated in church life, organizing masses and fundraisers for charity, but also organized social events for the youth in the church. In fact, CYO allowed me to participate in social events I might not otherwise have been able to, simply because it was a church organization. When I was fourteen years old, I was not allowed to go to a dance that was being held in the school gym for the grade eight students, though it was chaperoned by schoolteachers. However, I *was* allowed to go to a dance a couple of weeks later that was held in the basement of my church for the CYO and was chaperoned by church members. I'm not really sure how my mother differentiated between the two.

The school I was attending was a Catholic one, so I couldn't figure out what the difference was and why my mother wouldn't let me go to the school dance. I suspected it had something to do with inappropriate things happening between young, hormonal teens on the dark dance floor. I would have expected her to be more concerned about that happening at the CYO dance, where there would be boys not only my age but years older. Whereas only my thirteen- and fourteen-year-old classmates would be attending the school dance. I remember thinking it didn't make any sense that my mother would conclude that the CYO dance was somehow acceptable but the school dance was not. But the CYO dance was church related, and if the church approved it, so would she.

I had a positive experience of the Church as a young adult and had developed an ingrained "all or nothing" perspective, so to say the least it jarred me when I began to discover my own dissidence with the teachings, history, and perspective of the Roman Catholic Church. A clear shift took place my first year away from home, when I attended the University of Windsor. At first I still went to mass every Sunday, often running to the church on Sunday evening so as not to miss the last mass of the day. But somehow I didn't feel as connected to the Church as I had when I was at home. It sounded hollow when I said the prayers and responses during mass. They didn't sing the same hymns or sing the responses in the same way. And many priests' sermons just couldn't measure up to what I was used to with Father Jim and Father Murray. There was no comparison. I didn't know anyone there, and the experience felt empty.

Perhaps a large part of what was so important to me about the church back home was the people. Maybe it was the people all along who had kept me connected in the first place, so that now they were gone, or I was, it felt empty and I felt lonely. I don't know. But going to church became this thing I knew I should do but no longer had the heart for. At home there had been warmth and light and a sense of belonging; in Windsor there was a large, cavernous building. I felt guilty when I didn't go, but I felt empty and fake when I did go. Nothing felt right.

In Windsor, one of my closest friends was Jewish. According to what I had been taught, there was no hope for him because he did not accept Christ as Saviour: he was going to Hell. This was the first time I saw the consequences of my thinking. I had grown up in a Catholic home and had attended a Catholic school and church and my closest neighbourhood friend had been Catholic. I didn't belong to any sports teams or groups in the city, so nearly everyone I spent time with before Windsor was Catholic. My entire world existed within a Catholic bubble. Yet I couldn't believe that this person, who was good, kind, thoughtful, and considerate, was outside of God's love, that he was going to Hell simply because he was raised Jewish. That didn't make any sense to me at all. In fact, I didn't believe it. And right there, right then, my spirituality divided from my religion.

In the very fabric of my faith was its own undoing. So entrenched was the black-and-white perspective of "all or nothing" in my religious convictions that I believed I had no alternative. I could no longer be a Roman Catholic. "You accept all of it or none of it," my mother's voice rang in my ears and in my heart. So, because I had begun to believe things outside of Catholic teaching, I had only one choice— "none of it."

Perhaps this sounds like a simple-minded approach to my situation. After all, I was an adult by then. Surely I could have wrestled with the opposing forces and come up with a solution to my predicament that wasn't so abrupt, so final, so simple. Or could I? Yes, I was a reasonably intelligent, open-minded person who thought things through thoroughly and who didn't make quick decisions. But the simple approach had become the very essence of my belief structure. At that time I saw absolutely no alternative. So in the beginning, my Church did not leave me, I left the Church. My vision was expanding, as were my ideas and my beliefs. I felt compelled to broaden them all outside the denomination in which I had been raised. I became aware of what I expected. Until that point, before moving out of my childhood home, I wasn't aware of having any expectations of the Church. My focus was on what it expected of me. Then, somehow, I began to have expectations of it. I wasn't yet aware of any of the Church's more notorious crimes, so in my eyes it hadn't done anything yet to rock itself from its moorings. That came later when I became aware of its long trail of corruption. That's when the Church left me, but by then it was not a significant loss because I had already left it far behind.

The process of leaving the Church created a great deal of anxiety for me. I knew my mother would be disappointed and reproachful (through quiet guilt). I did not want to be outside her world, her religion, or her affection. I knew she would still love me, but I also knew that part of her approval would be gone forever. This was very difficult for me to reconcile. Though I had resented needing her approval in my teenage years, it was still difficult to accept losing some of that need.

But I could not deny that I was starting to see things in new ways and that I could no longer be a part of my mother's Church. I had stopped attending by then. I had even started feeling angry about what the priest was saying when I *did* go to church, to attend a wedding, a funeral, or Christmas or Easter Mass. Many sermons left me cold, or even worse, hot with anger or disgust at how the priests were interpreting the readings. As if they knew what Christ meant by this or that. I found their interpretations flat, uninspired, lacking in depth. And many of their sermons lacked grounding in the real world: they didn't address basic aspects of human nature or discuss how we could transform our lives through spiritual growth. They didn't deal with everyday experiences. It all sounded hollow.

I wanted them to tell me that they knew how difficult it was to be nice to people who act selfishly. Or how difficult it can be to not gossip because it's human nature to be curious about others and to want to hear "the dirt." They needed to tell us that the real reason it's not good to gossip, for example, is that it undoes the fabric of trust in our community and limits our ability to be open to other people's perspectives. Then let people draw their own conclusions that they need to not do it. Instead I heard a lot of "thou shalts" and "thou shalt nots" and warnings of fire and brimstone. Not very helpful or applicable.

The priests weren't showing me they understood the human condition, with all its faults and vulnerabilities. They weren't displaying understanding or kindness or humour, and they weren't telling stories that most people could relate to. They weren't giving us confidence that we could turn our lives around, that we could do better. I don't have respect for people in leadership positions who can't humble themselves to earn my trust; I can't trust people like that to lead me to a better place. I became disgusted at the kind of "leading" I was hearing in church.

As time went on, I also became more and more aware of how misogynistic the Church had been and still was. I began to experience my first feelings of anger toward the Catholic Church on behalf of all women. I began seeing the rules and the teachings in new ways. I began to notice the lack of authority women had, not just within the Church but in their own lives. The Church reigned over their reproductive lives while continuing to advocate the imagery of women as either virgins, temptresses, or whores. I remember coming alive with defiance and outrage.

It became difficult for me to hear the Scriptures the way I once did. I no longer had access to the wisdom of Father Jim and Father Murray; I was on my own now and distrustful of any religious teaching. I was jaded and unable to hear anyone talking about "God's will" or rules to follow to get to Heaven—it all sounded like a load of crap to me. I couldn't stomach it. Couldn't believe it. Didn't know what to believe. It was difficult for me to reconcile the teachings of love and compassion with the experience of binding control and strict adherence to unbending rules and doctrines that were cruel in their severity. Many beliefs and rules kept people outside God's love, inciting "believers" to judge and ostracize those they ought to have embraced, including homosexuals and single mothers. And while many individual Catholics are loving, kind, and inclusive, I couldn't belong to a group whose tenets were otherwise.

I think the Roman Catholic Church will always be a thing of my past. I really don't see it in my future. There are too many things that would have to be resolved before I could entertain the idea of joining again. And

the Church moves very slowly and changes very rarely, so I don't antic-
ipate that happening in my lifetime. The hardest part of being outside
a formalized religion is feeling that I'm not doing everything I should do,
or need to do, to be a good Christian. I don't think that going to church
is going to completely solve that one either. I believe very strongly in
the influence and healing power of psychology in a person's overall
well-being. Keeping things well thought out psychologically makes me
a stronger, happier, more giving person, but it doesn't complete a wholly
loving existence. To complete the picture, I need to believe in a power
or powers greater than myself—namely, true love and compassion. Living by Christian teachings gives that to me and my life.

   This is going to sound odd, but sometimes I have a comfortable feeling when I'm in a Catholic church and a mass is being celebrated. There
are twinges of being at home. And I long for simpler times. But I know
that time erases the distinct, difficult feelings and leaves the blurry good
ones. Even so, I miss the sense of belonging, of community. I miss contributing to a church and to my community through my church. I miss
the singing. I miss praising God with others out loud once a week. I do
praise Him regularly in my daily life, for the beautiful roses in my garden, when the sun shines brilliantly, for a cool fresh breeze blowing
through my window in the mornings. For all kinds of things. I stop and
say thank you. And I point these things out to my son, Dilan. I want to
teach him to be grateful for the beauty in life, which is God's gift to us.

   I also think it's important to take time to focus on the Scripture once
a week. To formalize it, to make sure we carve out some time for it in our
busy lives. Like when you pencil in down time for yourself or with a
friend because if you didn't you'd never do it. A long time could pass
before you'd get around to spending time with them if you didn't set up
a meeting. So it is with a church service, I think.

   I also want Dilan to have the same base in Christian teaching and
understanding that I have, because I believe in it. And because I want
him to have the kind of peace I've found in it. But I don't want him to
have to deal with the black-and-white perspective on things and the
torturing doubt and guilt of a Catholic upbringing. I want him to feel
loved and hopeful, to be open in his mind and in his heart.

   One church I have attended quite a few times is fairly progressive,
and the teachings are easy to relate to. They have some of the elements
of the talks that I so enjoyed when Father Murray and Father Jim gave
them. And the people seem genuinely interested in making me feel

welcome and comfortable in their church. But I'm not sure I could actually commit to this denomination. I still have some searching to do.

I'm very happy in my life right now but I also yearn for something to fill what is missing in my spiritual development. I would like to find a church where I will feel genuinely at home with the Christian teachings and approach, where I will be stimulated to think and feel beyond what I have thought and felt on my own. I want to find a church where men, women, and children are all respected and valued for what they can contribute. Where people are not just encouraged but expected to think for themselves, to challenge not only what they see in the world around them but also what they are hearing from the pulpit. I want to be part of a church that encourages respectful argument, that is understanding, kind, realistic, and demanding. One that wants people to develop in their spirituality to meet the difficult challenges of living today. I don't know if it exists. But that's what I want.

I will not pass on my mother's church to my son. I hope to find one that I believe will be right for us. And then, as Dilan grows, I will encourage him to follow his own spiritual path and to find a church that is right for him.

KEITH DIXON

The Ministry Revisited

I was ten years old when Grandma offered to teach her grand-children about the Bible. Five of us, three brothers and two cousins, walked to her house every Sunday afternoon for Bible study. We started with God creating the world in six days and then resting on the seventh. Next was Moses parting the sea for his people to escape the Egyptians. We memorized the 23rd Psalm and the Beatitudes. At Christmas and Easter we read the stories from the Gospels that got those holidays started. I believed all these remarkable things. To doubt them, I knew, might get God angry with me. That could mean big trouble.

The King James Bible was hard to understand and I grew bored very quickly. I told Mom I didn't want to go to Bible study. She said fine, but I had to tell Grandma myself. I was afraid to do that, worried she might get angry. She was always in a snit about things. She abhorred lying or stealing and ranted about people who drank booze or worked on Sunday. I worried quitting Bible study might just get her going on me.

By the time I was in high school Grandma was growing senile and had dropped Bible teaching. So I escaped having to confront her. Worse, perhaps, I had not looked honestly at the literal way of reading the Bible that Grandma had taught me. That was to come a few years later.

After four years of high school I enrolled at the University of Saskatchewan. I was extremely lonely that first year in Saskatoon. My home on the farm was two hundred miles away. I had knots in my stomach as Mom and Dad drove me to the door of Qu'Appelle Hall, the men's residence. As it turned out, those knots were mild compared to the anguish that rose with the approach of final exams. In between were days packed with studying, lectures, labs, and treks three times a day to eat at the cafeteria in Saskatchewan Hall.

My roommate Don and I were both engineering students. I had chosen that direction because I was good at the sciences in high school. Don had chosen it because his father was an engineer in Flin Flon. He chain-smoked to relieve his tension, and I immersed myself in my books. While eating meals we talked about the girls we saw in the cafeteria, but mostly we were obsessed with getting our work done. All this even though academic demands always made me anxious, and, for Don, engineering studies didn't come easy and making passing marks was very hard. We were one another's social life that first year.

The finals came close to pushing me over the edge. Free-floating panic exploded at thoughts of exams, expanding to irrational fear of routine things. I thought I was going crazy but was afraid to consult the campus doctor. In desperation I talked to my English professor, Dr. Tracy. He listened to my story and said, "I know what you mean. It's like falling off the edge of a cliff." I agreed it was like that, and he said he'd been through the same thing. I was enormously relieved to discover I was sane. If I wasn't, at least I could become an English professor and get away with it. Dr. Tracy's prescription was to take two weeks off studies and read whatever I liked. Textbooks or notes were to be packed away until the week before exams. It sounded like insanity. But I had gone to this man because I trusted him, so I knew I had to trust this advice. He lent me a book by Chaucer along with some poetry. With panic waiting to pounce at any moment it was hard to keep my mind on reading. But simply following his instructions gave me a sense of stability.

On the morning of the first exam my classmates were comparing notes and exchanging stories of how they studied all night. I felt doomed to fail. I only had time to go through my notes and textbooks once. I certainly had not stayed up all night cramming. As we waited for the door to the exam hall to open, my panic peaked. When I sat down to write, I was surprised I knew most of the answers. Much later, while on my summer job, I learned I had made As and Bs in all six exams.

That summer I got my first full-time job, with free evenings and weekends in the city. Back when I was a kid on the farm we lived eight miles from town. Sunday mornings we went to church as a family, but there was no way for me to get to the youth group events, so I never participated. Now Grace United Church was only a few blocks away. I joined the Young Peoples Union (YPU) and threw myself wholeheartedly into its program.

I returned to university and Qu'Appelle Hall that fall. Don was still my roommate, and we were now enrolled in our second year of engineering. Chemistry was to be my specialty. The summer had freed me from much of my anxiety, and I was still involved with the YPU at Grace United. Don looked askance at my new interest. He had no experience with church activities and couldn't understand my interest in religion. The friendship we had formed that first year faded. Though sharing a room, we went our separate ways.

In October, following the YPU crowd, I attended a Youth for Christ rally in Third Avenue United Church. The rally started like an ordinary church worship service. Then, just barely into the service, something began to happen to me. It was in no way connected to the service. The service instead became a distraction. Euphoria flooded my body, bathing me in warmth and light. It was much more than being incredibly joyful. There was a Presence that actually filled the sanctuary, my body, my thoughts, and, when I thought of the world outside, filled that as well. No boundary existed between my being and the Presence. I was one with It. Filled with awe, it dawned on me: *This must be God!*

The preacher, after the sermon, came down from the pulpit and stood by a front pew. He asked those who wished to "give their lives to Jesus" to come forward. That jolted me. I had never witnessed an altar call. I thought, "What a ridiculous thing to do! I don't need to go to the front. God is all around me. I'm staying right here!" I continued in my euphoria, but questions began racing through my mind. "When I go back to my room tonight how will I explain this to Don? Can I go back to my chemistry and calculus classes tomorrow as if nothing has happened? Do I really want to be an engineer? What would Mom and Dad think of me if I told them I met God?"

As the questions kept coming I knew I was finished with what I had been doing and that something new was about to begin. What was this new thing? The idea of becoming a minister arose in my mind. I knew practically nothing about being a clergyman. I had an inkling it was a profession where I could stay closer to what I had just experienced. At least it would be better than if I became an engineer. The idea appealed to me. As I built fantasies around it, it became ever more plausible. Finally I knew it was what I was going to do.

Before I left the church that evening I had decided to leave engineering and prepare to be a minister. A few days later I saw Dr. J.B. Corston, principal of St. Andrews Theological College, to tell him about my plans to become a minister. He wanted to know why. I told him about my experience in the church when God was everywhere. He looked uncomfortable with my story, the first of many signals I got that talking about this made people uneasy. He asked about my marks in engineering. I said I was making As and Bs. He suggested maybe I could serve God as an engineer just as well as a minister. I said I didn't want to. I wanted to become a minister. So he set my plan in motion.

The next five years were filled with studies. I finished my second year of engineering and then did fill-in classes to qualify for a Bachelor of Arts degree in order to get into a theological college. The BA completed, I was accepted by St. Andrews College in Saskatoon and completed a year toward a divinity degree. While studying for my arts degree I became involved with the Student Christian Movement (SCM), a non-denominational group that encouraged theological exploration and emphasized social involvement for Christian students. It was there I discovered a vitality in Christianity, a vitality I had not encountered in other churches.

I spent the summer of 1956 in Montreal at an SCM Student-in-Industry work camp coordinated by the Reverend Vince Goring. Reverend Goring was an Anglican priest who also served as the General Secretary of the SCM in Saskatchewan. Twenty-two participants came from universities across Canada. We lived together in a church hall in Point St. Charles, an old industrial area of Montreal, and found jobs in local factories. From among our numbers we selected a cook, whom we paid. Mornings started with a worship service conducted by work campers, in rotation. During the evenings we held discussion groups and Bible study and listened to invited speakers. Most important, we set to work on the details of living together. This process involved sharing chores and responsibilities and establishing daily schedules. We were introduced to the concept of wage sharing based on the Biblical concept of sharing possessions so that the needs of all are met (Acts 4:35). As students we needed enough money to go back to university. All but two work campers opted for the wage pool, and at the end of the summer everyone had adequate resources for another semester.

The effect on me was mind blowing! I discovered the powerful bond a group can create, but most significant to me was encountering a group of Christians eager to question every aspect of their faith, look for answers, and then to take the answers into the social arena and act on them. I emerged from that experience, theologically, a free thinker and, politically, a Marxist. Marx's *Communist Manifesto* seemed to me to be a logical expression for a Christian following Jesus' command to "love your neighbour as yourself."

Just prior to my second year of theological studies I co-directed an SCM work camp in Toronto. During that summer I met Wendy, a Toronto SCMer studying social work. By the end of the summer our relationship was serious enough that I decided to be near her by transferring my theological studies to Emmanuel College at the University of Toronto. I shared an apartment with two SCMers and met with a group exploring communal living. I felt little collegiality with Emmanuel College: it was just a place to get my degree.

I was ordained by the United Church in May 1960 and began my ministry in All People's Industrial Parish that summer. I served two congregations within the parish. One was the All People's Mission congregation in Thorold South, with services in English and Ukrainian. The other was a small congregation in Allanburg that had been there for seventy-five years. I worked as part of a team ministry, with two ordained pastors and one who was lay. A clergyman from Toronto came on Sundays to conduct the Ukrainian service. All People's Mission had been very active in the Social Gospel tradition and I was pleased to participate in that role. A strong support group of laymen within the parish made getting started in my first appointment challenging and exciting. But in spite of the good start, the course I had set for myself was not to last.

The first stumbling block was pressure from the governing Presbytery to move All People's from mission status to being a self-supporting congregation. If I yielded to that pressure, I would have to spend my time organizing fundraising campaigns. To resist that pressure I would have to convince the Presbytery that the Church still had a mission in an industrial community. That mission, I believed, was to make the Gospel relevant to men and women who worked factory shifts. I did this by becoming politically active and by encouraging the parishioners to be active, too. Christian commitment was more than attending baptisms, weddings, and funerals.

Another problem was that panic lingered just beneath the surface of my preaching. I had always been shy in social gatherings. Public speaking had not come easily for me. The larger the group of people, the more emotional energy I needed to open my mouth. At school I spoke in class only when interrogated. I was reluctant to hold up my hand for the teacher's questions, because that would mean having to speak out. Yet in spite of this reluctance others seemed to see me as a capable person. I had been Valedictorian at my high school graduation, and at eighteen I had been elected the first president of a farmers' union being organized in the district where I grew up. Part of me was flattered and needy enough to lap up the attention. But another part of me was petrified every time I faced the prospect of having to speak to a group.

To cope with this fear I learned to be well organized. I could not speak extemporaneously. I dreaded the blank mind that followed when my mouth opened. I wrote each sermon out in full. In the summer of 1965 the writing became harder and harder. The finished sermon was no longer ready Thursday. It was Friday and then Saturday when I had it done. Often I was finishing it off on Sunday morning. I did not understand why this was happening. I got other things done on time with no problem, but I blocked on writing sermons.

One particular Tuesday that summer I went to my study after breakfast to start the sermon. I worked at home since the church building had no office. Wendy was busy in the living room as I sat at the typewriter with the now familiar blank page in front of me. I could not think of a single thing to write. A decision interrupted the block. It was clear and sharp, with no qualifications. I was going to leave the ministry. The details could be worked out later. Ironically, that decision came as effortlessly as my original decision to enter the ministry. I got up from the typewriter and walked into the living room.

"I've decided to quit." I said.

"Quit what?" she asked, puzzled.

"To leave this job," I replied.

"You mean, as minister here?" She was still confused by my words.

"Yes. The ministry. I'm quitting the ministry."

Wendy dropped what she was doing and sat down. Her eyes were wide. I suddenly realized just how big the decision was.

Wendy had been raised in a home where her mother was very anti-church, and her father never mentioned a word about religion. She had found Christianity on her own through SCM and had never been involved with a traditional congregation. She found being part of All People's unsatisfying and the role of minister's wife extremely difficult. Our two sons had been born during those five years. She had withdrawn into the role of mother and wife, abdicating formal church responsibilities. I later learned from her that she was excited to hear me declare that I was leaving the ministry, though at the time she had never hinted as much.

I had to notify the congregation of my plans. I set December 31 as my last day, and announced it in a sermon. I can't remember what I said in that message. I do remember feeling guilty that I was somehow betraying them, betraying my own declared goals. I remember the terror that arose because of my confusion. I don't think I admitted those feelings in my message that morning. It was easier to hide behind rationalizations.

After the service, the congregation filed past me while I stood at the church entrance. I was engulfed in sadness as they spoke of how they would miss me. Whatever problems I was having with theology or the administration of the church, they were not of great importance to these everyday Christians. For them, theology was a non-issue. My being there was the most important thing to them. I was deeply moved.

I directed my anger toward the Niagara Presbytery. This church body, half clergy and half laymen, governed the congregations in the Niagara area. All People's Church had been a missionary project among immigrants founded forty years earlier by the United Church. Now the Presbytery was pushing for All People's to become self-supporting, and to that end pressure was applied to encourage us to use commercial fundraising strategies. I was already feeling that too much of my time was being spent on administrative matters. So my parting shot to the Presbytery, by letter, reflected my concern about its expectation. The only response was a chastising note from one clergyman saying it was inappropriate to say things like that to lay members, as it might upset them! Not one member of Presbytery called to ask how I was or if I wished to talk about my reasons for departing. I was hoping for dialogue with concerned colleagues, but instead I was left feeling ignored and abandoned.

I needed a job, and social work, teaching, and radio work all seemed like possibilities. I started with the Children's Aid Society, since my wife worked there part time. The director was a bit hesitant about having a husband and wife on his staff, but hired me anyway. I started as a social worker for "the Aid" on January 3, 1966. My plan was to stay a year and then reassess my direction in life.

That year gave me time to sort through what had just happened. I enjoyed social work, especially the congenial relations I had with the staff. I had time to review what had gone wrong in the ministry, which triggered both anger and anxiety. Within a year I was back coping with panic attacks even worse than the earlier episode at university. I consulted a psychiatrist and began digging into my past. When the baggage was eventually all brought to the surface I realized that the real trouble lay in the fact that I no longer believed the doctrines I had been taught in theological college. I was now relying on just my five senses to tell me what was true. Claims that could not be scientifically verified were dubious to me. The Bible had become for me a collage of historical, poetic, and mystical writings. Jesus had become an ordinary man, though a very insightful one. God? I was no longer sure He existed beyond man's imagination. My whole belief structure had come crashing down. For the first time I understood the real reason I could not preach sermons that last year: I did not believe a word I was preaching! At the end of that year I asked the Presbytery to remove my name from the role of clergy. They complied without comment. I remember someone telling me I could not be "unordained." "Once a clergyman, always a clergyman!" That riled me at the time, though now it seems funny.

It took nearly a year for the anxiety attacks to fade. During that time I explored the world of non-belief. Alongside my rampant agnosticism was an almost schizophrenic memory of what had happened to me that day in the Third Avenue Church in Saskatoon. The Presence I had experienced could not be denied. It was the most real thing that had ever happened to me. Because the "God" that the Church taught about seemed to have little resemblance to the Presence I had experienced, I disowned the Church's "God." The Church's claim that Jesus was the Son of God became incongruous because that God did not exist for me. Jesus, whose words still made a great deal of sense to me, was a man. A very enlightened man. But just a man.

Ten years later another spiritual shift began, very subtly and without conscious spiritual effort on my part. It was precipitated by the emotionally stressful nature of social work, and I was searching for ways to reduce that stress. So when my sister-in-law, Freda, said she had found Transcendental Meditation (TM) very helpful, I was interested. Nevertheless, I was uneasy that it might be a religion and asked her about the matter. Being a psychiatrist, she assured me there was nothing religious about it. So I took the TM training and began daily practice. The positive changes it created were so marked that I had no hesitation about continuing the twenty minutes of meditation morning and evening for the next ten years.

I had not taken seriously one of the cautions mentioned at the TM training course. They had told me that regular meditation can create major lifestyle changes in the practitioner. With the two upheavals I had already been through, I did not expect anything worse could happen. After meditating regularly for several years my interests did begin to change. I became fascinated with a variety of psychic phenomena, for instance, the idea that plants respond to human emotions. I started attending New Age workshops run by people who, a few years earlier, I would have considered totally flaky. The overall effect was to bring me to a place where I once again acknowledged there was a spiritual realm, though what I was discovering seemed very different from what the Church had taught me. For instance, the idea of past lives and reincarnation seemed so natural to me that, looking back, I wonder how my theological training did not turn over in its grave, or how my agnosticism didn't rise up in protest. At first I struggled to find scientific evidence for these claims. But soon, needing proof seemed irrelevant. I was discovering the intuitive way of knowing. The spiritual world was opening before my eyes, without distortion by the dark glasses of doctrine the Church had given me to look through.

I wandered around a smorgasbord of New Age offerings for five or six years, exploring fascinating psychic phenomena. I attended workshops where we experimented with seeing auras and moving objects with just the mind. I sat with trance psychics who let mysterious beings speak through them, answering any question I asked. I probed non-traditional methods of healing and discovered how much my mind could affect my body. I examined foods I was eating and became a vegetarian. The research waned when I felt myself approaching a dead end. I wondered, "Is that all there is?" I was searching for the profound and discovering trivia such as seeing auras and chanting affirmations. It didn't satisfy the need. It did, however, give me a hint about the direction I was to go. I received a message through a channelled entity (a psychic friend did channelling). I was to "look to the East." I didn't know what that meant in practical terms. I was soon to find out.

I felt I needed more instruction in meditation. I had taken the weekend course in TM and then practised for a decade without seeking guidance. Perhaps, I mused, I needed some personal help with it. I found a woman who taught meditation within the Buddhist tradition and began instruction with her. At the time I joined she was also facilitating a small group that met to discuss Buddhist precepts. I found the personal instruction very helpful, but the group discussion was confusing. My personal instruction had just begun when my teacher announced she was pregnant and was not going to be able to continue teaching. Shortly afterwards she told the group that a high Tibetan lama was going to be in St. Catharines and that we might all like to hear him speak. She said his tradition was different than her own but that the core teachings and practice were the same. The lama was His Holiness, the Sixteenth Karmapa, head of the Kargyu tradition of Tibetan Buddhism. This high lama is considered fully enlightened by his followers in the Tibetan Kargyu lineage, and they can show how he is linked, guru by enlightened guru, right back to the founder of Buddhism, Buddha Shakyamuni. His Holiness was going to be performing the Black Hat ceremony, a *puja* done only by the highest lama of that tradition. *Pujas* are spiritual rituals with external and internal functions designed to help participants advance on the path toward enlightenment. These details meant nothing to me at the time, but my curiosity was aroused and I decided to attend.

The Karmapa conducted the *puja* in the sanctuary of Mountainview United Church, all of which was another ironical touch for me! My daughter, Sheila, who was a teenager at the time, wanted to come with me. His Holiness entered the sanctuary after everyone was seated and waiting for him. My impression, when I saw him, was that he was in a trance. Buddhists there told me he had been in deep meditation preparing himself for the ceremony. Sheila picked up an energy from him that was so intense she had to leave the room. The ceremony was done entirely in Tibetan, so there was very little for my rational mind to process. It was a ceremony rich with symbolism, which I didn't understand, and the lama's face and voice were full of peace and serenity, to which I could easily relate.

My thoughts leapt about, pricked by curiosity about the *puja* yet going nowhere. At a deeper level of awareness, something else was happening. When the main ceremony was completed, an announcement was made that his Holiness would give Refuge to any who wished to receive it. I knew that taking Refuge meant that one had formally expressed the intention of following the Buddhist path. I had come intending to observe. Now, suddenly, on hearing this announcement, I knew I was to take the offer. I lined up with the others who had also chosen this moment to affirm their wish to follow the Path. Bowing before His Holiness, I was asked to repeat that affirmation. He then took a hair from my head and placed it on the shrine, which signified giving my body to the Path I had chosen to follow. I was given a Dharma name: Karma Lekshe Gytso, which, translated, I was told, means "Ocean of Profound Speech." I was now a Buddhist.

Meanwhile, I still had no teacher. The personal instruction in meditation I had been looking for was nowhere evident. His Holiness was not accessible as a personal guide. However, one of his attendants that day was Lama Namse, whom His Holiness had been assigned as his representative in Canada. Shortly afterwards, Lama Namse began giving teachings at a newly formed Buddhist college on the campus of Brock University in St. Catharines. I attended, hoping to learn more about what I had gotten myself into. Lama Namse taught through an interpreter, and since his English was limited, the learning process was slowed, placing limitations on consulting him about questions as they arose.

Lama Namse became my teacher, though there was no formal asking, which sometimes is part of the process in the Buddhist tradition. The way it happened was mostly a group process. Lama Namse travelled from Toronto to instruct at the centre in St. Catharines. A regular group attended his teachings. When we learned he might be amenable to moving to St. Catharines, we arranged with a Unitarian Church to rent their old house for a dollar a year. They asked us to pay the utilities and let them use the meeting rooms on Sunday for their classes. We established the Karma Kargyu Buddhist Meditation Centre of Niagara, and Lama Namse moved in. We all had a teacher, and each of us could say, "Cho Je Lama Namse Rinpoche is my teacher."

In the months and years that followed, Lama Namse initiated us into many of the *pujas* of his tradition, such as Chenrezig (the god of loving kindness), the Medicine Buddha, and the Nyungna (a purification ritual). He taught us the stories told about the Buddha, and about Marpa and Milarepa, the two holy men who had brought Buddhism from India to Tibet many centuries ago. He also started a small group of us on the Foundation Practice, the strenuous and intense meditation practice that leads to becoming a monk. It was a daily practice filled with mantras and prostrations. The mantras were all in Tibetan, which none of us understood, but we could pronounce the words from a book. A translation was included so that we knew what we were saying. The prostrations involved moving our bodies from a standing position to being flat on our faces on the floor, arms above our heads. The Foundation

Practice required doing ten thousand of these mantras and prostrations. It took me two years to complete the practice. Though I had toyed with the idea of becoming a monk, the motivation to do so never arose.

In 1985 Lama Namse returned to Tibet for a year. He invited members of our group to travel with him, and I accepted. Staying in Buddhist centres and monasteries with a lama as a travelling companion was the most memorable trip of my life. From the thriving new Buddhist spirit in the West, I moved back in history to where it had its roots and where it had been practised pretty much the same way for centuries. I was struck by how "spirituality" was defined differently by Westerners and Easterners. Westerners visiting India flocked to a monastery when a high lama gave a teaching. But there would be few Tibetans, if any, in attendance. However, if there was a special *puja*, something of importance in the Buddhist calendar (like the day of the Buddha's enlightenment), the Tibetan families would turn out in great numbers to pray and be blessed. Westerners view the Spirit through their minds. The Tibetans touch the Spirit through their hearts.

Back in Canada we were without a lama for a year, and when Lama Namse did return he decided once again to live in Toronto. We saw no need to maintain a house in St. Catharines that was used only one night a week. I offered my house as a meeting place. We decorated a large basement room, which became "the shrine room." For the next seventeen years, every Monday night, the group gathered to light candles, burn incense, and chant the Chenrezig *puja* for generating loving kindness. We talked and sipped tea. Lama Namse and other visiting lamas dropped in occasionally and gave a teaching. Fred, another member, and I took training at Karma Triyana Dharmachakra (KTD), seat of his Holiness in the United States, and were qualified to teach *shamata*, the beginner's meditation. Periodically Fred and I spoke to outside groups interested in Buddhism.

In 2002 I moved to Edmonton, Alberta, breaking with Buddhism for a while. That break was partly because there was no Kargyu group in the city, but also because my daily meditation practice had come to lack meaning. Meditation is the core of Buddhism. The lamas encouraged me to resist the temptation to stop meditating. The temptation is just the mind playing tricks, they said. I had appreciated TM's calming effects on my body when I first meditated, but the years of daily practice seemed to have produced little other benefit. I needed to take a break to assess where I was at, so I decided to stop my daily practice.

While in Edmonton my daughter introduced me to a group that met several times a week to hear teaching from a Western mystic, John DeRuiter. When I first heard John talk in Toronto, though he never would make such a claim, I had the feeling I was listening to the voice of the Buddha, or perhaps to the words of Jesus. His teachings and remarkable presence were what took me there. He used basic English, which was easier to understand than translations from Tibetan. He rarely addressed a whole group. All his teachings were one on one, with the audience listening. There was an immediacy of application that was clear to understand and very powerful. Nevertheless, after three years of listening to him, and hanging out with his followers, I experienced the same stagnation that had happened to me within Christianity and Buddhism. I remember not wanting to go to Grandma's Bible classes. It was there I felt spiritually stagnant for the first time in my life. I coped with the feeling by submitting without protest. I surrendered my personal freedom to think and to be who I am, and just went through the motions. I repeated that pattern when I got into the ministry, and then again in Buddhism. Most recently it has happened with John DeRuiter and his group. All of it forced me to look for patterns in the way I searched for and identified Truth.

It was an insight that provided me a great release. Instead of going on a blaming-the-world trip, like Grandma did, I look honestly for what is real and true. That truth has to carry either scientific objectivity or the inner knowing that comes from intuition. At the slightest hint of stagnation I look for where I got off the path of honesty, then try to correct my course.

Once I laid blame down, gratitude sprang to replace it. I'm delighted with how easily that happens. I still question the fundamental assumptions of Christianity, but I also find myself admiring the skill with which some Christians carry love into the world. I have concerns that centuries of repetition have distorted Buddhist teachings, but I can be prostrate in awe before the humble simplicity of a man like the Dalai Lama. I have misgivings about the dangers inherent in guru worship, but I rejoice when mystics like John DeRuiter tell me to take responsibility for my life and to surrender my decisions to no one but Truth.

Where does this bring me?

On my bad days the past grumbles at me from my life's receding horizon. I hear the pain and fear and confusion in its pleas, but I don't buy into the drama. It's just not real. On my good days I have a diminishing belief in doctrines and a growing delight in people. On waking I give minimal thought to my calendar and let today's sunrise take over. I eat and drink and touch and smell and hear and see and love and care, not because I must, but because I can. Out of that springs a quiet joy of Being.

From here on the path is blissfully uncharted.

JULIE RAK

Looking Back at Sodom
My Evangelical and Lesbian Testimonies

Every Christian knows the Bible story of Lot's wife as a lesson in obedience to God. This is how I remember it: When the Lord is about to destroy the cities of Sodom and Gomorrah for the sins of homosexuality and attempted rape, He decides to save Lot, Sodom's one just man, along with his family. The family is instructed not to look back at the city as it is being destroyed. An angel of the Lord drags Lot away and his daughters follow, but Lot's wife looks back and is turned into a pillar of salt.

During the fifteen years I was a member of evangelical churches, I heard a number of sermons about Lot's wife. The Old Testament itself never says why Lot's wife looked back. It never even gives her a name of her own. But evangelical Christians like to learn lessons from all the stories in the Bible, so all the sermons I heard about Lot's wife sought to fill in the blanks in the original story. The sermons reinterpreted the story so that a lesson "for today" could be learned. I heard that Lot's wife was punished by God because she had disobeyed his instructions. She looked back at the evil city of Sodom, with all its hedonistic pleasures (especially those which were homosexual), because she was really a hedonist herself. Lot's wife deserved what she got because she didn't listen to God or her husband. Most probably she secretly desired evil pleasures of the flesh.

The constant message was that if we disobey God's directives, punishment will follow. So the story of Lot's wife is a story of the folly of any kind of desire, especially for women. It is a warning to all wives who would disobey God or their husbands. It warns all evangelical Christians about the perils of disobedience, especially in our sinful world with all its temptations. In the New Testament, even Jesus himself warns his disciples about the Second Coming and the destruction to come. To prevent the disciples from being tempted by worldly things, and to stop them from returning to them when the time of destruction comes, Jesus says, "Remember Lot's wife" (Luke 17:32). I have heard this story used just this way in sermons as a warning to children not to be tempted by the sins of Sodom and Gomorrah by listening to secular music or by watching Hollywood movies.

I used to see Lot's wife like that: as a warning to obey God in all things and as a reminder to be more obedient. I was always reminding myself of this, partly because I really wasn't very good at obeying a whole range of commands and expectations within the evangelical fold. But I no longer see Lot's wife as some kind of warning. I see her rather as a beacon showing the way to another life, a monument to hard choices and sacrifices that women sometimes decide to make. To me, she is as the Russian poet Anna Akhmatova saw her in "Lot's Wife": a woman who looked back at the city where she had been happy and who was willing to give up her life and future for even one last glimpse of that happiness.

Evangelical Christians love stories. They like to hear "the old, old story of Jesus and his love" repeated over and over again, in hymns and sermons and especially in "testimonies"—that is, the life stories of Christian believers that tell of their conversions. Christian testimonies are about the victory of God over sin in the life of an individual. But in evangelical Christian life, any other stories about God and Christian life go untold and unacknowledged, at least officially. These stories should have their place in religious life even if they don't result in the happy ending of more wisdom and the desire to be more obedient to God and the church. When it comes to my own "testimony," this is how it went.

The year before I became a Christian was the most difficult year of my life. I had been living with my girlfriend of three years and going to university when my mother began to crack under the strain of living with my stepfather, a very abusive man. She attempted suicide after trying to leave him and was subsequently hospitalized. My brother also attempted suicide shortly afterwards. No other members of my family lived in Canada and I wasn't talking to my father at the time, so most of the challenge of caregiving for my mother fell to me. I became ill from the strain and dropped more than thirty pounds, though I still managed to attend school. During this time I left my girlfriend because she wouldn't "come out" as a lesbian and meet other women with me. I made the departure by starting a relationship with a man, who became my boyfriend. I decided I was bisexual and that though I was attracted to women I could have a boyfriend if I wanted to. I moved in with him and began work at his mother's bookstore, a rough place that happened to be the biggest seller of pornographic material in the city.

I had very little money and was so tired all the time. I often felt empty inside and just tried to exist day to day in the polluted, industrial city where I lived. My boyfriend was sympathetic, but I found it difficult to talk to him about my feelings. I wrote down how bad it felt but I told no one else what I was going through. By September 1988 my relationship with him was coming apart and I decided to move out. I moved into a household with three Christian women. My first reaction was that I had made a terrible mistake.

Very quickly I came to love and admire these women. One was training to be a nurse, one was an artist, and one was training to be a pastor. They seemed so happy and their lives had so much meaning and purpose. They didn't have to drink alcohol, as I did, to feel better about things. As time went on I wanted to hang around them and be like them. I began to think seriously about becoming a Christian, even though I had read the Bible through and knew God hated homosexuality. But that's okay, I thought. I already had a boyfriend so I was sure I didn't have to be a lesbian if I chose not to be. So one night I went upstairs and told my roommates that God had won out. They were so happy for me, and I was happy too.

My early Christian life was very exciting. I loved going to a local Baptist church with my friends. I read the Bible and went to Bible studies with the Navigators, a university Christian student group that had a great attraction for Baptists. Everything seemed so new and my life suddenly seemed to have meaning. I felt as if all the colours in the world were more vibrant than they had ever been, and I felt joyful inside all the time. I made many new Christian friends, though I could see I was different from most of them. I had not been raised in an evangelical church so I knew nothing about Christian music, or the games and activities Christian youth groups played, or what "the mission field" was all about. But I learned about these things, and a new world opened up. Most of my new friends weren't intellectuals, and reading material was kept to the Bible and Christian self-help books. But they were trying to live their lives with purpose and integrity. It was something I loved and respected.

For a decade this story about my conversion was my testimony. Every evangelical Christian (including me) knows what their testimony is because one day, an "unbeliever" might want to hear that story and perhaps be inspired to believe in Jesus because of it. But most testimonies are told for the benefit of other believers. In most of my former churches, during baptism ceremonies, people are encouraged to tell their testimony (usually it's on index cards) so that other Christians can be inspired by the story they hear. Since a testimony shows very clearly how one's life was changed by making a commitment to Jesus Christ, it becomes a way of making the work of God personal. I have seen many members of a congregation moved to tears when they hear these stories. And I have watched many of the people who tell them, as they stand up to their waists in baptismal water, cry as they relate the details of their lives and the reasons why they decided to make such a radical profession of faith. Most evangelicals know it isn't possible to live in continuous victory and joy all the time, but the basic pattern of the testimony—and the pattern of the Christian life I heard repeated all around me for years—*simply does not allow any other story to be told*. There is no room for ambiguity in this narrative about life and change.

But early on, some disturbing things did begin to happen in my Christian life, things that a testimony could not account for. I had started attending a Fellowship Baptist church that two of my roommates attended. I would happily ride my bike there in the summer, dressed in a skirt and blouse for the occasion, or I'd get a ride with one of my friends. Though the people in the church were kind to me, the pastor began to warn me not to be too independent. He said that even though there were women at the church who were bank managers and teachers, the Bible clearly said that women could not be leaders or teachers of adults in the church, no matter what their talents.

Most of the people in the church seemed to be more concerned about maintaining the building and running a church service than anything else. Church services started to bore me when so many of the sermons began to sound the same, or when we sang hymns from the last century about the same things, over and over. My church also distributed handouts from an American organization, Focus On The Family, headed by James Dobson. Among other things, Dr. Dobson, a psychologist by training, warned that dressing children in the "wrong" clothes for their gender would result in them growing up to be homosexuals. Most of the younger women I knew wore pants when they weren't at church, so this seemed ridiculous. I tried not to think about such things as it seemed to go against what the Bible said about judging others. Instead, to offset the negative side of religious life, I read all the spiritual books I could, went on spiritual retreats, did a lot of church work, and ran a women's prayer group with a friend.

I went to graduate school in another city to get a master's degree. I hoped I would then go to the mission field. I knew I would not get married: I was just too different from most of the other, more feminine and traditional women I knew. I had a wonderful time during my master's degree hanging around with Christian women who were much like myself, so I didn't think about church politics too much. Yet despite all the fun I was having, I was lonely. I enjoyed the company of my women friends and I even felt physically attracted to my best friend, but I shrugged it off as a temptation and decided to look around for a boyfriend.

Finding a suitable man in the evangelical world proved difficult. For one thing, there was that difference between me and other Christian women. And there are more women than men in evangelical churches anyway. I was highly educated, I liked to read, and I was comfortable in the non-Christian academic world. I was a music leader in my church and a leader in other ways, too. I had short hair, often dressed in black, and enjoyed hanging around in cafes. Women who were like me tended to become what was called "unequally yoked with unbelievers" by ending up with non-Christian boyfriends and husbands. This usually resulted in them "losing their faith," as it was called. Otherwise, women like me stayed single for the rest of their lives, serving God in some religious capacity. I just didn't look cut out for marriage and children. And I wasn't all that interested in the men I knew, all of whom looked like they were training to be accountants and engineers.

Despite my lack of prospects, there was one man who appeared to be a good date: my friend Michael. I had known Michael as an undergraduate and had even done a Bible study with him after I became a Christian. Michael was interesting. He had taken time off school to travel around the world, and even though he was in an engineering program, he liked to read books, too. He was Eastern European, with olive skin, a mustache, and a brilliant smile. He made me laugh and seemed to really love God. So I decided on him, and I asked him on a date. He accepted.

It began as a disaster. Michael took me for a walk on a railway siding (I was wearing white shoes, so this wasn't a good idea), where he told me that he thought dating automatically led to marriage. He wasn't interested in marriage, he said. I was surprised at this, but said okay, let's have dinner anyway. I went home disappointed, but after a couple of weeks Michael reconsidered and we started a long-distance relationship. I was his first girlfriend.

After a few months we decided to get married. I was really happy, and everyone I knew was happy for me, too. I planned to finish my master's thesis in the city where Michael lived so that he could complete his engineering degree. And then, we thought, we would go on the mission field. We didn't spend much time together in the months leading up to our marriage, but we didn't worry about it. There would be plenty of time to spend together after we were married. Besides, we were so tempted to have sex whenever we were together that it was better we stayed apart. This view of sexual activity came from our church tradition, which said that sex before marriage was wrong. As sincere believers we tried to obey this dictate. So we studied the Bible together when we saw each other, took walks, and dreamed about going on the mission field once Michael finished school. Looking toward married life, we took a marriage preparation course with our pastor. He stressed that I was to obey my husband and that Michael was to be my spiritual leader and head of the house. As usual, I tried not to think about how negative all this sounded, and hoped for a marriage where we would truly be partners. Michael said he wanted this, too, and I believed him. So, almost one year after we started dating, we were married. At my wedding I wore the same pair of white shoes I had worn on that first date.

Our ten-year marriage turned out to be a challenge for us both. From the beginning Michael and I fought about all kinds of things. We had so little money we had to stay with Michael's parents. Typical as it might sound, his mother and I never got along. We moved out and very quickly fell deeply into debt. There were student loans to be paid, and I had trouble finding a job, and all the while Michael continued with his studies. We were living in the city where I had become a Christian and been so happy. However, most of my friends were gone and things seemed so different without them. I finally got a job as a secretary at my former university. I had changed my name, and I felt as if my entire identity had changed with it.

School and church took up both Michael's and my energy, and our sex life became deeply unsatisfying. We went to my old church, but the sermons were all about our sinfulness and how we had to repent in order to fully experience God's love. There was more to worry about. I was having trouble experiencing the love of God no matter how much I prayed, and I often came home in tears because I couldn't figure out what sin I had committed to separate me from God. I begged Michael to switch churches, but he wouldn't hear of it. My loneliness continued. Although Michael and I had our share of good times, a rift developed between us, despite the counselling and self-help books we read so that we could learn to communicate with each other. Outwardly, we looked like a perfect couple. We even thought we were. But we also knew that marriage was a lot of hard work and sacrifice, like our relationship with God.

I finally got a better job at the university, and Michael finished his degree. He got a job near his parents' workplace, and we managed to save enough money to buy a house. I loved this house very much. It was a duplex with a beautiful garden and lovely old wooden floors. Without realizing I was doing it, I began to do almost all the gardening work and housework on the weekends. My job at the university turned out to be very difficult, and I found more and more reasons to stay late and work rather than come home. After much prayer and reflection, I decided to go back to school and get my Ph.D. in English if I got a big enough scholarship. I decided this would be a sign from God that I should go back to school.

I won a large grant and began school in the fall. Michael was jealous of my life at school, and he became more jealous as I began to succeed there. I loved being in the Ph.D. program and began to dream of being a professor one day. I enjoyed having new friends, and I worked in the teaching assistant and sessional lecturer union movement at the university. Then suddenly, Michael quit his job and decided to go back to school in order to become a Baptist pastor. I was shocked because he hadn't told me his plans beforehand, and we had so little money to send him to school. Secretly I was dismayed because I did not want to be a pastor's wife: the thing I disliked the most about Christian life was having to attend a traditional church. But Michael seemed so happy at the prospect that I decided we could manage, somehow. I told myself I was just being selfish and that such behaviour was sinful.

But things got harder. Michael started in a student minister position at a Korean church where no one spoke any English. I decided I could

not attend this church and so, against Michael's wishes, I started to go
to an inner-city church where some of my friends were working. There
I was able to combine my passion for social justice with my desire for spiritual growth. Most of the people at the church were young and idealis-
tic, and they worked with poor youth in the area. Soon I was a youth
worker and had teenagers hanging around our house all the time.
Michael joined me at this church after his student ministry time was
over, and he enjoyed it too. The work we were doing in the inner city
seemed so important, socially and spiritually. We loved the young pastor we worked with, a single man with fire in his eyes for God and a
wonderful sense of humour. We felt like we were living on the edge for
God as we ran a worship rock band, did youth work, and worked with
families in the area to help them in their daily lives. But as before, the sermons were all about our sinfulness and how we had to live good lives.
If we were having trouble, the problem was with us and our tendency
to disobey. Many of the people at the church didn't have much education, and some openly questioned whether I should be doing a Ph.D. at
a university, secular or otherwise. As usual, I brushed these comments
off and tried to forget about them. The two halves of my life felt like
they didn't go together, except when I thought about my work and my
life in terms of social justice and activism.

There were other problems, too. My husband became angrier, sometimes at me and sometimes at other things. He didn't seem to enjoy his
time at the seminary, and he was having trouble concentrating on his
work. He seemed happiest when he was leading planned activities like
Bible studies. I would ask him what was the matter, but he always said
everything was fine. As for me, I tried hard to pray and read the Bible,
but I began to feel that God was very far away. I couldn't sense God's
presence when I prayed, and I had read the Bible so many times in so
many translations that I was having trouble finding anything new in it
to contemplate. I blamed myself for what I figured was a rebellious attitude and kept trying. Michael began to insist that I pray with him every
night, even though it often felt as if our prayer and study time was
forced. I agreed only because I felt guilty about saying no. We had trouble studying together without fighting, and we seemed to have arguments every day.

And then, near the end of my Ph.D., I went to my first job interview
and was hired as a professor at a big research university. This was
unheard of in my discipline of English literature: there weren't enough

jobs to go around, and most graduates ended up teaching as underpaid, sessional lecturers. I was ecstatic and very thankful to God. Michael agreed we would move and that he would finish his degree in our new city. I wrote my Ph.D. thesis in four months, and we prepared to take up our new lives.

For both of us it felt like a wonderful new adventure was beginning. I loved my new job even though it was very challenging, and I made many new friends, including some lesbian friends with whom I felt very comfortable. It was exciting to be in a big department where so many people were supportive of me and of what I did. When I was with my friends from work, I felt like I "belonged" in a way that I had never belonged in Christian groups.

But my new life at school started to translate into a more difficult life at home. Michael didn't enjoy doing his degree in the new seminary any more than he had in the old one, but he did finish and took up a part-time assistant pastor position in a Baptist church. I immediately disliked his choice. It was in a vibrant area of the city, but it had a small and aging congregation strongly opposed to doing anything different from what it had done for the past thirty or forty years. I found myself extremely bored, and adding to the difficulty, Michael increasingly expected me to do church work while keeping up work at home. Tensions mounted because I felt that at the beginning of my new career, my position at the university should be the focus of my life. Michael also got very angry if I was even a few minutes late coming home from school. He asked me to try to convert my co-workers to Christ and did not seem to understand I didn't feel comfortable with such a request. I began to feel that the Christian life I led and the life I had at the university would never have anything to do with each other. I felt guilty. As always, I told no one about what was going on. I felt alternately happy about my new career, though physically tired and sick. I was overweight and out of shape. When I went hiking in the mountains with Michael, I could hardly keep up. And sometimes I thought maybe Michael liked it that way.

And that is when—without realizing it at first—I fell in love with another woman. She was an artist I knew who lived in another city, and we had met through my work. Like me, she was in an unhappy marriage, and we started to talk about our relationships and our lives. She was quite a bit older than me, but she was charming. Unlike my husband, she really seemed to like me for who I was. We became closer as time went on, and I would often find excuses to drive down and see her. I thought we were just good friends, but then one day I read a memoir about a woman quite a bit like me who had an affair with her best woman friend. To my shock, I saw myself in that story and I knew I was in love in just that way. I was horrified, but I felt compelled to find out if it was true. I talked to one of my lesbian colleagues at work about how I was feeling and she asked me point-blank: "Do you think you could be a lesbian?" I had no answer for her. I knew that before I was a Christian I had lived with a woman, but how could I possibly be a lesbian now? So I went to a counsellor to find out how not to be a lesbian and how to be faithful to my husband as well as to God.

In counselling I learned that the big issue wasn't whether I was a lesbian, but whether I was happy in my marriage. I had to admit I wasn't and that I had no idea how to change it for the better. My husband and I had been to a lot of counselling, but so much seemed to be wrong, and daily life seemed to be too much hard work for both of us. For the first time I thought about giving up, leaving him, and living as a lesbian. My heart filled with joy as well as fear. Could I really do such a thing? What would happen to me if I did? Michael and I went on a hiking vacation that summer. Michael liked to hike at his own pace, so I had plenty of time to think as I walked along the empty coastline by myself. I decided not to pray about things, because praying always seemed to lead to making decisions that were harmful to me. By the end of the vacation I knew what I had to do: I decided it was better to be a single woman than to pretend to be a straight one in a marriage. If I kept trying to pretend, I would eventually have an affair with a woman and commit an even greater sin.

I told Michael I was leaving him because I was a lesbian. It was painful to watch him move through disbelief, to shock, and then anger. He pleaded with me to reconsider, but I wouldn't hear of it. I went with him to our church and told the deacon's board so that they could decide what to do with me. They were sympathetic at first, but the senior pastor told me that homosexuality was not just a sin—it was an act that could not even exist in the mind of God. The pastor offered to do a Bible study with me to change my thinking, but I refused. It was decided I would have to leave the church and my denomination. The pastor wanted me to leave the church quietly, but I would not go unless some kind of announcement about my sexuality was made. I wanted to make sure the people of the church understood why I was going. Reluctantly, the senior pastor agreed to an announcement but said I could not write it myself.

So I left my husband and shortly afterwards sat through a church service and heard my statement of dismissal. Though it was deeply painful for me, and I felt very guilty about hurting and shaming my husband the way I did, I also began to feel happier and more peaceful than I had in years. I started to feel an inner strength and power I didn't realize I had. Other people noticed it, too. I started to work out and lose weight, and eventually I met a woman who has become my life partner. I attended a gay and lesbian church for a while and then went to an Anglican church, but gradually I stopped going. I still felt that I was a Christian, but I also knew in a very deep way that I had made changes in my life on my own without asking for help from God. I wasn't sure what this meant for my spiritual life. I had spent much of my marriage asking God for help, but help had not come. Was I just stubborn and a bad Christian? Or was the work of changing my life really just up to me and not God?

If I were hearing this story for the first time I would have some questions. Evangelicals often describe their conversion as a testimony in the style of Billy Graham's simple yet powerful conversion tool: the Bridge diagram. In the diagram, you must understand that your sins separate you from God, that your own effort will not "bridge" the gap between you and God, and that the sacrifice of Jesus on the cross is the "bridge" between you and God. You cross over on the Cross, from the darkness of sin into a life of light within the church.

There's a problem with this. When people convert to Christianity they often talk about how they didn't know they were living a life of sin. But the Bridge diagram requires them to acknowledge the sin. So they often say it is only later, when they "know" the truth, that they understand they were living a life in darkness and have now gone into the light. Any problems that arise from being a born-again Christian are a result of either disobedience or the actions of Satan interfering in the life of the Christian.

I could say the same thing about my marriage: I knew at times there was something wrong, but I didn't know what it was. It would be easy to explain this by saying I somehow "knew" I was a lesbian before I was married; that I turned away from this knowledge and then afterwards came back to the "truth." But the story of my sexual identity isn't that simple, just as the story of Christian conversion isn't that simple. I did not suddenly convert to lesbianism. I learned I really was a lesbian, attracted to women, through a series of blind alleys and false starts. It was a process of the denial of my desires, started at puberty, carried right through to my religious conversion. There were times I really had enjoyed dating men. There even were times I enjoyed being married. But my deepest and most satisfying relationships (whether they were romantic or platonic) have always been with women. I just didn't have the means—or now I'd say the *narrative* means—to put different events in my life together into a story that made sense to me. I can now conclude that I am better off living as a lesbian than living as an outwardly asexual woman who would have to spend a lifetime trying not to feel attracted to other women. But for a very long time I didn't know that the testimonies I made for myself could be different and that a happy ending for my religious tradition could not ever result in a happy ending for me.

When I now look at the story of my conversion I can see I needed to belong to a community, and that I was attracted to a community of women who in their own ways all had personal strength and power. In a sense, becoming a Christian was a way for me to become a kind of lesbian, since I had never been part of a lesbian community. I didn't always experience evangelical Christianity as an evil, confining system. Even in my testimony about my marriage I can see now why Michael became jealous and angry, and I can see that I got married so quickly because I bowed to community pressure to be like everyone else. So my conversion and marriage were not, as many people assume, a time of darkness that I left behind as I became a lesbian. Today the memory of what was positive in the traditions that I left causes me pain, even though I have no desire to return to the life I once led. I do not deny this pain now, nor do I deny the story of what I had to leave behind. That is the difference between my life as an evangelical and my life outside evangelical Christianity.

I could not have known years ago what my own narratives about Christianity tell me now. In the past I was unable to see how to choose a different story for myself. I had assumed that *not* following in the footsteps of Lot, as that story is understood by evangelical Christianity, would result in my death. Like his wife, I would have become a warning to others about the cost of disobedience. But once I "looked back" for myself, I found that there are worse things than becoming a warning to others. If the price of obedience is your dignity and integrity as a person, then obedience to a tradition that marginalizes the essence of who you are is going to result in spiritual death. A religion that refuses to consider the existence of complexity and ambiguity in its stories will blame its adherents for any problems they are having. So I will not end this story by saying I have "converted" to life as a lesbian from the "darkness" of straight married life in the church. I won't even say I completely understand what my faith means to me now because I'm not sure that I'm living in the light of faith, or of identity. I learned this instead: the lesson of Lot's wife is the lesson of true desires and of alternatives. There is more than one story for all of our lives, and we need to let all versions of our story grow within us, to teach us what we need to know.

JEFFREY W. ROBBINS

The Slippery Slope
of Theology

Sometimes looking back over the course of a life one realizes that decisions were made without a conscious choice ever being made. The classic example, of course, is falling in love. After all, where does one draw the line between dating and romance, between romance and falling head over heels in love? As much as we enjoy the feeling of being in love, is anyone ever prepared for its consequences? Does anyone ever know where it will lead? The differences between being attracted to another person, longing to be with that person, and then suddenly having one's life inextricably tied to that person by the bonds of love is one of the most profound and consequential things that will ever happen in a person's life. Yet at the same time, looking back one realizes it is not the sort of thing one consciously decides to do. Or at least whenever such a decision is made, it always is a leap into the unknown.

My story of faith—or perhaps more accurately, my story of a faith lost and found—follows a similar pattern. There are benchmarks along the way, moments when critical decisions are made that set one ineluctably on a path of transformation and release. But my decisions have sometimes turned out in unexpected ways. For instance, I can still remember as if it were yesterday standing alone on a suspension bridge in Waco, Texas. I had been on a weekend retreat of Bible study and communion, standing on the bridge with tears in my eyes and the clearest, most piercing sense of purpose and resolve I had ever felt before or since. At that moment I vowed to live in the likeness of Christ, to go wherever and to do whatever God willed, to study, to know, and to be transformed. I had offered up similar platitudes before, usually at the urgings of a minister, evangelist, or Bible teacher. But never before had this realization of the hard cost of discipleship hit me with such force. And never before had I been willing, as they say, to sacrifice all for the sake of Christ. It was one of those moments of rare spiritual clarity. Though I knew the intensity of the emotion would not last, I sincerely believed my resolve would lead to awe-inspiring, fearful, and joyous regions of the human heart.

I also believed it would change me. I thought I would be transformed from being the sincerely devout believer who was still plagued by nagging questions and questionable habits, to a man of real wisdom, spiritual insight, and moral character. I felt it was an obligation.

Then and there my thoughts wandered to the idea that perhaps someday I might become a saint, or a great mystic, or the highest of honours, a martyr for my faith. How else, after all, could I reconcile the intensity of that felt spiritual passion with the banality of ordinary, day-to-day existence? How else to explain the fact that when I prayed, earnestly and diligently, I typically discovered myself bored to distraction and struggling against sleep? How else could I make sense of Christ's promise in John 10:10 that I would live an abundant life? If this life did not provide the abundance the Bible promised, there must be something terribly wrong with me or with this life in general, because the alternative would be that the facts of life make God a liar. At least so I thought at the time, with the result that my fundamentalist faith was nothing but a death wish, a living contradiction pushing me unwittingly further and further into the depths of despair.

I liken this experience to that of falling in love because of the unexpected if not ironic effect this spiritual resolution had, which coincided with, or perhaps gave birth to, the awakening of my theological consciousness. In other words, by seriously resolving to live in the likeness of Christ, I was not only making myself vulnerable by willing myself into the crucible of God's grace, but also subjecting my religious convictions to a newfound critical scrutiny. I began asking myself to what extent my experiences bore the truth of my beliefs. And when the experience was left wanting, this necessitated a re-evaluation of the beliefs themselves. Unwilling (or incapable) of even entertaining the thought that my faith in God might be predicated on a lie, I set out on a theological journey for a faith that I could believe in and that was true to my own experience. I expected confirmation. What I got was entirely something else.

I did not foresee, nor could I have foreseen, where this journey would lead. But one conviction remained firm throughout, guiding me in my intellectual quest and offering some modicum of relief in those moments of most intense doubt. It was the idea—even more the hope—that if God were God, then I as a lonely sojourner had no reason to fear the truth. This bedrock conviction gave me the necessary licence to follow wherever my thoughts led. Only later would I discover that this pathway of a faith seeking understanding was the very definition of theology offered up and modelled by generations of Christian thinkers from the very dawn of Christianity. Beginning with Saint Augustine, the great patriarch of the church and the architect of Western Christendom, it extended through the great medieval theologian Saint Anselm and into the modern age with the Christian existential musings of Sören Kierkegaard. Eventually I would come to know and love these theologians from centuries past, but not before I wrestled with the personal story of another giant from the Christian tradition who was a man after my own heart.

I often remark, somewhat tongue in cheek, that Martin Luther cured me of my fundamentalist tendencies. Luther's biography is well known and doesn't need repeating here. What particularly resonated with me was how a person so consumed with God, so single-minded in his religious devotion, and so dedicated to the spiritual resources available from the church of his day, was nevertheless so terribly unhappy. He was a man so caught up in an endless cycle of sin, confession, and despair. Most of all, he was so afraid of a God that he, all too well, knew he should love.

A love under compulsion is no genuine love at all. On the contrary, as Luther would later remark, the more he was instructed to love God, the more he loathed Him. This was his Catch-22: Luther knew he utterly depended on the love of God because of how far he fell short of God's impossible demand for righteousness. Yet the more he sought God's righteousness, the more God appeared to him as a punishing tyrant or an overbearing father whom he could never hope to please. The more he tried, the further he fell short. What to do when nothing could be done?

I first learned of this story at about the same time I was making my spiritual resolution on that suspension bridge in Waco. I was a senior at

Baylor University, the world's largest and most prestigious Baptist university. I had chosen to attend Baylor largely because of its reputation as a conservative Christian institution. I wanted to study in a place where my evangelical faith would be taken seriously in the classroom and where there would be spiritual as well as academic training and resources.

Though I had two older brothers who also attended college, I was the first to leave our home state. I nevertheless left with my family's blessing and support, though not without words of caution from the ministers at my home church. As is the case with so many conservative evangelical congregations, my home church was not without its suspicion of outsiders. They had heard stories of how other young people, supposedly firm in their faith, had gone off to Baylor because of its Christian heritage only to return distanced from the church and skeptical of Christianity. Never mind that this seems an almost universally expected rite of passage for university students. The concern was that a purportedly Christian university should do more to shield young and impressionable souls from the potentially corrosive effects of the life of the mind. In this regard the state university in the hometown would have been better because the devil you know is better than the devil you don't.

At the time this concern seemed positively ludicrous. Plenty enough of my friends had decided on which college to attend with different concerns and ambitions in mind—whether it had a lofty reputation for academics or a more pedestrian reputation for athletics, or whether it was a "party school." My ministers' misgivings struck me at best as misplaced, at worst as offensive.

In any case, away I went, only now with a slight chip on my shoulder. My late adolescent rebellion did not take on the typical form of drugs, sex, and rock'n'roll. Instead I set out to prove not so much that I knew best but that I was in God's trusted hands. The provincialism of my former spiritual caregivers could not hold me back. Clearly it was no less Oedipal than standard teenage rebellion. But in my case it was cloaked in a genuine religious devotion, not unlike President Bush's famous statement to Bob Woodward that he answers to a "higher father."

During the first weeks and months at Baylor I dove into the religious life, becoming a leader in the Baptist Student Union and with the parachurch organization Young Life. I even decided to quit the varsity tennis team during the first month of the fall semester in order to commit more time to the various religious organizations I was involved in. I attended and led various Bible studies, and I went to worship services not only on Sunday mornings but also on Monday and Wednesday evenings. I led an outreach group for the homeless two afternoons a week. A group of us religiously minded students would go and sit with a group of homeless men under the Interstate bridge just to talk with them about their lives.

Somehow I also found time to study and attend classes, but that part of the college experience was only incidental. I scored well because I had to in order to maintain my scholarship, but the learning was segregated from the rest of my college experiences. That was until I hit a wall. At some point I discovered myself so busy and my weekly schedule so booked and formalized that I had absolutely no time to spare for friends or even my girlfriend. Literally every hour, every breakfast, every lunch, and every dinner was booked doing the Lord's work. I was only nineteen years old, yet I already had such an inflated sense of my purpose that I was too selfish to even consider the people I loved and who evidently loved me in spite of myself. At the end of my sophomore year of college, I suddenly realized how terribly weary I was, and for the first time in my life I admitted that I was unhappy.

When I look back on this manic religious activity and seek to understand it so that I might better understand myself, I see that it was not a guilty conscience I was seeking to relieve, but almost the opposite. I had such confidence in God and such belief in the Bible that I felt absolutely sure that doing God's work would necessarily translate into enjoying God's blessings, none more important than the promise of abundant life. I was God's agent. God's purposes, at least in my little neck of the woods, depended entirely on me. I was willing but ultimately unable to shoulder that impossible burden. Only then did the guilt set in—guilt for my own inadequacy, not for any single thing I did but for what I could not do, for what I was utterly incapable of doing. As ridiculous as it sounds, I now realize it was guilt for the fact I was not God.

Of course this was a great heresy, but I did not know that then. After all, I was too busy doing God's work to know the intricacies of church doctrine or the history of Christian theology. In my case, as the scholar of evangelical Christianity Mark Noll described it, "the scandal of the evangelical mind is that there is not much of an evangelical mind." While rebelling against the provincialism of my home church, resenting its suspicion of the world and, by extension, its lack of confidence in me, I had unwittingly internalized a central component of its fundamentalist psyche—namely, that only certain forms of knowledge and thought can be trusted. Which is not to say that fundamentalists are incapable of rational thought. Rather, they use circular logic. It begins with the view that all knowledge and thought must be in service to faith. It then ends where it begins: with a faith already known and secured in revealed Scripture, itself not subject to doubt or scrutiny. As a young college student I was studying science, literature, history, and even religion. I was becoming more knowledgeable. I was becoming a better thinker and a better writer. I was reading poetry, stories, and history, broadening my mind and my horizons. But none of this was ever allowed to infiltrate the religious conviction that was driving me to the point of exhaustion and despair. This was not just my problem, but something endemic to the logic of fundamentalist faith itself.

As a circular logic, it is also a tortured one. Two stories from my youth exemplify this best. First, long before the Left Behind series of books by Tim LaHaye and Jeremy Jenkins sold over 75 million copies and generated over 650 million dollars for Tyndale House Publishers, the 1972 end times film, *A Thief in the Night,* was seen by more than 300 million people. The plot of the film is fairly typical, if only because this film, together with Hal Lindsay's best-selling novel *The Late Great Planet Earth,* effectively established the genre of the dispensationalist thriller: ordinary people getting swept up in the cataclysm of the Tribulation, reading the signs of the times, and realizing, even if too late, that the Bible's warnings from the Book of Revelation must be heeded. This depiction of the end times has since become standard among fundamentalist and conservative evangelical Christians. It expects Christ's Second Coming within our lifetime and believes that this will inaugurate a period of great trial and suffering. This reading of the Time of Tribulation is based on a convoluted reading of the Book of Revelation.

What I remember most from my one and only viewing of *A Thief in the Night,* even more than the rise of the Antichrist, the Sign of the Beast, or the inevitable destruction of the planet, was the grey sky foreboding the imminent doom. It was a world absolutely lacking in colour, a world without hope. I sympathized with Patty, the young woman who served as the film's main character. Perhaps she was not blameless; even so, her fate seemed harsh and unwarranted. Of course, the evocation of this sympathy was exactly the point of the film and the reason for its great potency as a tool for conversion. As we watch the film we realize that but for God's grace, there go we. And most certainly we also learn to fear God, which according the book of Proverbs is supposed to be the beginning of wisdom. The point is that those who have failed to accept Christ within their lifetime are fully deserving of this awful fate. And as modern-day "hell houses" have demonstrated, this fear can be a powerful tool for evangelization.

But there are different kinds of fear; some teach humility and compassion while others are absolutely debilitating if not pathological. After watching the film with my youth group, I spent years with a debilitating fear of God. Though I was assured in my salvation (or at least had received numerous assurances from my parents, teachers, and ministers), I nevertheless obsessed over the prospect that I, like Patty, might be left behind. On the rare occasions that I returned from school to an empty house, my mind immediately returned to the film's imagery and sense of doom. Remembering the film's portrayal of news reports of planes falling from the sky when pilots and passengers suddenly disappeared at the Rapture, I looked to the sky or turned on the television for evidence that Christ had returned. Fearing the silence of an empty house, I would run to the park adjacent to my backyard, hoping and praying that someone, anyone, would be there. I asked why I had been forgotten, what terrible, unpardonable sin I must have committed; I wondered whether my parents and brothers enjoyed the bliss of paradise in my absence.

I know now, and probably even knew then, that these were all silly and irrational fears, but as a young adolescent, they were also uncontrollable and symptomatic of a tortured conscience. Only years later did I share these experiences and fears with others. My oldest brother understood them best. Like me, after viewing the film he too acquired this debilitating fear of God. He later told me that for months afterwards he would leave his bed in the middle of the night and sneak into my parents' bedroom, where he would sleep through the night at the foot of their bed entirely unbeknownst to them. The image was like that of our family dog, who would jump into my bed and crawl under my sheets shivering in fear whenever it rained or thundered. When the storms came, there was nothing I could do to console our poor, pathetic dog. It's a depressing thought that a film intended to save our souls by teaching us the fear of God reduced my brother and I to the same state as our family dog.

Like the first story, the second revolves around a film and its after-shocks. This time the movie was the Academy Award–winning *Philadelphia*, starring Tom Hanks as a gay man dying of AIDS. I was a teenager when AIDS first made the national news as a disease ravaging the homosexual community. At the time I saw the film, I had never known anyone with AIDS, nor had I known anyone who was gay or lesbian. Somewhere along the way I had absorbed the idea that the Bible taught that homosexuality was sinful in the eyes of God, albeit I had never given it a great deal of thought. Indeed, having had no knowing contact with anyone to whom this teaching applied, I had no reason to ever give it a second thought. That was why *Philadelphia* struck me so powerfully. I had grown up watching Tom Hanks play Everyman. I had seen him as Kip Wilson in *Bosom Buddies,* as the boy-turned-man in *Big,* as the widower searching for love in *Sleepless in Seattle,* and now here he was, a formerly vigorous young lawyer victimized by homophobia, ruined and reduced by AIDS, while all the time his character's loving parents and partner look on helplessly and hopelessly.

As I left the theatre I thought to myself what a shame it was that God must resort to such desperate measures to get humanity's attention. Without ever having given it a thought, I sincerely believed that AIDS had been sent as a punishment from God, that it was a last-ditch effort by a Deity quickly running out of options—a hard lesson, to be sure, but a necessary one to restore God's people to the path of righteousness. Then, all of a sudden, as in an epiphany, I was struck by a shock wave that resounded deep within my soul, by an overwhelming sense of horror at my own self for even entertaining such an inhumane thought. I knew then, and from that point forward, that such a God could not be worthy of my trust and devotion, let alone my love. Though it was only a movie that had so shaken the foundation of my faith, I knew that the suffering it depicted was real and profound. How had I allowed myself to become so callous, so doctrinaire, and so arrogant as to cut myself off in judgment of my fellow human beings? Where had my faith gone so terribly wrong?

In introducing my story of faith, I called it a story of faith lost and found. My encounter with Martin Luther remains the pivotal point on which the story turns. Like Luther, I discovered myself in a state of existential despair. I had grown weary of the cycle of sin and confession, which was nothing more than a narcissistic self-obsession. I had grown skeptical of the psychological dread associated with the dispensationalist theology of the Apocalypse. I had grown distrustful of a God who apparently saddled the already stigmatized with an even greater misery. I was searching for a God I could trust and a faith in which I could believe.

When reading Luther I discovered that my story was not my own, at least not in the way I had always imagined it. My story was not unique; rather, it belonged to a long and proud tradition of Christian thinkers who had also struggled with doubt. Augustine, Luther, or most explicitly Kierkegaard—they all described doubt not as a cause for shame and a sign of weakness but as the necessary companion to faith. This faith does not belong to the order of knowledge, so it cannot be contained by what is believed or what is taught. It is more experiential, more existential. In Kierkegaardian terms, true faith is an embrace of an infinite paradox.

That is why the circular logic of fundamentalist faith fails. It is an artificial delimitation of the world of thought and experience, one that ultimately betrays its own self-loathing. Think here of the two cases from above. In the first, an entire generation of evangelical Christian youth is exposed to what is essentially a horror film. Untold trauma has been inflicted in the name of the Gospel. How did the message that literally translates as "good news" get so distorted as to justify psychological torture? Had my good, loving, and supportive parents known how this film reduced their sons to the condition of the family dog, would they have still allowed or encouraged us to attend the youth services at the church? Had the youth minister known that instead of drawing people to God (which was surely his honest though misguided intention), it had the opposite effect of instilling a hardened spiritual rebellion, would he still have used this film as a ploy for growing his congregation?

The answers to these questions are not as simple as one might think. After all, for years afterwards, even as I was still scared by the silence of an empty house, I voluntarily read the books by Hal Lindsay and Frank Peretti portraying the spiritual warfare of the Tribulation. If Sigmund Freud was correct, religion functions as a substitutive satisfaction, as compensation for some perceived lack or inadequacy. What strange and pathological satisfaction did I receive from reading tales that I took with a deadly seriousness and that simultaneously scared me to death? If it is true that *A Thief in the Night* was psychological torture inflicted on me involuntarily, then how do I explain the continual torture I inflicted on myself? Did I find these tales of the Apocalypse satisfying because of their portrayal of vengeance for the ungodly, or were they penance for my own depravity? Did I read these stories because they vindicated me by testifying to my special role as a spiritual warrior in a cosmic battle between good and evil, or because I somehow enjoyed the anxiety they inevitably produced? Regardless of the answer, the circle remained closed—closed from the outside perspective that might have put the whole scenario in some critical, if not comical, relief.

Turning again from *A Thief in the Night* to *Philadelphia*, here is where we see how the tortured theology of self-loathing extends beyond the self to a posture of inhumane moral superiority and judgment toward others. Beyond the psychological trauma inflicted by a fundamentalist faith, this points to the source of religious violence, or at least to a cruel indifference. How did a religion purportedly built on a faith in Jesus become so cavalier and self-righteous in the face of human suffering? When and how did its moral pronouncements take precedence over its duty to serve? How could I have forgotten that Jesus was a scandal during his own time for his association with sinners and tax collectors? These were all questions I finally began to ask myself. While slow in coming, once voiced or at least entertained in the mind's eye, they struck me with a force that was undeniable. The world had crept in and had penetrated my elaborate defences. The self-enclosed circle was broken. From that point forward my prayers to God would have to be a prayer for the world, and my thoughts about God would have to withstand the scrutiny of my experience in the world. Without realizing it, I had become a theologian.

Albert Camus once wrote that "beginning to think is beginning to be undermined." For Camus, this was the challenge issued by existentialist thought and the crisis of the modern mind. Historically and theologically speaking, this challenge began long before the school of existentialism. As the crisis of the modern mind, it has its roots in the Protestant Reformation, and more specifically in the figure of Martin Luther. Until I discovered Luther and the world of Christian thought and history that he opened up to me, I was a hamster in a cage spinning the wheel in intense and sincere efforts that always led to the selfsame truths. After

Luther, and like the Protestant world he helped inaugurate, I faced a different challenge—namely, the question of what to believe and whom to trust. In becoming a theologian, I liberated myself from the hamster cage, but I also found myself on a slippery slope where everything and everyone was put into question. Once I began to think, the security offered by a self-certain faith was no more.

My fundamentalist posture toward faith was indeed undermined as I began to critically reflect on my experience, but that is not the whole story. The long and arduous task of thinking my way out of fundamentalism was surely not as clean and direct as I am presenting it here. That is the drawback of any narrative; the storyteller must impose a certain logical order or structure on a vast and sometimes contradictory array of events, experiences, and thoughts. As I look back on my life, I know that these were the watershed moments that tugged at my conscience and opened my eyes. But at the same time I was never without a certain reticence or caution.

Over time I grew increasingly skeptical of basic evangelical tenets, such as the inerrancy of the Scripture and the exclusivity of Christianity. Yet while eventually I would be repelled by the militancy and wilful ignorance of fundamentalism, in no way did this translate into a rejection of the living and dynamic faith as revealed throughout the pages of the Scripture, nor did it lead me anywhere near to repudiating Jesus. On the contrary, no matter how far-ranging the critical questions I was willing to ask, no matter how far I slid down that slippery slope of theology—whether exploring the integrity of the world's other faith traditions, the theology of the death of God, or postmodern deconstruction—the basic truth remained that when I conceived of God, when I imagined the fullness of human potential, and when I dreamed of what society could become, Christ was not so much the answer as he was the image through which my answers were inevitably filtered.

I am not saying this is the way things should be, nor am I saying this is the way others ought to think. Or that those who see the world and imagine possibilities differently are somehow wrong or misguided. I am simply saying that is this is the way it is for me. For that, I am unapologetic; indeed, I am eternally grateful to the living witness of Christ as preserved within the all too human tradition of the church for providing such an inspirational, but equally challenging, image toward which I can strive. By confessing Jesus as the Christ I believe I am claiming no more and no less than his earliest followers were—namely, that they had been seized by the living witness of this man to such a degree that he changed the way they imagined both God and the world. The rest—whether the politically motivated doctrine of the Incarnation, the impenetrable doctrine of the Trinity, or the regrettable medieval innovation of the necessity of the atoning sacrifice that turns God into a bloodthirsty tribal chief—the rest, I consider accumulated time-bound baggage that the Christian faith would be better without.

To return to Camus' observation, I could adjust his formulation slightly by saying that the wisdom of theology is the mystery of God. As a mystery, God remains unknown and fundamentally unknowable. Beginning to think theologically, therefore, undermines one's confidence in what is, or even can be, known of God. Of course, this is the age-old caution against idolatry that belongs to all the monotheistic faith traditions, a caution forgotten time and again by nearly all religious believers, most especially those who have been trapped by the logic of fundamentalism. To be a fundamentalist is not only to accept the laudable responsibility of knowing what you believe, but more dangerously, believing that you know with an absolute certainty. In my first sincere, though naive, efforts to practise my faith, too often I fell into this trap of confusing faith with knowledge, claiming to know things by faith about which I had no real experience and had never given any real thought. When I prayed to God from that suspension bridge many years ago, I had no idea then that my prayer to live in the likeness of Christ would eventually lead me to question so much of the religion that bore Christ's name. As I look back now, the irony is almost enough to make me believe in providence. As my mother is so fond of saying, "When God closes a door, he always opens a window." The securities offered by a self-certain faith have been closed to me, but not without opening a window into the integrity of the human experience, and by extension, into the soul of the mystery of God. Thus, I still think that something of what my mother says is true. It is just no longer as altogether clear as it once was that God is the gatekeeper.

JACOB SHELLEY

Life Stages

It wouldn't be accurate to suggest I was raised in a manner consistent with archetypal fundamentalism. At least, not by my parents. I grew up in a home where my father encouraged critical thinking and allowed for the challenging of beliefs. It was the church, more specifically the Pentecostal church my family attended (part of the Pentecostal Assemblies of Canada), that attempted to pull me into fundamentalism.

Of course, it was never presented as "fundamentalism," and there would no doubt be some resistance to the label by my fellow churchgoers. Nevertheless, couched in language of spirituality and authenticity, the rhetoric of Pentecostalism closely resembles that of fundamentalism. It was in this environment that fundamentalism influenced me. Within the walls of the church I was exposed to the closed-minded, uncritical thinking of infallibility, inerrancy, and absolutism, among other sure-tell signs of fundamentalism. I was one of the fortunate ones ("blessed" if you will) whom the church graced with the opportunity to know "truth." The only problem I faced was that this truth was destroying me.

I was brought up in the midst of fundamentalism; even so, I struggle with identifying myself as a former fundamentalist. At most I was a fringe fundamentalist who never really belonged in their ranks. So my story is not about leaving fundamentalism as much as it is about leaving the notion I had to be a fundamentalist. My liberation was from the overwhelming pressure and from the superimposed conviction that I ought to believe as everyone else. That I ought to adopt what was

121

presented as infallible truths. In reality, I had serious misgivings of such things. At minimum, I questioned why a particular set of propositions was more truthful than any other set.

Despite the skepticism, even the cynicism I had toward the fundamentalist ideologies constantly paraded as ultimate truth, and despite the tremendous internal conflict I experienced, I nevertheless attempted to be part of those around me. I attempted to tow the party line, to assimilate in thought and in action. To become what I was told I ought to be. In this regard, I was a fundamentalist. I learned to suppress my discomfort with and incredulity toward fundamentalist dogma, dismissing such reactions as signs of my sinful nature. My misgivings, I tried to tell myself, were the consequence of a lack of faith, of spiritual immaturity. One more prayer, another devotional reading, a song sung with earnest—these were all that separated me from the spiritual epiphany that would allow me to escape from the shadows of persistent doubt. Doubt was not to be tolerated; doubt betrayed the influence of sin and evil. It got to the point that I began to understand the disquiet in my soul—which tormented me incessantly—as none other than the Evil One.

To my detriment (though hindsight reveals the benefit), I was unable to embrace the notion of the Evil One as my archnemesis, armed with a pitchfork and resembling a horned devil. This is not to say I did not feel afflicted, subject to the temptations offered by the vices of life. I succumbed to the carnal pressures on a regular basis. The problem was that I knew precisely whom to blame for my infidelity: it was none other than myself. I was the evil one. I was the very thing that prevented me from experiencing the "fullness of God's glory."

It is hardly surprising I was an angry and angst-ridden teenager. After all, those around me were proficient in "God-speak" and seemed to have some deep spiritual connection that I was lacking. Not to be outdone, I learned to play the roles, learned to sing the songs, and became quite skilled in God-speak myself. Ironically, I was never interested in the drama classes offered during high school. Perhaps there was already enough acting in my life. Nevertheless, it would be misleading to suggest that I was not sincere in my efforts. I truly strove to become a "godly man," one who "shone Jesus' love." Only I was not as concerned with convincing others as I was with convincing myself. Perseverance became the anthem of my life. If only I could just focus, concentrate on praying for just a few minutes more; if only I could fall in love with reading the Scriptures; if only I … and so it continued.

I had become a spiritual junkie searching for the next hit that might deliver me into ecstasy. And just like the junkie coming down from a high, my return to reality—particularly the reality of who I was (not who I was trying to be)—was a painful experience. But instead of searching for needles or dealers, I scoured for the next church meeting, social event, or spiritual experience that would allow me to lift from my shoulders, for a moment, the self-induced state of denial. The altar was where I searched for my next high, my preferred dealer being any minister, worship leader, or fellow believer who could provide me with the necessary fix. All the while, like a junkie sickened by his own pitiful actions, I was internally conflicted. This manifested itself in outward anger, frustration, and a word I have come to appreciate, "angst." My dissatisfaction with those around me stemmed from the dissatisfaction I felt with myself.

The story of my liberation from fundamentalism is the story of my struggle to realize that, in spite of what I had been taught by the church, I need not believe as they did. Nor did I have to accept God as they presented him, or any theological matter. The pressures associated with developing a "personal relationship" with Jesus dissipated, along with the pietistic obligations that relationship entailed. This left me free for the first time in my life to truly seek after God, and not the prepackaged ideologue *cum* deity that had been presented to me.

The story of my liberation from the pressure to conform to fundamentalism is best divided into five stages, which I will affectionately label as follows: The Early Years, The Guilty Years, The Angry Years, The Painful Years, and The Years to Come. Some might interpret this journey as an easy stepping away from Christian faith, but that would be a serious misunderstanding. An escape from fundamentalism (mine or anyone else's) can be arduous and painful. Moreover—and again, contrary to what the faithful might believe—leaving fundamentalism doesn't necessarily lead to agnosticism, atheism, or skepticism. Why is it that questioning, searching, and doubting are associated with faithlessness? For many who strike out on this journey there remains comfort in the promise that Yahweh made to Israel, delivered through the prophet Jeremiah: if we seek after Yahweh, we will find Yahweh—not, however, Yahweh as constructed by fundamentalism, but Yahweh who claimed, "I will be whatever it is that I will be." Leaving fundamentalism doesn't mean leaving faith—if anything, it allows for a sincere pursuit of faith.

The Early Years

I am the second of seven children, all whom have names taken directly from the stories of the Bible. It seems appropriate I received the name Jacob. The name means "deceiver." While Jacob of the Torah deceived his father in order to receive his father's blessing, I was content trying to deceive myself. But my story did not begin in self-deception. Instead, it began quite contently. I look back on my childhood with great fondness, even amidst the constant bickering that comes with having six siblings.

My early years were immersed in the church and steeped in faith. As a child I desired to become a pastor, and it was generally agreed it was my life's calling, my destiny. I would follow in the footsteps of many of my ancestors. Several members of my father's family had been pastors; my father had attended Bible college (one that I would later attend) and had been a pastor for a few years. For a long time I believed I had no choice but to do the same. I grew up listening to the inspirational stories of my great-grandfather, Fredrick Shellistowski, who would brave the cold Ukrainian winters to travel on foot to neighbouring villages to preach the Gospel. Likewise, how could I ignore the stories of my great-grandmother, Mary Melnichuk, who dashed back into her blazing house to save her most sacred possession, her Bible?

While not all my ancestors had been Christian, few stories had been passed down that did not include some element of the miraculous, the sacred, or the sensational. What's more, at several points in my life I had been taken aside and had a "word" spoken into my life. One of those times, I was attending a children's camp and my counsellor took me aside to share a vision he had about me. I never put much stock in such things; even so, they had an impact on me. Who could forget someone telling you that God had given them a vision in which you were doing great things?

All of this had a powerful influence on my childhood. At a young age I had already adopted a lifestyle centred on church activities and Christian friends. There always seemed to be some reason for me to go to church. It was my second home. The Early Years were a time of happy enjoyment; attending church and church events and lending a helping hand came without a second thought. They were years not yet engulfed in turmoil. Like most children, I was content to trust the guidance of others. But this was to come to an end.

The Guilty Years

I cannot say exactly when the transition began to take place, but it would have been early in my adolescence. It was the age of coming into my own intellectually, spiritually, physically, and of course sexually. The parallel between my burgeoning guilt and my burgeoning sexuality was more than clear. The guilt, however, was also the consequence of my growing recognition that the world had more than one dimension. This subtle shift occurred on multiple levels. One of the earliest incidents I can recall happened during my early teens. Since I lived only a few kilometres from the church, I often walked or rode my bike to the services. On one particular walk, I was tormented by thoughts of how I could know for a fact that God existed. Did God exist, or was he simply a conjecture, an elaborate scheme? While no answers came that day, it may very well represent the beginning of my descent into what I refer to as "the Guilty Years."

I don't recall exactly what catalyzed these thoughts. I just had the overwhelming sense that my beliefs, and my justifications for them, were no different from other beliefs, and from other people's justifications. I considered my beliefs true and absolute, but didn't most people who believed other things? What separated me from the Buddhist or Muslim? I simply believed my truth to be Truth, and their truth to be confusion. My thinking, especially for one brought up to accept fundamentalist dogma, was not only distressing but also a sure sign that I was distant from God. Had I talked about this with my peers, let alone with any religious authority, I would only have been told to pray more fervently, to read my Bible more often, and to have stronger faith, along with other antidotes that were quickly becoming unsatisfactory. So I tried hard to keep these thoughts buried, but that only allowed them to fester. Instead of trying to work through my struggles, I simply tried harder to be the ideal Christian. I prayed harder, read my Bible more, and raised my hands higher while singing louder. Yet I still struggled, believing my heart to be the root cause. However hard I tried, I couldn't escape the thoughts that were infecting my consciousness. The guilt quickly followed.

My guilt was not helped by my growing doubts about the tenets of the Christian faith. What made the Scriptures true? Why must one speak in tongues? Who says that the "gentle voice" inside the Christian is the Holy Spirit and not a self-centred ego? These were only a few of the many questions I was beginning to struggle with. At first I tried to keep my struggles within the bounds of "proper Christian thought." That is to say, I forced myself to believe that the answers to my questions were found in the Scriptures, or through prayer, or in the guidance of the church. What became especially troubling was that even when the church provided answers, I was dissatisfied. The answers simply led to other questions. If I could only *believe* ... But I could not, and it was my own fault.

Then there was the struggle over my burgeoning—and often overpowering and alarming—sexuality. Learning to interpret new feelings and thoughts, attempting to decipher the smiles and glances of blossoming young women, and trying to reconcile all of this with the spiritual imperative of chastity was overwhelming. Now both my mind and my penis were out to get me. I can begin now to understand how poorly the church has dealt with human sexuality. This is unfortunate, as sexual development is an almost universal experience as well as an extremely formative time in one's life. At my church, sexual activity was often mentioned from the pulpit, but as something to be avoided until the confines of marriage. Rarely were there any open discussions.

In fact, there were *no* open discussions. One youth pastor maintained that remaining sexually pure was easy—after all, he and his wife had done it. I sat at the back of the church thinking, "Great, but it's too late for me, so thanks for nothing!" I had already failed to maintain my purity; not only that, but I was compromising the purity and thus the salvation of an innocent young woman. Throughout my teen years I heard countless warnings from the pulpit that young women should avoid the advances of horny young men, whose intentions were sinful and lustful. I was guilty by virtue of being male. Yet this did not coincide at all with my experience. Though I was a willing participant, my sexual encounters were invariably initiated by the girl. I was too afraid to make the first move. I vividly remember the fear mingled with excitement as one of my girlfriends coaxed my hand onto her breast for the first time while we watched a movie. This particular girlfriend used to sing in the worship team. After youth services we would park in her car and make out. This involved "Christian sex"—which can range from groping to "everything but." As long as virginity was maintained, a sense of purity could be sustained. The emphasis on purity simply resulted in a redefining of what constituted purity. For example, a friend of mine once maintained that he was still pure and virginal even though he had already engaged in what would normally be considered intercourse. In his mind, the fact that he hadn't ejaculated meant that he had not had sex. Only later in life did I come to realize that almost everyone, in some way, had experimented sexually. It seems that my pious youth pastor's purity was anything but easy and was certainly not the norm. This recognition did not help me feel less guilty.

Is it any wonder that I associate guilt with this part of my life? Besides believing that all my thoughts were heretical and ungodly, I was being told that my sexuality—something I could not control—was evil unless reserved for the marriage bed. Don't forget, masturbation was also strictly forbidden. There was no option for relief, unless of course I found a bride. How could I be anything but guilty? My eyes were magnets for breasts. Women were everywhere, and I enjoyed that fact. Between the girls I saw daily at school, in the media, or simply in my mind, my hormones were absolutely raging. And for this I felt guilty. What's worse, I truly thought I was one of the few who actually struggled with these thoughts, which only increased my evilness. I was the pervert that stared, hoping for a glimpse of skin or perhaps a bra. I was the pervert that acted on these feelings. I was the only one who would give my left arm to simply *see* never mind touch a breast. I was a warehouse of guilt.

Hormonal thoughts were in constant battle with oppressive religious guilt. I thought myself to be such a disappointment. I was not only letting down my family and friends but also disappointing God. In spite of all efforts, I couldn't stop the thoughts, be they sexual or heretical. I tried, but of course the Catch-22 was that in trying to not think about sinful things, I was invariably led to thinking of them, especially sex. I could not escape, and I believed that my lack of faith was preventing me from becoming the person I thought I had to be. Yet I was beginning to recognize that I had little choice in the matter. My sexuality was burgeoning irrespective of my prayers; my unorthodox thoughts persisted despite my pious acts. That I felt guilty, therefore, is not at all surprising. That the next stage of my life I associate with anger is also not surprising.

The Angry Years

The guilty years and the angry years are intertwined. At times my reaction to how I was feeling—mentally and physically—was guilt; eventually, that guilt began to manifest itself as anger. This is hardly surprising. After all, I was experiencing great turmoil and angst. Either I wasn't trying hard enough, or I lacked faith, or I was simply a bad person. I am well aware that every teenager spends a few years swamped with insecurity and anguish. But my efforts to be a "good teen" only contributed to the problem. Faith apparently did me more harm than good.

I was facing a crossroads. Was I the problem? Or did the problem lay elsewhere, perhaps even in the teachings of the church? I was convinced that the problem was me, so I began a fervent campaign to eradicate anything in my life that might be acting as a hindrance to faith. I spent countless hours praying blessings on those who had caused me the greatest harm. I went out of my way to show Christian love to those I disliked most. Volunteering for events became the norm. For a little while I even managed to display some discipline in life (though, typically, my efforts to pray and read the Scriptures were often thwarted by sexual impulses and distractions). If only I could atone for my thoughts, perhaps God would reveal Himself in my life.

I often heard pastors speak of the "still, small voice" we sometimes hear in our hearts. They often attributed it to the voice of God. Apparently it was the Holy Spirit convicting me, or perhaps revealing some lesson I needed to learn. The problem was that the still, small voice seemed to be against me. It would remind me that I was trying to escape who I actually was by trying to become who I thought I had to be. When I attempted to dismiss my struggles as sin, the still, small voice would pipe up and suggest it was a ridiculous notion. When I felt ashamed for questioning the claims offered in a sermon as infallible truth, it was the still, small voice that encouraged me to keep pushing deeper, to ask more questions. I began to fear that God was playing some sort of mean trick on me, testing my faith. Therein lay the dilemma: I could pray, asking God for guidance in the matter, but unless he showed up in full blazing glory I could not help but question the voice. Was it truly God, or was it my own sycophantic way of dealing with a growing chasm between the party line and my own beliefs?

The Angry Years were not solely the result of my own wretchedness. I was struggling with the person I was becoming, and at the same time, all around me, I was beginning to witness the fragility of the Christian faith. When you spend time with those who wear a badge of religiosity on their breast, you cannot help but be exposed to profound hypocrisy. In particular, I was becoming detached from those who were leading the church, be they pastors, youth leaders, or worship team members. This is not to say that the average churchgoing believer was not contributing to my disillusionment—such people certainly were. After all,

I was surrounded by people who were attempting to reconcile their religious beliefs with the other pressures of life. For example, members of my youth group who were consistently holy at church events were different people at school. One moment they were weeping at the altar, the next moment they were drunk at a bush party. But right or wrong, I held our leaders—and those who professed their religiosity the loudest—to a higher standard.

I was becoming more and more aware of the social phenomena surrounding religious rhetoric. In my religious environment, the slogans pitched by the religious were often taken (just like advertising slogans are) as statements of truth. In addition, rarely were the faithful equipped with the necessary tools to critically evaluate these statements, let alone licensed to do so. We were instead conditioned to equate religious and spiritual language with holistic and spiritual living. To my detriment, many around me accepted God-speak in good faith. A favourite approach was to suggest that the Holy Spirit was responsible for thoughts, ideas, and judgments that otherwise would have flowed freely. For example, it was curious how Christian teenagers looking to start or break off a relationship with a boyfriend or girlfriend were suddenly endowed with an acute ability to discern the voice of the Spirit: "I feel the Lord has led me to you," or alternatively, "I don't think the Lord wants us to continue going out." Most troubling was the use of spiritual rhetoric either to buttress claims of authority or to discredit those—such as myself—who were dissatisfied with the rigid fundamentals and who were questioning their legitimacy.

These two uses of spiritual rhetoric worked in tandem. The guardian of truth—be it a pastor or a parishioner—would denounce the questioning of a fundamental as contrary to the will of God and in almost the same breath position himself in such a way as to make a claim of authority, mainly spiritual authority, over the one who was asking questions. All too vividly I recall many encounters where my faith was questioned by those who were my obvious spiritual superiors. These conversations often ended with promises that I would be prayed for. Some would describe these disagreements as dialogues motivated by an interest in the collective and mutually beneficial pursuit of truth. Not in the slightest representative of honest dialogue, in reality, these were exercises in proselytizing.

The more I was exposed to the posturing, the angrier I became. I deemed it a righteous anger, the by-product of the incredulity I felt toward those who could so easily profess spiritual niceties but whose hypocrisy was more than evident. Yet my anger was misguided. That is not to say I lacked cause to doubt their sincerity. After all, hypocrisy is the lifeblood of fundamentalism. Nevertheless, the anger I felt was not ultimately rooted in the actions of others. Rather, their actions only mirrored what I was desperately trying to avoid admitting: my own culpability. I was angry at those in the church because they represented an accurate depiction of who I was becoming. Initially, this led to increased anger. But with the realization of who I was becoming came a painful awareness: I was not, nor did I seem capable of being, the person I "ought" to be. The anger easily transmuted into pain, and the angry years became the painful years.

The Painful Years

When it comes to suffering, it's obvious that mine has not been the worst witnessed by humanity. Yet I wouldn't be telling my story honestly if I did not describe the profound pain I felt. It was not physical agony, and I am unable to point to any significant symptoms (aside, perhaps, from anger or aloofness). But it was painful. It was the suffering that came from realizing who I actually was. It was the overwhelming pain associated with accepting myself. Not surprising, I only truly began to accept my newfound self after I left home to attend college. It was an opportunity to recreate myself. It was not easy, given that I chose to attend a Pentecostal Bible college for a one-year program. While I remain indebted to the college for my experiences there, and more specifically for the friends I made, it was a difficult time. That year only reaffirmed for me that I did not belong in the confines of Pentecostalism, and likely not within evangelicalism either. Sometimes I wondered about the faith overall. One poem I wrote during my time at the college expresses my feelings well. The poem asked why it was that I was cursed. I had begun to realize that my thoughts were not my own doing, at least not entirely. So why could I not believe like the rest? Why could I not believe the things everyone there told me I had to believe? My realization, as one line succinctly puts it: "I believe my lies and not theirs."

The painful years continued as I moved on to a Bachelor of Arts, majoring in religious studies. The pastor of my church warned me that going to university to study religion was dangerous and could be a really good way of losing my faith. I responded angrily to this, frustrated with such a simplistic understanding of faith, one that reduced it to the status of loose change that might inadvertently be misplaced. I was also insulted by the insinuation that I lacked the intellectual integrity to grapple with difficult questions. There was also a sense of discomfort, knowing that I did not fit in. I was slowly being separated from that which I had been attached to at birth. These were incisions not from the blade of a knife, but from the sharpness of thoughts. Those around me viewed the changes I was going through as a "phase" or something that could be prayed through. With each encounter it became more and more clear—people did not want to discuss things with me. Instead they wanted to set me straight. They did not approve of me or my ideas. They sincerely believed that I had been fooled by the sleight of hand of some clever professor, some ungodly thinker. My growing fondness for thinkers such as Nietzsche and Kierkegaard was associated with a rebellious spirit. It was a painful time because my very person was becoming unacceptable to my Christian elders and peers. *I* was the problem. Yet I believed, just like Nietzsche, Kierkegaard, and others who struggled with their beliefs, that I was engaged in a similar journey. I was truly seeking to understand the issues and ideas that were swirling around me. I had wholeheartedly invested myself in finding truth. In my church, all of that counted for nothing. What mattered to them was that I did not believe like a Christian should.

The truth of the matter was that they were right about my beliefs: I no longer thought like them. But I was also coming to realize that I possibly never had. Following the feelings of guilt and anger came the painful thought that my life so far had been nothing but an elaborate lie. After a sudden break-up with a girlfriend, I had a further opportunity to evaluate my life. At that point I had been engrossed in post-secondary education. With the break-up, insecurity suddenly arose. Indoctrinated in me, despite my doubt and skepticism, was the notion that God, if he were properly revered and feared, would bless the faithful. Though unconvinced and entering hesitantly, in the desperation of the break-up I decided to give one more kick at the can of righteous living. The rationale underlying the decision was that perhaps my unfaithfulness and utter sinfulness were the reasons why the relationship had failed. It was another kick at the can even though I was completely aware of my dissatisfaction with the beliefs and ideologies circulated by the church. It was abundantly clear to me that I could not be the person the church told me I ought to be. In the fragility of dealing with hurt emotions, the guilt I had felt for many years revived itself. I was responsible for the break-up. If only I could honour God with my actions; if only I could read my Bible; if only ... and so it began one final time.

It was easy to fall back into the old patterns. Within a short time I had made significant "changes" in my life. I even had people approaching me with the observation that I was a new man. The outward appearance of righteousness is easily feigned. Yet there remained a nagging voice—the still, small voice I spoke of earlier—that was not fooled. So when someone commented on how the Lord was doing wondrous work in my life, the still, small voice would remind me that everyone was fooled, except for God and me.

A realization very important to me during this time was that, while I had uprooted the fundamentalist notions that had been planted deep in me, I still believed in God. To be sure, my understanding of God was very different from the God taught by the church. But I had come to appreciate God as a dynamic entity, one not easily captured by propositional statements. In any event, my outward appearance of righteousness was not fooling Him.

From the outside, it may seem as if I was being intentionally deceptive, utilizing a feigned spirituality to promote my own interests (at that time, it would seem, the acquisition of a new girlfriend). The terminology used by fundamentalists to describe my condition would have been "backslidden." For them, I needed to rediscover my salvation, to "rededicate my life to Jesus." Given my failures to live up to their understanding of the "victorious Christian life," I had doubts about this approach, but years of being instructed that this was the proper and only way of living a godly life had left an impression in the deepest corner of my psyche. This reminds us again of how potent the incantations of fundamentalism can be. I was a self-professed skeptic, one who had spent years dissatisfied with the teachings of the church, yet in a weak moment, I defaulted to the oppressive teachings of the church. To borrow a biblical analogy, I was like a dog returning to its vomit. With such internal conflict it was only a matter of time before everything crumbled.

The events of those few months could no doubt be the subject of several chapters. It was an important experience for me. Since my time in Bible college I had liked the idea of "better to be hated for what you are, than loved for what you are not." Now I was learning to adopt this as a mantra. Ironically, the system that attempted to teach me truth and honesty led me to be untruthful and dishonest about myself. It was likely the first time I truly accepted that it was better to be hated for who I was, despised for what I believed, than to be loved for falsities and untruths about myself. It was a liberating feeling, but nevertheless infused with pain. What made this realization even more painful was that it would not remain in the abstract. My decision would soon lead me to be truly hated for who I was.

To put it simply, my beliefs and ideas led to a situation in which my wife and I were treated with contempt and scorn by her family. It has been a horrific ordeal, spawned out of distrust toward me based entirely on what I believe. When my wife and I did not comply with her family's demand that we postpone our wedding indefinitely—because God had not given them a peace about me—it resulted in a volatile and abusive situation. Why? By this point I did not sing in church, did not attend prayer meetings, certainly did not use spiritually laced rhetoric, and was not afraid to push the boundaries of accepted norms. All of this led to accusations, name calling, character attacks, and much more. This has had far-reaching implications, affecting friendships and other social relationships. Now, four years later, despite some attempt to maintain civility, my wife's family has again disowned her—this time because she has finally grown weary of their assault on my character. In fact, it was a letter in which she beseeched her parents to accept her decision to marry me and asked them to accept her for who she had become that resulted in the bulk of her family—in the name of God, peace, and love—cutting her out of their lives. Their righteous indignation has also led them to reject any interaction with our newborn daughter, their only grandchild so far.

I was also ostracized from the church I was attending at that time. Though rooted firmly in Pentecostalism, the church, which was integrated with the university campus, touted itself as a new kind of church, open to new ideas, accepting of everyone. Of course, I found this not to be true. No doubt members of that church have (and still do) point to me as the problem. Yet all I ever did was disagree. In the toughest time of my life, dealing with the evil inflicted by my now in-laws, this same church, which always identifies itself as a "true community" (not like those other churches!!), was not a place of refuge. Though some friends tentatively stood by us—albeit insisting that they were not interested in taking sides—the church's leadership never stopped to inquire into how my wife or I were holding up. In fact, a few months later when the church became engulfed in controversy and I encouraged the leadership to maintain their integrity, it was interpreted as an attack and I quickly became the pariah. I was even banned from the church's web forum—several times. Unfortunately, the church was more concerned about maintaining its image as a new kind of church than with actually being a *church*—a community that cared for people. Being hated for who I was, was not much fun.

The Years to Come

I cannot write much more without speculating. What I do know for certain, and what I am eternally grateful for, is that I know I am no longer alone on this journey. During the stage I identify as the painful years, I had the pleasure of meeting a lovely young woman whom I would later marry. What is special about this relationship is that my wife has never prevented or discouraged me from seeking answers. In fact, our relationship has been premised on formulating better questions, not as individuals, but in partnership.

The painful years have ceased. For this I must give credit to some very special friends. In the years of struggling to find who I am, I have found friends who have been willing to accept me, others who have encouraged me, and some who have travelled alongside me. One fellow traveller is the editor of this book. I have never had the privilege of being one of his students; nevertheless, we have become close friends. I am not sure if our stories would suggest it, but we have journeyed down similar paths. Fortunately for me, he is only one of a few close friends. Indeed, it is better to be hated for who you are than to be loved for what you are not; better yet is to be loved for who you are.

I hesitate to stop writing. I have just begun to scratch the surface, in part because it is an ongoing story. Though I have struggled with the fundamentalist beliefs taught to me since early childhood, only in recent years have I been able to say I have been completely liberated, left free to question and challenge, think and explore, without fear of condemnation. No longer do I struggle with an archetype Christianity to which I feel I must conform. Yet it would be irresponsible to suggest that the journey is without difficulties. Life always presents new challenges to overcome. But these challenges are far easier to face when one has confidence in oneself. How fortunate for me that I have a wonderful partner and good friends!

I hope this story will help those who are within fundamentalism, or who are associated with someone who is, to acquire a clearer understanding of the struggle of leaving fundamentalism. My encouragement to those within would be to not fear questions. Life is not about answers, but about questions. As Kierkegaard noted, life is about passionately pursuing what could be, not simply focusing on what is. Take opportunities to challenge old ideas, to read new books, to think forbidden thoughts. Do so without fear, knowing that if we seek God, we will find God. More than likely you will be surprised where God is found. For those reading this work out of interest, or because they know someone currently within the fundamentalist camp, please understand that the problem is neither with people nor with faith. Where fundamentalism errs is in turning God, faith, and Christianity into a static system of propositions that must be accepted. Faith is a wonderful thing; dangerous and frightening are the constraints some people place on faith.

I hope my story helps others discover that life is not about the destination, but the journey; that it is not about the answers, but the questions. As Nietzsche wrote, truth can be reached *in* many ways and *by* many ways. That is a notion worth living by.

ANDREA LORENZO MOLINARI

"More Catholic Than Thou"
One Man's Journey Through
Roman Catholic Fundamentalism

I am a Roman Catholic theologian. My story is about a lesser-known type of Christian fundamentalist, namely the type who espouses an ultraconservative brand of Roman Catholicism. My opinions about these fundamentalist Catholics have been formed by exposure to them at the Franciscan University of Steubenville, Ohio, and by later encounters with them over the course of my fifteen-year career as a theologian and lay minister. To understand my strong opinions with regard to this type of fundamentalism, I must explain my own spiritual development as a Roman Catholic, my subsequent early experiences with Protestant evangelical fundamentalism, and my initial encounters with these Roman Catholic groups.

Both my parents were Roman Catholic, yet they came to it by different paths. My father immigrated to the United States from Italy and was a cultural Catholic. Roughly, that means his relationship to the Church was one of polite toleration—he would sit patiently through the droning recitation of a dead language (Latin) that had a fleeting connection to his mother tongue (Italian). Otherwise, Catholicism played almost no part in his life. My mother, on the other hand, was a convert from Methodism.

It was my mother who fuelled my interest in the Christian faith in my early years. At her insistence we went to church every Sunday. Each night before we went to bed, she took my sisters and me up on her lap and read a story to us about some Bible hero or heroine. In my earliest memories I hear her telling Bible stories about Joshua, Gideon, Samson, and David. She also emphasized prayer, both formal and spontaneous. She taught us to weave prayers into the fabric of our lives, whether it meant pausing to say grace over our meals or taking time to speak to God about our day just before we climbed beneath the bed covers.

She also insisted that I attend our parish grade school. This, too, had a strong impact on my spiritual development. At that time (the early 1970s) there were still a number of sisters teaching in grade schools, and I remember always having good relationships with them. Theirs was a simple Catholic piety, steeped in daily attendance at mass, saying the rosary, and acts of charity. I remember their kindness and gentleness with great affection.

Likewise, I fondly remember our parish priests. When I was little, it was still common for several priests to be assigned to one parish—a luxury that does not exist today. With priests and sisters a plentiful commodity, it was quite common for them to handle many of the ministries now managed by either professional lay people or volunteers. For example, the usual candidates for the parish youth ministry were (1) the youngest priest on staff (usually fresh out of seminary) and (2) whatever sister or sisters he could move to action by pleas for help. In the early 1970s at my home parish, that young priest was Father Steve. All the kids loved Father Steve. He was very young and energetic. He came to visit our classrooms, played ball with us on the playground, presided over all school masses, and came to see us during religion class. He used to tell us stories about Jesus and about how much He loved children. To us, he *was* Jesus.

In many ways I am still a product of the optimism that flowed out of the Second Vatican Council. For those unfamiliar with it, the Second Vatican Council (1962–65) was called by Pope John XXIII with the intention that the Roman Church bring itself up to date, address contemporary problems, and take part in discussions of the major questions of the day. This decision by John XXIII was a surprise, as he had been elected pope as something of a stopgap measure. The council produced a series of documents regarded as authoritative, which addressed diverse issues such as modern biblical criticism, the relationship of the Roman Church to non-Christian religions, the relationship of the Church to non-Roman Christians, and the role of the laity within the Church. Sadly, here in the United States the Church did a poor job of explaining the council's teachings to its people. Today, the average Roman Catholic who remembers the transition from the pre–Vatican II to the post–Vatican II Church and who is asked about the changes the council brought will probably mention the vernacular mass and the fact that the priest now faces the people during the mass.

Like the rest of my generation of young Roman Catholics, I was told that God loved me. We were also presented with a younger, hipper Church that said "you are okay." Unlike the young Catholics of the 1950s and 1960s, my generation was not steeped in the question-and-answer indoctrination of the Baltimore Catechism. We were not taught Church doctrine. After Vatican II the catechetical pendulum had swung decisively from legalism and content-focused formations toward a more emotive, feel-good focus on community. A healthy balance was attempted, and largely realized: on the one hand, a gradual and systematic introduction to the teachings of the faith; on the other, a healthy cultivation of the spiritual life rooted in prayer, liturgy, community, and service. I differed from most of my Roman Catholic contemporaries because of the importance my mother placed on teaching the Scriptures and on personal prayer, coupled with the sisters' and priests' emphasis on God as a loving and forgiving Father who called on us to live in community.

I had my first brush with fundamentalism when I was nine. My father had grown up as an ethnic Catholic, but his faith held little importance to him. He had been a chief petty officer in the Italian Navy until he married my mother. He immigrated to Michigan (her place of birth) and took a job as a factory worker at General Motors. While working there he was approached by a Pentecostal man who began to talk to him about Jesus Christ. He then introduced him to like-minded factory workers. Like many Catholics, my father knew little about the Scripture, and he had never heard anyone frame Christianity in phrases such as "having a personal relationship with Jesus" and "accepting Jesus as your personal Lord and Savior." For him, Christian faith was a spectator sport. Yet here was a man who was asserting that he could and should get in the game.

This was very foreign to my father. As a general rule, Catholics tend to participate in the faith more as a result of familial and cultural gravitational pull than by personal choice. They are baptized as infants, and someone else decides they will be Christian. They are introduced to the

Eucharist when they are too young to really grapple with its significance. Now my father was being asked to choose Jesus, probably for the first time in his life!

I am certain my father's decision to embrace Pentacostalism had to do with the evangelical sense of community. He had come to a foreign country without knowing the language and in doing so had separated himself from his entire family and previous way of life. He had taken a job in a factory where a man was little more than a living cog in the industrial machine. Aside from his immediate family, he had few friends. Suddenly he was presented with a group of men who gathered around him and supported and encouraged him to live for God—a concept that must have been lying dormant in his heart because of his exposure to Roman Catholicism. Not long after encountering his new friend at the factory, my father "gave his life to Jesus" by answering an altar call at a local Pentecostal church. My mother was pleased because for the first time my father was taking an interest in matters of faith. Her own experience with Methodism and attending other churches left her open to attending other church services, with the caveat that our family not cease its weekly attendance at mass. In retrospect it is ironic that it was my mother, the convert to Catholicism, who was responsible for my continued involvement in the Catholic Church. Not long after being "saved," my father began attending a Saturday morning men's breakfast sponsored by an organization called the Full Gospel Business Men's Fellowship International (FGBMFI). My father decided to bring me along with him, and from that time on (my ninth to seventeenth years) we rarely missed Saturday meetings. During those years nothing had a stronger impact on my spiritual development.

The FGBMFI meetings began with an exuberant praise and worship service. This was completely foreign ground for my father and me, but both of us adapted quickly to the concept of singing more than one song at a time in a religious service. As a young adolescent, I was amazed by the energy and excitement of praise and worship. In this service the men used various instruments from guitars and drums to synthesizers. At that point my experience with musical instruments in church had been limited to the pipe organ.

The men actually seemed to enjoy singing, unlike in my home parish, where the women shouldered the responsibility for that ecclesial ministry. The praise and worship service led to a period of Charismatic-style gifts such as "speaking in tongues" and various displays of healing. This was completely wild and unlike anything I had seen before. The Pente-costals in the group lost no time pointing out various New Testament texts where such spiritual gifts were taken for granted (e.g., Acts 2 and I Corinthians 12). This scriptural argument made sense to my father and me. For Catholics, such assertions resonated with the miracles associ-ated with the saints down through history, especially with those linked to the various Marian shrines (e.g., Lourdes). After the Charismatic-style worship wound down, the men who led the meeting called everyone to prayer and then offered a blessing over breakfast. After breakfast the officers dealt with weekly business such as membership and finances. The treasurer took an offering, and the president got up and introduced the guest speaker.

It was during this second half of the meeting that my father and I experienced our greatest struggles. The FGBMFI organization described itself as "interdenominational," which meant it encouraged men of every Christian church to attend. Doctrine was supposed to be left at the door. In practice this refusal to discuss doctrine referred more to mainstream church doctrine, as the vast majority of the teachings presented as Chris-tian bore an uncanny resemblance to Pentecostalism. In the late 1970s and early 1980s the American religious landscape was dominated by funda-mentalist preachers like Jimmy Swaggart, Oral Roberts, Kenneth Copeland, and Jim Bakker, who advocated a "Prosperity Gospel" brand of Christianity. According to the teachings of these highly visible televi-sion evangelists, God wanted little more than to bless his children with every good thing on this earth, from fancy suits to a beautiful wife to a stretch limousine. They relied on scriptural texts such as Deuteronomy 28:1–14, which promise God's financial blessings on those who obey God's commandments. All a Christian needed to have to activate this del-uge of blessings from Heaven was simple faith in God.

In practical terms, a Christian needed to assert his faith by giving to God (preferably to the ministry of the preacher making the appeal), with Him rewarding this act of trust by multiplying back this monetary gift many times over. These preachers emphasized in particular the virtue of giving far more than one could afford. They appealed particularly to the many factory workers who had been laid off by General Motors. These preachers often pointed to the story of the widow who gave her last two coins (Mark 12:41–44). A favourite verse among these preach-ers was Luke 6:38—"Give, and gifts will be given you. Good measure, pressed and shaken down and running over, will be poured into your lap; for whatever measure you deal out to others will be dealt out to you." God was presented as an investment broker in the sky.

To my father's credit, he was never taken in by these promises of worldly wealth, though he readily accepted the concept of tithing. From the time he accepted the idea of a personal relationship with Jesus, my father began to tithe his gross income to charity. Despite periods of unemployment and moments of great financial insecurity, he did this without fail for twenty-eight years, until his death in 2005. He gave to charities without regard to denominational affiliation and without ever claiming his charitable gifts on his income tax. When asked about deductions for his charitable giving, he quoted the words of Jesus to me: "But when you give alms, do not let your left hand know what your right is doing" (Matthew 6:3).

Looking back, I realize that my father was doubly inoculated against the "Prosperity Gospel." First, he had known great poverty as a child. He was born in 1937 in Genoa, Italy, and he had endured the ravages of the Second World War as a child in an area of Italy that never fell to the Allies. As a boy he had become well acquainted with starvation and extreme want. His experience of poverty and his sense of God's protection during such dangerous times would not allow him to accept that poverty was somehow a sign of a lack of God's favour. Second, his Catholic "DNA" would not allow him to accept the principles of the Prosperity Gospel. Whatever its failures, the Catholic Church had exposed my father to St. Francis of Assisi (*Il Poverello*, "the little poor man") and countless other mendicant saints. My father used to shake his head when these preachers spoke of their fine cars and fancy houses. He pointed to Jesus' words in Luke 9:58—"Foxes have their holes and birds their roosts; but the Son of Man has nowhere to lay his head."

Despite our difficulties with the Prosperity Gospel, my father and I did enjoy the FGBMFI meetings. The sense of community was infectious, and the other men made a great effort to be welcoming and supportive. For the first time in both our lives, we experienced church as a place where we mattered as individuals. As a young adolescent I was deeply affected by the men who attended these meetings. Even though I was almost the only young person who attended the meetings, I was welcomed with open arms. It was like having a whole roomful of dads and uncles and older brothers, all of whom made their faith their first priority. Whether they admit it or not, young people are always looking for role models. I was no different. I am certain that their example and loving acceptance provided protection against many of the problems that other teens struggled with.

Despite our aversion to the Prosperity Gospel, my father and I enjoyed the biblical teachings offered at these meetings. During my years in junior high, we began to read the Bible together every day. For the first time, I was being challenged to read and interpret the Bible. My father and I spent hours huddled over the kitchen table, debating the meaning of certain passages. I realize now that despite his complete lack of formal theological education, my father had a balanced and enlightened view of Scripture. Moreover, his respect for my theological ideas (even when they differed with his) gave me confidence to formulate my own opinions without fear.

That was my spiritual life and its development through high school. My family continued to attend weekly mass, but my real spiritual feeding came outside the Catholic Church. I still had love in my heart for Roman Catholicism, but I felt a certain frustration with the blandness of its liturgies, the vacuous character of the vast majority of its homilies, and its apparent apathy about teaching doctrine. Yet I still felt a connection to the Catholic Church despite my general disappointment and dissatisfaction with what it seemed able to offer me. I realize that there was (and is) a great tension here. Even now, as a theologian, I still feel this terrible tearing. I still find most of the Roman Catholic liturgies I attend to be depressing and boring, events that leave me angry and frustrated rather than spiritually fed or renewed. Yet then as now, I felt a connection that somehow transcended this frustration. I recognized what it was then as summed up in the phrase "the saints." What I mean by this is a sense of the heroes and heroines of the Faith. Despite all its flaws, somehow the Church had succeeded in telling me about Francis of Assisi, Peter, Laurence, Agnes, Perpetua, Cyprian, and John Chrysostom. Somehow the Church had succeeded in showing me their faces and suggested (ever so obliquely) that they could be helpful guides, spiritual mothers and fathers for me as I struggled with my faith in the here and now. As much as I felt disappointed by the Church, I couldn't bear to walk away from my heroes and heroines. I feel the same way today.

Moreover, as I began to think about things like college and possible careers I felt a strong desire to serve the Church. I realized that in order to do so effectively, I would need to study theology. My thought process was simple. I was a child of Vatican II, essentially uninformed about the Church's teachings. When my Protestant friends told me that Catholics worshipped Mary, or when they attacked the Roman practice of sprinkling an infant at baptism, I couldn't defend myself. They wouldn't dare attack my knowledge of Scripture, as they knew that even though I was a Catholic, I was easily their match. But I hated feeling ignorant of my own Church's teachings. How could I be something if I didn't even know what that something was?

I looked at a number of Roman Catholic schools but quickly ruled them out for financial reasons. I even consulted with my parish priest. Sadly, he was not knowledgeable about which universities could offer me an affordable Roman Catholic theological preparation. Then one day I was talking with several women I knew at church and expressed my frustration at trying to find a school. One recommended the Franciscan University of Steubenville. She told me that unlike many Roman Catholic schools, this university only taught what the Catholic Church teaches. I was sixteen at the time and too young and naive to be outraged by such a blatantly ignorant statement, an insult to the many fine Roman Catholic departments of theology that serve the Church across this country.

I took her advice, applying to the University of Steubenville in the fall of 1984. I was accepted and began my studies in the fall of 1985. At that time the school was strongly associated with the Charismatic Movement. It hosted annual summer youth conferences as well as other conferences aimed at its fervent clientele. As a result of these conferences, several of the priests associated with the school had developed a degree of fame within the Charismatic community. Of these, none was more famous than Father John P. Bertolucci, a magnetic author, evangelist, and television personality. (Sadly, he was publicly removed from ministry by his home diocese of Albany because of sexual impropriety during the sexual abuse scandals several years ago.) The other major figure at the university in those days was Father Michael Scanlon, TOR, who was president of the university and who led a Catholic Charismatic community. Most of its members were university graduates and other Catholic Charismatics who had come to Steubenville in order to live in community. The community was located in and around the city of Steubenville. At the time it was scarcely distinguishable from the university itself.

Even though I had already been exposed to Charismatics, the university was unlike anything I had ever experienced. Gradually I realized there was something really different about this place. The university was unique in that there was an odd kind of peer pressure in play. It was a peer pressure to be religious, and it involved daily attendance at mass, participation in Charismatic-style prayer groups, and adherence to the teachings of the Church. I remember reading articles written by Father Scanlon and listening to his talks, during which he spoke in glowing terms about this "positive peer pressure" and how beneficial it was to the university. Disturbed by these things, I approached him and asked him how he could see people succumbing to peer pressure (even "good" peer pressure) as a desirable thing. I asked him, "If people only do 'Good' because they want to be accepted, then how strong is their commitment to the Good? Isn't it merely a matter of forfeiting one's autonomy and accommodating oneself to one's environment?" Father Scanlon mumbled something or other about forming good habits and walked away. I wasn't satisfied with his answer.

This administration-encouraged peer pressure generated a strange spirit of competition, especially among the students. I was part of many conversations (perhaps better, "interrogations") during which I was quizzed as to the catholicity of my views. Indeed, I was a bit of an odd duck at Steubenville. I was Catholic yet my spirituality was Bible-centred. My familiarity with the Bible set me apart; I was suspected of being Protestant. In general, the spirit of competition I encountered was centred on who could be the most authentically Catholic in their views. In other words, a certain bizarre "more Catholic than thou" attitude seemed to prevail. It was not enough to just be Catholic. One had to be Catholic in a certain way. The result was an interesting hybrid: Charismatic-style teaching of the kind with which I was familiar from my days with the FGBMFI, coupled with what I would call "hyperorthodoxy."

This hyperorthodoxy was characterized by one-upmanship, with the most rabid students going to great lengths to demonstrate their adherence to the Church. It was not enough to attend church on Sundays. One needed to attend mass every day. The holiest of the holy were those who sacrificed for God, imitating a monastic lifestyle by attending early morning mass. Frankly, I just didn't have the desire to get up that early. I figured that if God wanted my presence at morning mass, he shouldn't have made me a night owl.

I heard people make derogatory statements about those who only attended weekly mass. I smile today when I remember those comments, knowing full well that any university student who makes the effort to attend mass while away at school should be commended, not disparaged.

As I recall, devotion to Mary, Jesus' mother, was a particular lightning rod for many of the students. Most Catholics have at least a nominal Marian spirituality. At Steubenville, however, it was not enough to simply respect Mary. One needed to venerate her by daily use of the rosary. One might already have a fairly strong devotion to Mary that included various Marian devotions such as the rosary, the scapular (a pair of small cloth squares joined by shoulder tapes and worn under the clothing on the breast and back as a sacramental), and Marian novenas (a period of public or private prayer lasting nine days to obtain special graces or to offer a special prayer intention), but even this was not enough. To be truly Catholic, one needed to wear a rosary ring or actually carry a rosary on one's person at all times (apparently so as to be ready to rattle off a decade of the rosary at a moment's notice). Scapulars and Marian medals needed to be worn in plain sight so as to make clear to everyone at all times that one was unabashedly Catholic and pro-Mary. My question at the time was the same as it is now: Why is there a need for such militant expression of Marian devotion? Various theological leaders, including the Marian theologian Mark I. Miravalle, encouraged this extreme behaviour.

In general, this devotional climate at Steubenville was sanctioned by the administration—that is, by Father Scanlon and his priestly and theological followers. As noted earlier, the university was tightly linked to a Catholic Charismatic community in and around Steubenville, whose members had chosen to live in Christian relationship with one another. In many ways this ethos had seeped into the university campus, mainly through the creation of "households." Basically, a household was a Christianized fraternity or sorority (without the wild parties), centred on daily prayer and other devotionals. These households were the principal means by which the university administration implemented its policy of positive peer pressure. Households with names such as "Earthen Vessels," "Little Flowers," and "Lion of Judah" were established in the various wings of the campus dorms. Which household one joined was determined more by the dorm to which one was assigned than by personal choice. For example, a particular dorm had three floors, each with four wings. Thus the dorm had twelve households. This system relied on the yearly influx of lonely, scared freshmen to fill out each household's numbers. What could be better for incoming freshmen than to be welcomed into a household that would take them under their wing and show them how to conform to the ideals established by the university?

Yet this convenient religious cocoon often isolated and ostracized those who couldn't fit into the box. Maybe religion had been forced down their throats at home. Maybe they were wrestling with deep emotional scars. Maybe they just weren't that religious. Those who couldn't fit in became outsiders, and the isolation was palpable.

Basically, the university had one path for developing young people's spirituality, and God help you if you didn't walk down it. The pressure to conform was intense. Frankly, this myopic approach to Catholicism, touted by these hyperorthodox as "authentically Catholic," actually ran counter to the diversity that has always characterized the Church. Certainly, there are limits to the Church's inclusiveness. There is heresy, and there is defined Church teaching. But within that which is acceptable there is a whole world of freedom of expression. For instance, when St. Francis of Assisi founded his order, the Friars Minor, he demanded that his brothers not own books of any kind. At virtually the same time, St. Dominic was founding his Order of Preachers. Theirs was an order of priests and brothers who were expected to battle heretics. For them, books were an absolute necessity. Yet both the Franciscans and the Dominicans were active in the world. Different from (and predating) both these groups were the Cisterians, who lived a cloistered life of work and prayer. Yet strangely, all three were and are Catholic, coexisting in the Church to this day. The irony here is that by being rigid and narrow, those who claim exclusive ownership of what is Catholic are actually betraying Catholicism.

This effort to rigidly define how one should live Catholicism is what I found intolerable at Steubenville. And this same rigidity seems to characterize most of the ultraconservative Catholics I have met. An example: In my third year of professional ministry I accepted a job at a suburban parish in the Archdiocese of Milwaukee. The parish was 150 years old but had never had a professional youth minister. Within two years I had managed to assemble a good group of volunteers and establish a fully functioning youth program that offered activities for young people from grades five to twelve. Our offerings encompassed social activities, retreats, lock-ins, catechism classes, and even a weekly youth mass offered every Sunday evening.

Then a small but vocal ultraconservative faction in the parish went to the pastor and opposed my work. They took issue with the fact that during the weekly youth mass the priest was calling the teens up to stand around the altar and hold hands during the Eucharistic prayer.

Never mind that the teens were actually attending mass—their posture had to display the appropriate traditional reverence! Furthermore, they were unhappy that I was addressing issues such as peer pressure, sexual morality, and substance abuse. They felt it was not the role of the Church to discuss such issues. This discussion should take place at home. In addition, they took umbrage with my approach to teaching the teens Scripture, which included the use of comparative texts (e.g., contrasting the Flood story in Genesis to that found in the *Epic of Gilgamesh*). They found my application of modern biblical methods of interpretation offensive: the Bible should be read literally. Their view was that the Church should teach nothing but doctrine, which was to be found in its pure form in the various papal encyclicals. So they approached the pastor and demanded that I teach the teenagers the encyclicals of John Paul II. In other words, they wanted me to read through these documents line by line and exegete them as one might do with Scripture.

For the record, I admired John Paul II even though I could not agree with all his positions. I respect the fact that he took positions and that he stood for something when it would have been much easier to remain neutral and not expose himself to criticism. That said, I never thought his writings were especially suited for teenagers. Delicately put, the man had doctorates in both philosophy and theology and his writings are deep and complicated. These encyclicals were written for theologians and pastors, not teenagers! Even more to the point, in the main they did not address issues of key importance to the average teenager. I explained my objections to the pastor (who agreed) and to these parents. But my arguments did not satisfy them, and they continued to badger the pastor until he decided he had had enough and opted to discontinue the youth program altogether, effectively ending my employment.

This incident illustrates some of the many flaws in the conservative Catholic approach. First, like those people at the University of Steubenville, they have no tolerance for diversity or for differences in emphasis and approach. Their way is the only way. Second, in my experience these ultra-orthodox are poorly informed. For example, their shock that I might call on the *Epic of Gilgamesh* to illuminate a discussion of the biblical flood demonstrates an appalling lack of awareness of what is normative according to the Roman Catholic Church. Had these parents bothered to look at the materials I offered them, they would have read the Pontifical Biblical Commission's *Document on the Interpretation of the Bible in the Church* (1993) and seen that the Church encourages the use of a whole host of modern methodologies in Scripture study. Third, these people exhibit a complete inability to contextualize theology. They read papal encyclicals from the 1890s or the 1950s as if they were recent writings. These are the same people who bemoan the fact that Latin was discontinued in favour of the vernacular. For them, Latin is the sacred, pious language of the Church. They do not understand that the Church adopted Latin in the first place because it was the language of the people (at least in the West), and that before Latin, most of the early churches conducted services in Greek (instead of Jesus' tongue, Aramaic!). They argue vociferously that people should kneel during the Eucharistic prayer, despite the long tradition in both the early and medieval Church of standing. There were no pews in medieval cathedrals! The Reformers introduced church pews once the emphasis on the liturgy of the word began to result in long-winded sermons.

I am sure it is clear by now that I have little use for fundamentalists. What I find especially irritating about them is that they seem to approach life as if they already know all that is worth knowing. They have already made their decision about a person or situation based on their preconceived notions; they do not bother to ask themselves why a person or situation is the way he/she/it is. It seems to me that it is jumping the gun, to say the least, when one makes up one's mind before hearing all the facts. Since a person is rarely if ever presented with all the facts, it seems best to take an approach to life that allows one to adjust and adapt one's ideas based on new information.

On the other hand, I think I understand people's impulse to seek definitive answers to life's most difficult questions. This same desire for the good is what created myths like Santa Claus. Yet the Santa Claus myth doesn't explain how Christmas gifts only seem to appear under the trees of children whose parents have adequate financial resources. (For some reason, Santa never seems to get around to the slums of New York, Milwaukee, or Los Angeles.) It is the tension between the way we wish things were and the way things actually are that I believe motivates the impulse to religious fundamentalism.

From a religious and philosophical point of view we may wish that we had all the answers, that things were black and white, that this universe had logic and a formula. In reality, we find that we have more questions than answers, that grey seems to be the colour of choice for this present reality, and that many times there seems to be a terribly random and chaotic character to events. The truth is that things are not simple here on earth. They never were. Perhaps that is where saints as "heroes and heroines" can be of most help to us. They provide us with real examples of real people who faced real problems yet managed to remain faithful to God despite all they suffered. That example of determination in the face of adversity is of much greater practical service to us than a religious "snake-oil salesman" approach that promises (but ultimately can never deliver) easy answers to life's complex questions.

BEVERLEY BRYANT

Inching Along

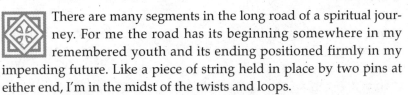There are many segments in the long road of a spiritual journey. For me the road has its beginning somewhere in my remembered youth and its ending positioned firmly in my impending future. Like a piece of string held in place by two pins at either end, I'm in the midst of the twists and loops.

Unlike Buddhists, with whom I'm currently striking a slight acquaintance, we Christians see these two end points as remarkably significant. You are born, and there is a finite amount of time before you die. During this time you must make peace with God by accepting Jesus, throw your lot in with Him, and in doing so be saved. Should you fail at these "acts" during your life on earth, your soul will be lost and you will spend the rest of eternity without God.

At various points along my own journey I have rationalized that eternity without God is only a bad thing if you actually believe in Him. A similar thought is that Heaven and Hell only have significance for believers. Let that sort of talk slip out in certain fundamentalist circles and you get a knowing lift of the eyebrow or a barely discernable tightening of the lips. At risk, as the believers see it, is an acknowledgment of the Truth.

Truth. A capital "T" word, to be sure. For fundamentalists this word embodies what is absolute. Truth is what you can know. Truth is written in Scripture, firmly held, and not a question of debate. Truth exists. Fundamentalists know it, and if you don't then you're outside the circle.

I have been guilty of the same sort of fearless judgment that is so pervasive in the world of God-fearing believers. After all, who can dispute a message from the Lord God Almighty, especially when a believer has a "transcendent moment" characterized by speaking in tongues? God moves in mysterious ways. Perhaps, but I soon came to understand that raw human emotions can contribute to such spiritual "gifts."

I was five, in Sunday school in Edmonton, with my thin dime clutched tight in my small, sticky fist. When other children dropped their coins, their parents would sit in affected nonchalance as the coin rolled its way down the sloping floor of the sanctuary, finally to finish its descent in an increasingly loud and furious spin. I held on to my offering, watching the minister's twenty-something son hold his brow in fervent prayer. "Oh," I thought, "to be so caught up in God!"

Soon enough, my brother and I would leave the grown-ups and congregate near the front to hear a whimsical story about the meaning of God in people's lives, mostly intended for adult listeners. Then we would make our way up, up, into the spires of the old church, into the church's strange little rooms, the result of some early-twentieth-century architectural quirk. There we would attend Sunday school, participating in whatever craft had been chosen by the curriculum. To my selective adult memory, mostly what comes to mind is colouring a picture of a handsome Jesus tending a cute, white, fluffy lamb. Or a garnet-robed Mary Magdalene bathing His feet. These images now seem bizarre, yet at the same time something about them remains pleasant and special to me.

Sundays were fun, especially when the Waffle House was on the post-church agenda on the way home. Our parents were pleased to have their moment of fitting into the picture of a perfect, churchgoing, middle-class family. We children were thrilled by the treat of a pile of crispy waffles, whipped butter, and golden syrup poured from those funny little jugs with the slidey lid.

Another childhood memory about church is the Christmas pageant. The image has us being quite dressed up, running around the vast, echoing church halls and basement common rooms, preparing for the event or celebrating its completion. Our church had even sponsored various children to attend from the local orphanage. Our family played host to a small, dark-haired boy in a white shirt and ill-fitting pants. My brother and I were quite taken with this bit of Christian charity, and we did our best to impress on this poor boy that we were the real children and he was just pretend for the night. The whole scenario now makes me cringe, but I'm sure we felt, as a family, very self-righteous and Christian. We were, after all, doing our duty and helping out the less fortunate.

.A better memory of those pageant days is my firm knowledge of Luke 2:8–12 (from the King James Version of course, the version many Protestant fundamentalists consider the most authoritative): "There were shepherds abiding in the fields, keeping watch over their flocks by night, and lo the angel of the Lord appeared before them and the glory shone round about them and they were sore afraid." That memory is spiritual glue—it will probably always continue to stick with me.

Despite some intervening years when we didn't attend church regularly, our family's white, middle-class Canadian version of Christianity had been firmly planted in me. But by the time I reached high school, my family was firmly in the grip of evangelicalism. We had joined a Presbyterian church in Ottawa, where my mother had a conversion experience—she found herself saved from depression and an imminent fall into alcoholism. My father had a strong faith but wasn't as emotional about it as my mother. He went along and did his duty in a quiet way. My brother was deeply involved in the teen group and seemed to have found a place of comfort. I watched their transition and tried to attend a few events, but I never felt quite part of the scene. Youth groups were for "good" kids, and I wasn't really part of that scene. I was in high school and was having more fun in the here and now.

My lack of participation and failure to find a home in any of the church-based activities left me feeling more and more on the outskirts of the family. I don't remember exactly when I stopped going to church, but as soon as high school was over, I was out, anxious to be gone, to leave the parental nest and live with my boyfriend. Neither the church nor Christianity figured prominently in any of this, though I'm sure it did from my parent's point of view. A lot of prayers for me were said.

My desire to leave only deepened. By the time I finished university I wanted to be even farther away. My roaming took me out to Vancouver and then on to the Middle East. Finally, six years and many thousands of miles later, it seemed safe to return to the fold with a husband at my side and lots of stories of fun and adventure away from home.

I returned to Toronto full of a desire to fit in, to settle down and have a life planted in the bosom of family and friends. I remember being quite overcome the first time my husband and I went back to my parents' house. I felt so welcome, so at home, so loved and accepted. It was marvellous. There's a thread here, a little loop on the string that explains a lot. Much of my journey, in and out of religion, in and out of my parent's house, in and out of my family, is about love and belonging. Human beings will do amazing things to belong. Just ask any teenager, or their parents! Like anyone else, my desire is always to be known for who I am, to be accepted, to be part of the group and to fit in. But there is a parallel story to tell. I now believe that at the root of my feelings of non-belonging, or disenfranchisement, was an evolving awareness that I perhaps was gay.

I was not one of those young people who say, "I always knew I was gay." It's only now that I'm older and have begun to piece together the story that I can look back and say, "Yes, I had a serious crush on that girl," or, "It's no wonder the bar scene didn't attract me." It wasn't till I was in my mid-twenties and living in Vancouver that I had my first same-sex relationship. It was more angst and agony than anything else. It ended with me in a state of confusion as to whether I was really "gay" or had just happened to fall in love with a woman.

It was soon after that relationship ended that I went to the Middle East for four years of adventure and serious partying. I found a strong gay community there, but I stayed on the periphery, making some friendships with openly gay men and women but keeping my sexuality firmly on the hetero side. It was during that time that I met and married my husband, the man I brought back to Toronto, both of us ready for a fresh start.

Religion had no particular place in our lives, and my parents despaired of my "uncommitted" life. But I was happy and we soon had our first child. Around this time we reconnected with some Saudi friends, a lesbian couple who lived in the United States. After a few trips to see them, moments, forces, and feelings conspired and I was in a crisis, feeling so attracted and in love with a woman. By now I was pregnant with our second child and fully aware of the mess I was in.

This set the stage for the re-entry of Christianity into my life, but this time in a clearly fundamentalist form. Its vehicle was a Charismatic woman a few years older than me, who had what seemed to be a direct line to God and who demonstrated the gifts of the Spirit on a regular basis. My friendship with Julie (not her real name) developed over the months of my second pregnancy. She was the older sister I craved, and probably the approving mother I needed. I felt young and gauche around her. She was strong, competent, and attractive. To me, her life was orderly and focused. I wanted what she had.

My growing interest in the spiritual life she enjoyed developed alongside our friendship. She had an active, daily connection with God. She went to church and prayer groups where the Lord spoke to her and through her. She was walking in the gifts of the Spirit. When she sang and praised the Lord it was a wonderful thing to see. She prayed and spoke in tongues. When she prayed for me I felt healed, blessed, and touched by the hand of God.

On other days I would call my lesbian friend and confess my attraction to her. I rethought all of my previous lesbian experiences and began to seriously consider that I was gay. Throughout all this, my relationship with my husband was deteriorating. It was a relationship that played a sad second fiddle to everything else going on in my life. I was overwhelmed, depressed and trying to cope with a new baby.

Are you getting a sense of the blackness, the chaos, the hopelessness? It was all there, and it was huge. Now picture a beam of white light entering the scene, a message from Almighty God, who has the power to change all things, who loves us, who wants nothing but His best for us. Imagine this God speaking to me through my loved one, Julie. Imagine me hearing that it didn't have to be this way, that homosexuality is not God's "Best" for me, that it can go away, that I can have the love and devotion of my husband and fulfillment in the pure friendships of Christian women. That I can live a life ordained and sanctioned by God Himself. In order to have it all I need only be Born Again. If I commit myself to God I will be victorious over this work of the Devil.

Sign me up! Can you picture the flood of emotions, the tears, and a room full of righteous women praying for me and for victory over my special problem? Can you picture my determination to put my past life and all my sins behind me? To Answer the Call?

My poor husband, he gallantly went along with me. We became a churchgoing, Bible-studying family. My goals were no longer material or temporal. My lesbian friend in the United States got dropped cold. I never even called to explain. I couldn't. I felt that if I did I could be lost again. My life was for the Lord. I wanted to stay home and raise my children, even sacrifice all and send them to Christian school. I went to Bible study in the day and Bible study at night. I prayed, I learned about God, and I began to use my gifts in His service.

Of course I called my mother right after my living room conversion, with Julie there praying for me and leading me through the sinner's prayer. "Here I am mom, one of the Flock now! Isn't it wonderful?" The prodigal daughter had returned, and they, so to speak, killed the fatted calf. The hallelujahs floated to Heaven on the thankful prayers of my family. At last I would join the rest of them in Heaven when this earthly life was over.

Heaven, the goal of all Christians?

Yes, that's what I'd been taught from the earliest days in the small rooms of my Sunday school. Believe in God. Believe in the Lord Jesus and follow Him and you will go to Heaven. The added piece I hadn't heard before was specific to this fundamentalist/Charismatic brand of Christianity: God supplies power to overcome our everyday struggles. "Victorious living"—another phrase I had never heard before—was possible for me. Victory over homosexuality, victory over gossip, victory over coffee, victory over adultery, victory over fat, victory over scarred relationships, victory over any manifestation of the devil. God can act and will act in this life. In the now. He is present and accessible.

Some who are reading this might say I'm misrepresenting the Gospel, but I can only tell you what I heard. My earlier understanding was that belief in God is important so that we could do good here on earth, have a Fatherly ear to pray to, and ultimately end up with our eternal reward: Heaven. But here was a Gospel preaching a great life in the here and now, with power from God for everyday struggles. Even better!

There is another component that really pulled me in tight. There had always been a strong intellectual aspect to my family's Christianity. For years my parents had a poster on their wall that read: "In order to know the mind of God, you must first explore your own." It was an advertisement for a conservative Christian seminary in the United States. This was a fundamentalist stream of a different sort, one that firmly believed that the Truth could be known by study and diligent pursuit. I wanted both. I could be a Charismatic *and* an intellectual, all the while being a Christian! For me it was saying (albeit a little contrary or extraneous to my "Spirit" experiences) that there is an intellectual pursuit that is extremely complex and engaging. In retrospect, I think it was this intellectual rendering of Christianity that so appealed to members of my family. I attempted to incorporate this aspect into my Christianity and managed to take several courses at a nearby seminary. I was on my way to my Masters of Divinity.

End of story, right? Girl goes on to get her degree, successfully brings her intellect to bear on the works of the Spirit. Happy family, saved from the curse of homosexuality, spiritually secure, and intellectually satisfied. What could possibly change now?

I entered the world again. By this time our financial needs had pulled me back into the workplace, where I began to carve out my role and place with my career. I started a job, and I met people who had an interest in some of the things we had been talking about in our Bible study group. I began to work as a public health nurse; in that environment my interactions with people were not as purely clinical as in hospital nursing. We were working with new mothers, with seniors, with school-children and teenagers. Our focus was their health, and an essential component of good health was dealing constructively with emotions and interpersonal relationships. This interpersonal stuff was very similar to the intrigue I had with my religious experience. We were talking about concepts like forgiveness, letting go of old issues and ideas, paying debts, and keeping a clear conscience. In my new work world I was meeting people who spoke this language in a secular sense, but who spoke about it intelligently, with greater depth and understanding than the women in my Bible study group.

There was one woman, Loretta, who spoke this language with great clarity and intelligence. She sat a couple of desks down from me, and shortly after we met I knew that the desires and feelings I had experienced before were resurfacing. I was both horrified and ecstatic.

The next three years were a daily mix of emotions. I was happy and engaged when I was with her, guilty and anguished at home. I was torn between my belief that my feelings were wrong, that I was being tempted by the devil, that my faith was not strong enough, and the overwhelming sense of completeness I felt when Loretta and I were together. I rationalized everything. We were friends; there was nothing sexual going on. Yet I just knew that I was alive when I was with her and struggling to be okay when I was not. There had never been a woman who rushed to work on Monday mornings the way I did.

I remember going every day to walk around a nearby lake and pray. On one particular day I cried, I sought forgiveness. I wanted it all to end. I felt tortured and was ready to confess my feelings for this woman and to go and ask for prayer to heal me of my endless obsession.

But we were going away that weekend—"the girls," friends from work, four of us for a weekend at a cottage. I was to share a room—and a bed—with the woman I was in love with. Nothing overtly sexual happened, but by the time the weekend was over it was clear that my feelings were not borne in isolation. The fact that this woman returned my feelings was a turning point for me. We were in love and, of course, within a few weeks in unimaginable turmoil. That month placed both of us on a path toward each other and a new life.

On a parallel course with the dissolution of my life as a heterosexual married woman was the dissolution of my status as a Christian, at least as a born again, fundamentalist, Charismatic Christian. Fundamentalists are highly tolerant of past sins, and they believe in forgiveness, but they are not at all tolerant about ongoing sin. Simply put, they see it as the workings of the devil in one's life. Yet I could not see my relationship with Loretta as evil. I had to distance myself from that notion very quickly in order to maintain any semblance of emotional health. I stopped attending church and dropped my Christian friends as quickly as I had dropped my lesbian friend in the United States. The main thrust of my guilt was associated with my relationship with my husband and my children. It was a genuine guilt—real, tangible, and stemming from how much we were hurting each other. It wasn't a God-sanctioned guilt associated with the sin of homosexuality. I was determined not to expose myself to those who would see it that way.

Sometime after the break-up, Loretta and I attended a church downtown whose members were openly gay and that preached a Gospel that was inclusive of homosexuals. We even went to a "coming out" group associated with the church. It was a good place for us, and I felt that I was able to reclaim my place in the church. I remember taking my mother there for a service. I was teary, emotional, and quite impossibly proud of myself as we filed forward for Communion. Once again I was trying to convince her I could really be a part of her faith in God. Yes, I was gay, but damn it I could still be a Christian. Maybe not as good a Christian as her or my Charismatic friends, but there was still a place for me.

There was an edge of anger that continued for the first years after my break-up. Loretta and I used to talk about a period of tearing down: my life and status as a white, middle-class, heterosexual married woman. I wasn't that any longer. Only white and female, but now separated and homosexual and only barely clinging to middle class.

I adopted a belief that life was about choices, and making them fiercely whatever the consequences. I went through a period starkly different from the "victorious life" of my fundamentalist period. In those past days, outcomes had been guaranteed. As long as you believed and did the right thing (or even did the wrong thing with appropriate contrition), you could reasonably expect God would work it all out for you. But when you're on your own, free floating in an immense and chaotic universe that operates on causes and effects of your own making, it's a stark contrast.

I spent years feeling no sense of awe or wonder, no awareness of the beauty and occasional synchronicity of the world. I was bitter. I had tried to live the dream and it had turned to ashes at my feet. But if that's the way it had to be, then so be it. Life is about choices and consequences. There is no grace, or guiding power, or ultimate plan. You live your life, good things happen, bad things happen. I was adrift, yet satisfied with that position.

My association with the church, however loose, was over. I would still make the occasional family-induced trip to a special service at Christmas or Easter. When I go I feel the tugs, have the teary eyes, notice the desire to belong. But is seems to be a club I am no longer part of. I think that the desire to belong, and not to have to deal with my sexuality, was what drove me during my time as a fundamentalist. But the truth is I had to deal with that part of my being. And I couldn't do it within a fundamentalist approach to Christianity. Could I have found a niche in a lesbian or gay friendly corner of some other denomination? Quite possibly. Do I want to advocate for gay rights within the Church? No, that doesn't seem to be my role now.

The church was not a core part of my life. I had a church-based upbringing, then many years of absence and a brief time of fundamentalism. I thought that perhaps it was the lifeline that could pull me onto the so-called conservative side of the world. I could then be like everybody else. But of course that wasn't really true, because being a fundamentalist or evangelical Christian puts you in its own grouping. For instance, I've since heard that people I casually knew were leery of my pins and crosses and daily Scripture verses. Of course they were!

I can look back now and wonder what the fuss was about. It's probably way more cool to be a lesbian than a fundamentalist Christian. But I'm minimizing the issue. It was not cool to be a lesbian who left her husband and family, traumatizing the children, shocking her family, and enduring their questions, the most troubling being: "But was it really necessary?"

If a fundamentalist road could have saved me from that path, perhaps I would still be on it. But it wasn't able to do so. For me, that road was an elaborate form of escapism from the issues I had to face.

I didn't stick around to gauge any reactions. I don't know what prayers were offered up for me. I didn't stay to defend my choice; I cut off all contact with any people with whom I had associated. I dropped the seminary courses, I dropped a friend I had there, and I dropped any association with the church we were attending. I think the pastor tried to reach out to me, but I was not interested.

It was over.

It has been almost ten years since I went through the divorce from fundamentalism. I still have an uncomfortable, somewhat separated relationship with the church. There are parts that still pull me in, but not the fundamentalist, "victorious living" parts. It is too sure of itself. It has lost the mystery of exploring the nature of our relationship with God. It's too caught up in Absolute Truth and the Only Way to Salvation. This absolute certainty about life and its meaning, about what is right and wrong, now seems to me to be a serious form of abandoning the need to grapple with the real complexities of life.

The intriguing pieces of my spiritual journey are from my childhood and young adulthood. The more mainstream parts. I pass by the bookshelves in my mother's home and my eyes scan the titles. Part of me wants to be there again, discussing theology with the grown-ups, listening to the words of the pure and upright. There's a joy and righteousness in following the narrow path and in answering the call of God.

But that path is not mine. I tried to use Christianity, especially the fundamentalist stream, to help me evade a part of myself that I didn't want to have to face. For a while I thought that having to be a lesbian was a tough road. Sometimes it still is. But I am now more myself and more in touch with who I am. I had to deal with those issues and make those difficult choices about my life and relationships. Fundamentalism worked its escapist magic for a time. It was a period I had to go through. I had to have one last-ditch effort to fit in and one more opportunity for acceptance. It didn't happen, and I'm now more "me" than I've ever been.

I'm now finding my way back to a spiritual life. During my dark and angry days I thought it was gone forever. I think I can find it again. There is a beauty and a quality to life broader and more illuminating than the pathways of our everyday existence. Finding those moments, getting those glimpses of grace and beauty, is vitally important.

I'm still inching along my string. I know there will be loops and curly pathways ahead. But I'm confident I will find my way. There is an order and goodness to the universe that, despite my apparent lostness, will complete the good work begun so long ago.

GLENN A. ROBITAILLE

From Fear to Faith
My Journey into
Evangelical Humanism

 In my nearly fifty years of profound spiritual and religious involvement I have learned one very important thing: spirituality is a blending of who we are (from our own social location, enculturation, personality, and temperament) with the Numinous (transcendent, ineffable, and unknowable). Since human beings are radically different, spirituality is always going to be as individual as the people who are spiritual. The human spirit is a snowflake or a fingerprint, identifiable in its similarity but always unique.

Religion, as a structure for discovering and expressing spirituality, has always resonated with me. My earliest memories are a montage of images involving rosaries, makeshift altars, homemade vestments, and bread pressed down and sculpted to resemble a communion host. As a child I would celebrate mass in my bedroom, with my prayer beads wrapped around my belt and the top of my dresser carefully organized to resemble what I had observed in the church. I baptized my first convert to Roman Catholicism at the age of nine. I was not entirely sure what an Episcopalian was back then, but my young friend was that. And whatever that was, it wasn't part of the "One True Church," which is what the Roman Catholic Church was, so I was taught. After several long discussions on the likelihood of his eternal damnation, I invoked an obscure ordinance that allows lay people to baptize others in cases of necessity and in the absence of a priest, and initiated him into the faith. It seemed the natural and reasonable thing to do.

In short, I am a believer in God. I have been for as long as I can remember. Sometimes I see God as personal and intimate, other times I see Him in almost Deistic terms—the divine "wind up the universe and let it go" notion popular with the transcendentalists like Walt Whitman and Ralph Waldo Emerson. It is a curious blend to be sure; but the angle from which I observe reality has been defined, and while it can be sharpened and tuned, it is what it is.

Leaving fundamentalism has not been an easy process for me. My conservative armor began to crack in my mid-twenties when I realized that my view of truth had been channelled along the sight lines available to me from my limited vantage point. In many ways my Catholic upbringing and my innate spiritual curiosity set me up for dogmatic thinking, and paradoxically enough, for a reaction against dogmatic thinking.

As a youth I sat engrossed in catechism, drinking in every word—receiving, reflecting, reducing. The lesson had a meaning and the meaning an application. God's Law was being imparted, and within the Law, Truth. If the Catholic Church impressed any one point on me, it was the idea of salvation not existing outside the Truth, and Truth not existing outside the Church. There was only one true way, and Roman Catholicism was that way. And if it was not the way, then another way—another dogma, another "one true church"—existed. You were either exactly right or you were hopeless and eternally wrong.

I have had several defining moments in my life, moments when my understanding or direction radically shifted. One of the earliest occurred on a particular Saturday evening when I was twelve. For reasons I can no longer remember, I lost my temper with my older brother and verbally wished him a fiery recompense in Hell. Had I done this on a Friday I would have gone to confession Saturday morning and received absolution. With the next opportunity for confession being a complete week away, I found myself in the precarious position of having to navigate a refusal of the Eucharist on Sunday without drawing my father's attention to that avoidance.

In my understanding of Catholic theology at the time, to receive communion after committing a so-called mortal sin constituted a sacrilege. It required the absolution of the bishop to be forgiven. Since cursing my brother qualified as such, and having no access to a bishop, I laboured to find some creative method to avoid communion. Instead I found myself caught between my father and mother in the queue leading up to the altar rail. In the end, fear of my father's querying won out over my fear of God, launching me into four years of abject terror for my soul. Sunday after Sunday I piled one sacrilege upon another as I continued to take the "Body of Christ" profanely and with full thought and intent. By the time the evangelicals got to me I was ripe for the picking.

My first real exposure to evangelicalism came in 1970 during the early days of what has since been dubbed the Jesus Movement. I was inspired to look at the phenomenon through the example of my tenth grade history teacher, an Elder in the Open Brethren and a man of deep faith. What attracted me to him was his air of authenticity. He seemed to possess a genuine interest in me as a person, and a seeming unflappability in the face of the constant ribbing he took from staff and students alike. Over time I embraced his message of "grace through faith" on the promise that, in so doing, the slate with God was clean.

It is the idea of saving grace that most appealed to me. As this man and the Open Brethren see it, it is not the works we do, or don't do, that determine our acceptability with God. It is a simple matter of faith. If you believe and have faith in Christ, God in his mercy accepts the death and resurrection of Christ as payment for your sins and you receive his "unmerited favor." In churches that have been influenced by John Calvin, this favour is eternal, unchanging, and unconditional. If you name the name of Christ and invite him to be your Savior, you are freed from the penalty of sin and assured an eternity in heaven. This is quite different from Roman Catholic theology, where a state of grace has to be maintained by participation in the sacraments. For Catholics, to die outside the state of grace, at best, means eternal separation from God; at least years of suffering in Purgatory—a place of temporal suffering and cleansing. In my case, my ongoing sacrilege meant eternal damnation. Salvation by grace through faith was an "emancipation proclamation" for me. After four years and countless hours of existential agony, I felt forgiven. I had been saved.

I cannot deny that I experienced a profound benefit in that very Protestant experience. When fundamentalists use the term "saved," they are referring to being saved from the fires of Hell and eternal separation from God. At that time in my life I could relate very well to the concept. And in a very real sense, I needed to be saved. I was caught in the undertow of a dismal theology that predicated forgiveness for sins on performing the right action, and it was sucking the life right out of me. I was barely treading water, hoping and waiting for a passing ship that never came, begging God for a forgiveness that could only be granted through the proper prescription, on my own lacking the means to fill it.

I learned through this experience that people who are drowning are not distracted by protocol, nor do they spend an inordinate amount of time checking the credentials of the rescuer. The first hand in the water will be the one grasped. Once the crisis has passed, it becomes another matter to evaluate the long-term meaning of the event. That may or may not mean the sharing of a new and longer road. As it turned out, the hand that rescued me was not all that different from the one I had already known.

Fundamentalism could be defined as *a preoccupation with a narrow and exclusive view of salvation coupled with a compelling need to disseminate that belief to others.* Soteriology (the doctrine of salvation), in fundamentalist circles, focuses solely and exclusively on the afterlife. Historically, one could say that Christianity as a whole has had this focus. Even a casual survey of religious history reveals an "other worldly" emphasis as integral to what Christianity has been about. Resolving the issue of Heaven or Hell is almost coded in the souls of those raised under the influence of the Christian message. It then stands to reason that my first spiritual conflict was around the issue of salvation. The first conflict for many people of faith is one born deep within the survival instinct that finds its energy in fear. "The fear of the Lord is the beginning of wisdom," says the Psalmist. Before wisdom can exist, respect must be growing. It is quite likely I had that part of the routine down pat.

My fundamentalism began to unravel as I was reading about "the crippled and deformed" in Leviticus 21. According to this passage in the Jewish Scripture (called by Christians the Old Testament), no one suffering from a deformity of any kind—the dwarfed or hunchbacked, the blind or the lame—is permitted to "go near the curtain or approach the altar of the Lord." Many similar texts exist in the Bible, but for some reason, on that particular day, something moved within me. The idea of people being found unworthy to approach God on the basis of a physical defect entirely outside their control was so repugnant to me that I could not imagine it being reflective of God. I found myself saying, "If I believe this to be true, what am I saying God is like?" It was my first real attempt at higher criticism, the interpretive filter through which I came to view all beliefs from that moment forward.

For the most part, fundamentalists teach an "if God says it, then that settles it" approach to hermeneutics (the word used by theologians to describe the science of interpretation). We do not critique the Bible; the Bible critiques us. Methods of higher criticism are employed by theologians to consider such issues as context, history, authorship, redaction (the refining of material through editing), and literary style in an attempt to get at what Scripture is trying to tell us. In the fundamentalist circles I travelled, deconstruction of the Scriptures would be anathema. For them, only a modicum of historical grammatical methodology is entertained. In short, applying moral reasoning in evaluating the truth of a text is not acceptable. The Scriptures stand over us; we do not question them. After reading Leviticus 21 I found myself on the other side of the microscope and armed with a qualifier, a critical question.

The substance of this critical question flowed from my emerging realization that *all good theology begins with the character of God.* I was likely influenced in this thinking by my reading of Aristotle, who postulated that one could make certain deductions about the unknown based on what is known. If you start with what is, you can walk backwards toward causation and form reasonable hypotheses. This seemed to make sense to me as I looked at what Scripture says about God. For instance, if, as I had been taught, God sanctions a practice like genocide, as the destruction of the Canaanites would suggest, then I must also conclude that the character of God is genocidal. If I believe that God ordered genocide, then I must also conclude that genocide is in the nature and being of God. I took this a step further and began to question my own character based on these beliefs. If I accepted God as genocidal, what did it say about my character if I would worship God solely on the grounds that God is more powerful than me? While fear may be a good starting point for wisdom, it did not speak well of my character if the only reason I possessed faith was to avoid angering God.

Coming to these recognitions did not give me a lot of joy. I found it easier to navigate life with certainties, well or ill founded. I am not sure anyone likes ambiguity, and perhaps fundamentalism thrives on that very reality. It is natural to want to "know truths" rather than have to wrestle with uncertainty. Nevertheless, for me, loving God and liking God seemed connected. I simply did not like a God who could take such a cruel outlook on the physically disadvantaged, or who would see ethnic cleansing as an appropriate measure for removing potentially negative influences on one's culture.

Conservative theologians try to rescue such passages, and I gave them every opportunity to do so with me. I read no less than twelve conservative texts on biblical interpretation by respected authors. Usually fundamentalists point out that the Hebraic mindset was a leap forward from the nations around them, all of which likely would have abandoned the infirm or simply killed them. Canaanite culture was characterized as so depraved that complete elimination was the only way to safeguard the rest of society.

"Selective flooding," I like to call it. Instead of flooding the whole world, smaller pockets are targeted for elimination. I found it very hard to separate the biblical examples of selective flooding from the ones that occurred in my lifetime. If God did order the extermination of the Canaanites, man, woman, and child, what is God like? The God I was seeing through that corrective lens began to strongly resemble Adolf Hitler or Idi Amin. I needed a new archetype. Predictably, given my attachment to Christian thought, I looked for that archetype in the person of Jesus.

In December 1976 I turned off the radio and television, set aside books and periodicals, and entered a two-year, self-imposed retreat with the sole purpose of seeing Jesus as he truly was. I called it a character study of Jesus. Armed only with the Bible, I began to read the gospels critically, examining not only the words and teachings of Jesus but also his behaviour. Who did he relate to well? Who did he criticize? What kinds of things did he emphasize? What made him angry? In many ways it was more psychoanalytical than polemic. I wanted to know what the biblical record had to say about Jesus and, if I believed it to be true, what the God who resembled Jesus would be like.

An important shift in my understanding occurred when I realized how Jesus revised significant Old Testament doctrines at various points in his teaching. Repeatedly in the Sermon on the Mount he said, "You have heard in times past ... but I tell you ..." Jesus made a distinction between what had been said and what he was saying. One could speculate that what was said in times past did not line up with what he saw as the will and intent of God. He seemed to present these views as an inadequate blending of where the people were spiritually at the time the Hebrew Scriptures were being written, with how they understood God.

I came to believe that when Jesus revised these beliefs, he did so using a principle: What is good for the human being? A better way of describing it would be the "agape" principle, the principle of love. Jesus best illustrated this concept when he was challenged for allowing his disciples to pick grain to eat on the Sabbath. He said, "The Sabbath was made for man, not man for the Sabbath," meaning that the Sabbath was given because God values humanity. The intent of the commandment in Jesus' teaching was to benefit humankind. Human beings needed one day of rest in seven. That was the premise. God did not need humankind to keep an arbitrary rule. It was better for humanity that they eat the grain on the Sabbath if they were hungry than it was to suffer unnecessarily to keep a rule just for the sake of keeping a rule.

As I examined the Hebrew principles that Jesus challenged, I found that love was underneath the adjustments Jesus made. It was the principle of promoting human well-being. In Jesus' mind, things are not right or wrong because God says so; God says so because certain things are harmful to the human being. Find what is good for the human beings involved, and more often than not you will be sitting squarely on what Jesus saw as the will and purpose of God. That is what I came to believe.

The focus of fundamentalism is on narrow definitions of obeying God's will as defined and prescribed by the fundamentalists making the rules. Jesus' emphasis was more or less an expansion of the two great commandments: "Love God with your whole heart, soul, mind, and strength," and "Love your neighbour as yourself." Even though these are the two principles Jesus identified as being the most important in the Law, they were rarely emphasized among the circles I travelled.

Throughout my foray into fundamentalism, my influences were heavily given to the legal model, which viewed the Christian life through the lens of justification. According to this model, faith is about appeasing God. God is perfect and cannot allow imperfection to coexist with him. Human beings are not perfect, therefore some remedy must be found. In nearly all cultures of antiquity, appeasing God involved sacrifice and death: it was all about the blood. When these images are seen as archetypal, they cast significant light on issues of human shame and the resulting suffering that comes when people live according to their baser instincts. When they are seen as literal, God is portrayed as an anal-retentive, obsessive-compulsive tyrant. God becomes someone more concerned about the wrong kind of people invading the neighbourhood than about understanding, encouragement, or grace.

It took a few years for me to assimilate this recognition into my functional awareness. When I finally did I was twenty-eight years old and the pastor of a growing evangelical congregation. I could no longer accept the literalism that had created such a conditional and abusive view of

God. If I believe God demands perfection and will only accept imperfection if it is covered in blood, what am I saying God is like? The question triggers the image and sound of a chainsaw.

I have been fortunate, in that the denomination in which I have served since 1979 is considered moderately evangelical. The Brethren in Christ Church does not include the inerrancy of Scripture in its Articles of Faith, nor does it advocate for a single hermeneutic in the interpretation of Scripture. The Brethren in Christ are an offshoot of the Radical Reformation, which means that individual conscience plays an important role in the way most parishioners approach faith. It would have been so much more difficult for me professionally had I attached myself to the Open Brethren or another more fundamentalist denomination. I have had some room to think and grow, enjoying the encouragement of a few denominational leaders as I have presented some of these ideas in the broader church.

Struggling with fundamentalism had another profound impact on my life. About the same time as I relinquished my conditional and abusive view of God, I began studying counselling theory. Years before I finished a doctorate in the field I began serving in a psychiatric hospital as a fee-for-service chaplain. Theological abuse was not officially identified as a category back then, but the evidence of it in the psychiatric population was undeniable. I began working with individuals one on one, inviting them to think about the implications of their beliefs and what those beliefs might say about the nature and character of God. At the age of forty-five I left pastoral ministry to pursue pastoral counselling as a vocation. I have remained in it since, balancing a private practice with a full-time chaplaincy at the Mental Health Centre Penetanguishene in Ontario.

I remain strongly attached to the Christian images of crucifixion and resurrection. As a mental health professional I am profoundly aware of the impact of guilt and shame on the human psyche. The impulse toward atonement and redemption has been part of the human drama throughout all of history. Healthy human beings believe that wrongs must be made right and that restitution must be made. Being able to accept responsibility for one's failures is an innate requirement of a healthy personality. The archetypal image of a God-man dying in our place to make restitution for our sins is powerful and healing. When embraced it has the power to allow grace and mercy to flood our awareness, creating energy for self-acceptance and love. When it is literalized, it merely reinforces the very doubts that gave rise to such archetypal images in the first place: the idea that we are inadequate, unlovable, vulnerable, and without inherent worth.

As a fundamentalist, my focus was mainly on pleasing God, discovering God's will, performing God's requirements, and avoiding God's disapproval. Today I would describe myself as an *evangelical humanist* with a focus on being a channel of God. If I believe God is compassionate, merciful, and loving and that he values human beings, then what does that mean to me as a believer? How does God manifest Himself through me? It meant I first had to let go of the illusion that truth resides solely in a twentieth-century North American Christian view of the world. Back in the 1980s I began reading the sacred works of other religions, the *Bhagavad Gita*, the *Upanishads*, the *Dhammapada*, the *Koran*, and the *Tao Te Ching*. While the same challenges exist in these writings as in the Christian and Hebrew Scriptures, I found them full of wisdom and encouragement. Studying them has increased my self-awareness as well as my understanding of other traditions.

As a fundamentalist I was preoccupied with issues of *immanence*, with personifying and reducing God to someone manageable and understandable. In my present understanding I am far more intrigued by issues of *transcendence*. This transformation was recently illustrated to me while I was walking along the shore of Georgian Bay on a particularly starlit night. As I gazed up at the stars and contemplated the millions of galaxies represented by each one of them, I was struck with the improbability—indeed the miracle—that a speck of dust existing on a speck of dust in the universe could perceive its own existence. My very next thought was how thoroughly arrogant and useless it was for any one speck of dust to think it could conceive an iota of truth about anything universal from the limited perspective available to it. Almost simultaneously I was overwhelmed by an extreme gratitude that, by some miracle, this speck of dust had the gift of being able to contemplate and, to some degree, appreciate a possibility so superlative and beyond definition as to defy words in describing it—that is, the existence of God. Good religion is that which inspires human beings to reach out beyond themselves in understanding and love. It possesses power born of humility, and from a deep desire to become something we cannot fully understand yet long to be. Within that longing rests the divine spark.

In my youth I desired that God be within me. Faith was an overt grasp at acceptance and love and a polysymphonic apology for being human. Over time I have come to realize that *I* am *in* God; and whether or not that reality expresses itself in a tangible way is entirely up to me. Spirituality is a blending of who we are (from our own social location, enculturation, personality, and temperament) with the numinous (transcendent, ineffable, and unknowable). I am Christian, and quite content to "let God be God." It is not necessary to explain it any better than that.

I have often said that I have ten good questions for every religious answer that can be proposed. Perhaps this is the greatest difference in my spiritual evolution. Where I once traded in supposed certainties and sought grounding in perceived absolutes, I now revel in the great mysteries of existence. I no longer fear the ambiguity. Rather, I let it enrich me.

JAMES FIESER

The Jesus Lizard

I do not believe in God, but for many years I did. My story begins in 1970 when my older brother placed an ad in the local paper: "Guitar for sale, $25." It was a cheap spare that he wanted to unload. I was twelve at the time, and like my brother I spent many afternoons practising guitar, harbouring a fantasy of some day playing in a rock band. As my brother practised some riff on his guitar, I'd listen through the wall and play the same thing on mine. "Stop copying me!" he'd yell from the other room.

In response to the newspaper ad, a man of about thirty stopped by to look at the guitar. "Hi!" he said. "I'm Bill Jones, pastor of Westside Baptist Church." Bill was from Alabama—with a heavy Southern accent to prove it—and had been sent to our city of Johnstown, Pennsylvania, as part of the Southern Baptist Convention's effort to infiltrate the North. He didn't buy the guitar, but he stayed a couple hours talking to us. "I'm trying to form a Christian rock group that will present the message of Jesus in the language of today's hippie youth," he said. "How does the idea sound to you?" This was long before the invention of contemporary Christian music, so the concept of a Christian rock group was pretty radical.

"We already have a church," my brother said.

"You wouldn't have to leave your church," Bill replied. "As long as you love Jesus and play music, that's what's important."

"Where would the band play?" my brother asked.

"We'd perform around town at special events that we'll call 'Happenings,'" Bill answered. "We'll set up psychedelic light shows, burn incense, and do other things that might lure hippies. Between songs, we'll weave in the story of Jesus, and at the end of the evening have an altar call. Discuss it with your parents and let me know."

Bill left, and my brother immediately began pestering my parents about joining the band.

"I don't know about all this," my mother said. "I'm not too comfortable exposing you kids to drug users."

"Bill's a preacher, mom!" he said. "What bad could happen with him there?" After some coaxing she agreed.

So our band, The Eternal Trip, was formed with Bill, my brother, and a couple of other recruits. I was too young to join, but as a consolation I got to be the band's roadie, helping drag their equipment around from one Happening to the next. Their first few gigs were unpolished, and I once heard someone comment, "The Eternal Trip—it's a bad trip!" But they soon smoothed their rough edges and began to draw large crowds. While they performed, I sat in the back, mesmerized by the swirling lights, thundering music, and strange people who looked like they'd just walked off the cover of a Grateful Dead album.

During one happening a bearded guy with long, straight hair down to the middle of his back sat next to me on the floor. He became a little agitated and said to me, "I'm having a drug flashback. Please tell me everything's okay."

"Everything's cool, man," I told him. "Everything's cool. Just be cool." He soon calmed down.

"Thanks," he said, "you helped a lot." Later that evening he went up front to give a testimony of his faith. Taking the microphone, he said, "I've been into the drug scene for years. I've smoked hash, dropped acid, and even shot up heroin. I'd be lying if I said that it wasn't fun, but after a while it started to feel empty. I needed something more than an artificial high. I then learned about Jesus and accepted him into my heart, and it's the best thing I've ever done. He's given me a spiritual high like I've never had before. While things have not been perfect since then, I at least know where to turn when things get tough."

His story profoundly affected me, and I realized I needed what he had. Something was missing from my life, and Jesus was the answer. During the altar call at the end of the evening, I went forward. Kneeling with Pastor Bill, I said the sinner's prayer: "Lord Jesus, please forgive me for my sins. I accept you into my heart as my personal savior and ask you to take control of my life."

With those words I became born again and was assured a place in heaven.

A few weeks passed, and our family joined Pastor Bill's church. I wholeheartedly embraced my newly found relationship with Jesus and immediately wanted to share my experience with others. One thing I needed to develop was a compelling testimony—the believer's most effective tool for witnessing. Listening to dozens upon dozens of testimonies, a common theme emerged among them: the testifiers were drowning in a sea of self-destructive behaviour from which Jesus rescued them, giving them true happiness. The more shocking their pre–born again lifestyles, the more effective their testimonies seemed. I didn't have anything that even remotely resembled the life experience of a former drug user. In fact I was a pretty well-behaved kid. In time, though, the Holy Spirit guided me in finding the right words with which to share my faith. The most important thing about the experience of being born again is realizing the supreme sacrifice that Jesus made for all of us, not just for serious drug users. In fact, it seemed to me that the testimonies of converted hippies were mainly brag lists of how daring their drug experiences had been. As I witnessed to my friends about the cleansing blood of Jesus, they too became saved, and many joined our Baptist church.

Within a couple years the hippie movement died out and The Eternal Trip disbanded. I devoted an ever growing portion of my time to fellowshipping with my new church family, studying the Bible and witnessing for Jesus. One crucial event involving my father shaped the growth of my faith. A quiet man of strong convictions, my father was locked into a sales job he passionately hated. He regularly thought about quitting, but with four children to support, he couldn't risk our family's financial security. So he suffered in silence, and when the stress reached a critical point he was prescribed tranquillizers. He routinely increased the dosage as his body adjusted to the drug, which sometimes made him sleep longer than usual. One summer morning my mother loaded our station wagon with kids from the church youth group to drive us all to a church camp two hours away. Concerned because my father was still asleep, she asked Pastor Bill's advice about possible dangers.

He asked her, "Is your husband snoring?"

"Yes" she replied.

"Don't worry, then," he said, "I deal with people on drugs all the time, and he'll just sleep it off."

With that she drove off. A couple hours later, Pastor Bill had second thoughts about his advice and stopped by our house to check on my father. When no one answered the door, he let himself in and made his way to my parent's bedroom. There he found my father, dead.

My mother returned a few hours later to find our house surrounded by police cars. Pastor Bill drove to the camp to pick me up. On the way back he said, "I can't pretend to replace your dad, but whenever you need someone like a father, I'll be there for you." It occurred to me that over the past few years he had already assumed a dominant place in my life as a model of spirituality. Other kids were being shaped by their father's personality, hobbies, and vocational aspirations. I felt that the Holy Spirit was working through Pastor Bill to shape my spiritual life. With my father now gone, this was all the more true. When my mother remarried the following year, Pastor Bill remained my spiritual model.

By the time I entered high school I felt the Lord calling me to the ministry, where I could devote my life to spreading the good news of Jesus. In many ways I was already a novice minister. I formed a high school Bible club with my born-again friends and challenged our school's policy of prohibiting public prayers. My efforts met with ridicule, which just fired me up for the Lord all the more. Most important, I achieved a long-time dream of being in a Christian band, sort of like The Eternal Trip, where I could minister to people of my own age. A folk rock trio, we called ourselves The Song of Hope. I played lead guitar and sang backup vocals. By this time the contemporary Christian music scene was well established and there was a broad network of venues where we could perform—from traditional churches to beatnik-like Christian coffee houses. Largely because of Barry, the rhythm guitarist who wrote most of our songs and sang lead vocals, we gained a respectable following. Our musical style varied according to Barry's moods. On his more upbeat days he felt that all styles of music were gifts from God and could be used in his honour. On his more morose days he felt that rock music and distorted guitars were inappropriate vehicles for glorifying God. So one day we were a loud Christian rock group, the next day a more subdued Christian folk group. Working with Barry was often frustrating, but once he was on stage he sang like an angel and had a spiritual glow that everyone found magnetic.

One evening we played in a small Pentecostal church. This was my first exposure to Charismatic Christian spirituality. After our performance the pastor laid hands on me, as they put it, "to baptize me with the Holy

Spirit." My heart pounded as he first tried casting demons out of me. "Demons are everywhere," he explained, "and before the Holy Spirit can fill you, you need to clean your vessel of them." Even with his best efforts, though, no demon fled from my soul. He then tried to slay me in the spirit. With the palm of his hand against my forehead, he pushed me, but I just stood there praying. He then tried to get me to speak in tongues, but all that came out of my mouth were the English words "Praise you Lord Jesus! Praise you Lord Jesus!" When the evening drew to a close, he said to me, "Don't give up—these things occasionally take time."

For the next few months I struggled to understand why I couldn't experience the Holy Spirit as Charismatic believers do. The issue resolved itself when I attended a large Christian music festival. At some distance from the main stage there was a canvas pavilion with a sign out front reading "Healing Tent." Inside I saw twenty people standing in a line shoulder to shoulder, eyes closed, saying "Praise you Lord Jesus!" A healer laid hands on someone to slay him in the spirit, with an assistant standing to the side to catch the willing victim as he fell backwards. The healer moved to the second person, with the assistant also catching him as he was slain. Like an assembly line, they moved down the row till eventually all twenty people were lying on the ground. The Charismatic experience instantly lost its appeal, and I was again happy with the spiritual relationship with God that I already had.

My days with The Song of Hope ended when I graduated from high school and went off to college a few hours away to major in Pre-ministerial Studies. It was sad to leave the Christian community that had been so important to me for the past several years. While my college was filled with conservative Christian believers, it wasn't quite the same. The college itself was affiliated with a traditional Presbyterian denomination and displayed an intellectualism that was completely new to me.

One of my classes that semester was Old Testament History. On the first day of class the professor told us, "You may wonder why you need a course on the Old Testament when you've been going to Sunday School all your lives. Let's find out how much you really know." With that he passed out an exam that sampled the kinds of questions we'd be expected to answer later in the semester. "During which Egyptian dynasty did Moses live?" "Who was the first king of the Northern Kingdom?" "In what year did the Babylonians conquer the Southern Kingdom?" Of the twenty questions, I couldn't answer a single one. I overheard a student say she got eighteen of them correct. Prior to college, I had read the Bible devotionally; now I was being forced to approach the Word of God academically. I quickly befriended other Pre-ministerial majors, who had a much better grasp of Christian theology than I did, and they patiently coached me on my Bible courses.

During that first semester I also took Introduction to Psychology, a subject I knew nothing about. The professor emphasized the role of the brain in human behaviour. This part of the brain, he explained, was responsible for sensory perception, and that part of the brain for motor action. Emotions, rational thinking, and memory were all products of brain activity. He also stressed the extraordinary mental abilities of higher animals like chimpanzees and gorillas and how they could use sign language at a level beyond the speech abilities of human toddlers. One day after class I asked him, "If my thoughts are just a product of my brain activity, what is my spirit? What part of me lives on in heaven when I die? How am I spiritually different from a chimpanzee?" He replied, "I'm not going to answer those questions for you. It's your job to resolve them for yourself."

Back at my home church, Pastor Bill moved on to an administrative position in the Southern Baptist Convention. His successors at the church were not especially good shepherds, and I became increasingly disillusioned with "spiritual leaders." From my college dorm, I wrote a letter to Pastor Bill expressing my worries. His immediate replacement in the pulpit was a rather weak public speaker, and few members of the congregation liked him. When the deacons refused to increase his salary he threw himself on the ground, pounded his fists on the floor, and screamed out, "No! No! No! You can't treat me like this! I work hard here and deserve a raise!" Then during Easter Sunday service he devoted an entire sermon to attacking members of the congregation for their lifestyles. He was fired, and for a time the next preacher seemed fine. Behind the scenes, however, he was romancing my older stepsister. The trouble was, both were already married with children. One day the two ran off together, with my stepsister leaving her husband and infant daughter. A few days later, the pastor's daughter compelled him to return home. He subsequently resigned. In my letter I asked Pastor Bill to intervene and help save our church from disintegrating. I never did mail the letter since rumour had it that Pastor Bill was purposefully distancing himself from the old congregation.

The conduct of yet another preacher further weakened my respect for the Christian ministry. During a visit home I strolled around our local mall and passed by a piano store. Inside I saw the Charismatic preacher who laid hands on me the previous year. Walking inside I greeted him and asked, "What are you doing here?"

"I left the ministry and now work here selling musical instruments," he replied.

"What happened?" I asked in surprise.

"After a while I was no longer sure about the truth of what I was preaching," he said.

"But you were seeing miracles and other acts of the Holy Spirit on a regular basis," I said. "How could you call that into question?"

He answered, "I just wasn't sure anymore that it was real."

"How did that affect members of your congregation when they learned about it?" I asked.

"Many gave up their faith and stopped attending church," he said.

"And how did that make you feel?"

"Quite bad," he said, "but I couldn't keep pretending."

"Don't you still at least believe in God?" I asked.

"I just don't know," he replied.

That summer I spent three months in Israel with my Old Testament History professor and twenty other students. To prepare us for the trip, the professor said, "A year in college is like sandpaper in smoothing off student's rough edges, but a summer in Israel is like using a coarse woodfile." He was right. My immediate purpose for the journey was to gain a better sense of the country's ancient history and archeology, which I accomplished. Yet what took me by surprise was encountering such a vast array of unfamiliar cultures—conservative and secular Jews, Arab businessmen and Bedouins, European tourists, Christians of every denomination. One afternoon I was visiting the Baha'i Temple in Haifa. I was inside standing before the main shrine when a Baha'i walked in, holding the hands of his two young children. As he stood before the shrine, a look of joy came over his face and tears streamed down his cheeks. He was evidently having a religious experience. What troubled me most about this was that it seemed as genuine and sincere as any Christian experience I ever had or witnessed among my Christian friends. Christianity was the true faith, and I couldn't understand how a believer in a false religion could have an authentic spiritual experience. It then occurred to me that perhaps *his* was the true religion, and *I* was the one who was misled.

While I was in Israel a flood swept through my hometown of Johnstown, killing eighty-five people. My college roommate, Alan, was also from Johnstown and was directly affected by the flood. After a heavy rainstorm, water had covered the valley where he lived. Alan and his family went to the top floor of their house and, looking out the window, saw their car wash away. When a dam broke, a wall of water crushed their house and washed Alan fifteen miles downriver. He prayed all the while for the safety of his family. He survived, and by a miracle his dog was found alive high in a tree. Unfortunately his mother and three younger siblings drowned. Alan felt that God wanted him to survive, and he bore no ill feelings toward God for the fate of his family. But while he wasn't bothered by the good Lord's handling of the situation, I was. I felt it was odd that while Alan prayed for the safety of his family, all that was granted was the life of his dog.

Over the next year I began wondering whether God really answers prayer requests as often as believers claim. Alan's prayer for his family was a dramatic example of a fruitless request. The emptiest of all prayer requests, I thought, were prayers before meals, when people routinely ask God to bless the food and have it nourish their bodies. Even the best believers get sick and sometimes die from contaminated food. It seemed to me that the success rate of prayer requests was no better than random chance. In that respect, prayers for special favours were no different from gambling and perhaps equally sinful. That's no small issue, considering that the bulk of all believers' prayers involve asking God for something. I was still committed to Jesus, but now I felt that Christians typically misunderstood God's hands-on involvement in the world. In many ways my change in attitude about prayer was liberating, since it freed me from desperate pleas for divine intervention.

After two years I transferred to another college. It was another private Christian school, but much more liberal than my previous one. There I was able to explore different theological ideas without being ostracized. I was less confident now about my ability to serve in the ministry and decided to major in philosophy. I also began dating a young woman named Rebecca who had a similar fundamentalist background and who, like me, was affected by the broader world of ideas that college presented. She also was a philosophy major, and we spent much of our courtship debating philosophical issues about religion.

One of my courses at the new college was Introduction to Geology. The first day of class the professor told us, "Geology is built upon the theory of evolution. To understand the rock you hold in your hand or the ground you walk on, you need to see it within the context of the earth's evolutionary development. Biology, chemistry, and even physics are exactly the same. Whether you believe evolution or not is irrelevant; what's important is recognizing the impossibility of modern science without the theory of evolution." Like most fundamentalist believers, I was critical of evolutionary theory and felt it undermined the account of the world's creation in Genesis. But at that point I wasn't in a position to brush aside a theory so foundational to science. I thought perhaps that God had used evolution as a tool of creation. That seemed more plausible than rejecting evolution completely.

One afternoon I wrote a letter to a friend from my old college, recounting all the theological issues I'd been wrestling with over the years. As I wrote, it occurred to me that many of my Christian beliefs had radically changed. I told him that the concept of a disembodied human spirit made no sense to me; that the religious experiences of non-Christians seemed as genuine to me as those of Christians; that it was pointless to pray to a God who was reluctant to communicate back; that religious traditions are constantly fighting scientific advances. But amidst my struggles, I added, I had remained devoted to the divinity of Jesus and the inerrancy of the Bible, burying my doubts beneath my faith. But as I itemized my doubts in the letter it struck me that almost every aspect of my original faith was now causing me problems. It was like I was holding on to a whispy ghost long after it had been drained of its substance. I put down my pen and read over my words again and again. After five minutes I picked up the pen and wrote, "I hereby evict Jesus from my heart." With that I abandoned all belief in God, the afterlife, and everything supernatural.

I went to Rebecca's dorm and told her about my decision, unsure of how she would respond. "Just like that?" she asked.

"Yes, but it's been creeping up on me for some time," I said.

"Well, now that you live in a Godless universe, don't you think life is meaningless?" she responded. "All you have is the hedonistic here and now. That's got to be pretty despairing."

"I don't feel any despair," I said. "Life seems more vital now that the world is not just an appendage of some unseen spirit realm. I know who I am now better than I did before."

"But surely you must feel morality is meaningless if there's no God monitoring us and punishing offenders. What reason do you have for behaving ethically? Why don't you just go rob a bank?"

"I'm not sure belief in God has any real impact on moral behaviour,"

I told her. "Believers regularly sin in full knowledge that God is watching them. The reason I wouldn't rob a bank—then or now—has more to do with disappointing my mother and having the police catch me. Nothing has changed on that front."

"What about life after death? Doesn't it bother you to think that when you die you'll rot?"

"Of course I'm worried about dying," I said. "But aren't you, too? I don't think belief in heaven is an antidote for our natural instinct to survive."

She paused, then said, "You know, you don't have to throw the baby out with the bathwater. Maybe there's something you can salvage of your faith. You could explore any number of more liberal interpretations of Jesus and the Bible. Maybe you should try those before embracing atheism."

"I don't think I can do that any more," I said. "Fundamentalism presented me with a very rigid either–or option: either I believe Jesus is God incarnate, or I reject God completely. After living and breathing that perspective for so many years, there's no middle ground I can accept. The whole idea of Christianity now seems as preposterous as ancient Greek mythology. That leaves me with atheism as the alternative." My debate with Rebecca continued on and off for about a week. At the end of it, she also abandoned her Christian faith for atheism.

During the semester break, Rebecca and I visited Johnstown. Throughout my two years away at college, my Christian family and friends had continued to provide me with a sense of belonging I never quite got in college. I was worried about how they'd react to my recent deconversion. To my surprise, my mother listened respectfully to me and just said, "You may change your mind again down the road." The reaction from my old friends in The Song of Hope was less compassionate. The group was recording an album, so I visited them after one of their practices. Barry greeted me by saying, "So, Jim, I understand you got too smart for God."

Catching me off guard, I thoughtlessly replied, "It's more that God got too dumb for me."

"That's blasphemy!" he retorted. "How can you say that about the Creator of the universe who is infinitely wiser than any human? You're much worse off than I expected."

"Look," I said, "I was speaking rhetorically. I don't believe in God, so God couldn't literally be dumb."

"Are you saying you lost your salvation? That God reneged on his promise of eternal life to you?"

"No," I replied, "I'm saying the whole story is a fairytale."

"But you experienced Jesus!" he snapped. "I was there as a witness to the fruits the Holy Spirit bore through your life. How can you deny that?"

"That's part of the trap," I replied. "Believers are trained to interpret every positive experience as the working of the Holy Spirit. If the sun is shining, if you're happy, if you get a good job, it's all the work of God. Non-believers have the same kind of experiences but they don't drag in the supernatural."

"If Christianity is just a fairytale as you claim, why would anyone choose to believe in Jesus?"

"There are a few lures," I told him, "a kind of get-rich-quick scheme. Right off, Christianity offers a quick path to knowledge. With just a few weeks of Bible study a new believer presumably learns the most important secrets about the universe and the human struggle. That's pretty appealing. It then offers a quick path to power. Armed with your newly found knowledge you can exercise it over others, scare them with stories of eternal damnation, and intimidate them into converting. Finally it provides a quick path for community bonding. New believers have an instant family who profess to love them. That love, though, lasts only as long as you agree with the party line. If you don't, then you're branded as a backslider or heretic and shown the door."

"Is that how you feel about us?" he asked. "Are you afraid your Christian friends will abandon you? We love you through Christ, Jim, and we won't give up on you. Jesus will bring you back into the fold."

"But I no longer belong in the Christian fold." I said.

"Well, that's your choice and you can't blame us for that. If Christian knowledge, power, and community bonding are so bogus, do you have anything better to offer?"

"Not yet," I told him, "but it begins with a more scientific outlook on the world."

"You're just swapping faith in God for faith in science. Can't you see how ridiculous that is?"

"Here's a story that might better explain my situation." I told him. "Long ago an amateur explorer set out on a journey to find the Jesus lizard—a small reptile that supposedly could walk on water. He trekked through mosquito-infested jungles, sweltering in the tropical heat, sometimes going for days without food. Months passed with no sign of the elusive creature. Morally defeated, he sat down by a stagnant pond to lament his misdirected efforts.

"Just then a lizard scampered into the pond. Rapidly kicking its legs, it slowly rose to the water's surface, and, taking giant glides, traversed the pond without sinking. There it was, defying the natural order of everything surrounding it. The explorer was transfixed by the experience and vowed to alert others of the existence of this living miracle. Its very presence, he believed, was proof of an invisible and perfect world beyond the tangible one. With boundless energy he told everyone about his experience, with many moved by the story. Critics, though, argued that the Jesus lizard was a purely natural phenomenon, which the explorer would realize if he approached the matter more impartially. Accepting the challenge, the explorer immersed himself in the latest theories of hydraulics, fluid mechanics, and surface tension. He eventually agreed that the Jesus lizard phenomenon might be explained by known laws of physics. By that point, though, having become an important symbol in the religious lives of many believers, the mythology of the Jesus lizard had taken on a life of its own. Realizing he could do nothing to reverse what he'd started, he stayed silent on the issue for the rest of his life."

Barry fidgeted impatiently while I spoke, and then said, "Nice story, Jim, but how does that relate to you? Are you saying you discovered Jesus and created Christianity? What's your point?"

"No, I'm just saying that in many ways I was like an amateur explorer making extravagant claims before I did my research." That was the last I saw of Barry.

Rebecca and I returned to campus. About the time we should have become engaged, she transferred to an elite college ten hours away. Within a few weeks she broke up with me. Her departure was destabilizing for me since I felt that we had been on an intellectual journey together. Ultimately, though, our split was even more undermining for her. When she dropped out of school for financial reasons, she stayed in the area, living in squalor. She even worked as a prostitute for an evening, but found from that single experience that it was not the job for her. Fortunately, she eventually got back on her feet and finished college.

When my senior year was over I went off to graduate school to study philosophy, eventually earning my doctorate. My dissertation was on David Hume, the great skeptic. Like Hume, I felt that philosophy's principal function was to debunk outrageous claims that people make about reality. I'm now a tenured philosophy professor at a mid-sized university. Though God and religion always come up in discussions, I avoid telling students my personal views on the subject.

My entire fundamentalist experience is a part of my past I'd prefer to forget, but that has proven difficult. With today's political climate being driven so strongly by fundamentalist Christian forces, there are too many unpleasant reminders of my earlier life as a born-again believer. What's worse, I'm forever being cornered by fundamentalists who try to power-drive me into their community. My usual response is to tell them about the Jesus lizard.

LEIA MINAKER

"Are You a 'Real' Christian?"

On a recent business trip, driving to Calgary from Edmonton, as I was eating breakfast in the crowded hotel lobby, a middle-aged woman approached, danish and coffee in hand. She asked if she could share my table. I nodded, and she sat down. Small talk somehow led to the topic of children's books. She mentioned the *Narnia Chronicles*, and I smiled, recollecting the days when my four siblings and I would sit in the living room while dad read us the famous series by C.S. Lewis. When she asked, "So, are you a Christian?" my mind raced with possible responses: "Yes, but you probably wouldn't consider me a 'real' Christian"; "Yes, but we probably disagree on pretty much everything," or perhaps, "Wow, this orange juice is fresh!"

So instead, I merely nodded, and she chattered on. At some point in the conversation I voiced my criticism of the common fundamentalist Christian catchphrase, "Love the sinner, hate the sin," which in reality is merely code for, "Ewwwwh ... homosexuals are just gross!" I remember her defensive look and her words, "You know, this bleeding heart liberalism isn't even *Christian* ... anyway, I've got to go. Nice meeting you." With a strained smile, she got up and left.

Though we had spoken for only a short time, I often think about her. I think about how our conversation would have been different had we met three years earlier. Had I met her then, I likely would have felt I had met a kindred spirit—a fellow Christian with whom I would spend eternity in Glory. I sighed, wondering whether I would ever meet a kindred spirit over breakfast in a hotel lobby.

I grew up the eldest daughter of a good Christian family. Perhaps you've met people like us. We were the family who sang on worship teams, led Bible studies, held prayer meetings, and attended Marches for Jesus. Besides reading us the *Narnia Chronicles*, Dad led family devotions in the mornings. On Sunday afternoons we'd have visitors for lunch. Dad would cook a huge pot of soup or spaghetti sauce on Sunday morning and go to church looking for new people he could invite to share lunch with our family. On countless occasions more than ten people crowded around our six-person kitchen table. Laughter, music, and affection were abundant in our home.

I look back on my almost idyllic childhood with fondness. Growing up with one older brother and three younger sisters meant there was always something to do, always another imaginary world in which to play, and always a sibling with whom to share the chores. Depending on the day, my brother and I would catch frogs and snakes in the field across the street or play Lego and Barbies. Being the eldest girl, I did my best to teach my younger siblings the proper way to live, the proper Christian doctrine to adhere to, and the proper example for them to emulate. My youngest sister—ten years younger—was an eager student. Looking back, I realize I was a strong willed, independent, and fairly bossy child who loved to mother my younger sisters.

I was raised within a very secure world view and felt safe growing up. I knew that no matter what happened, God would protect my spirit, which was, of course, the most important thing. God loved me, Jesus was my friend, and the Holy Spirit gave me peace and courage to carry on in the face of adverse circumstances. My fundamentalist upbringing afforded me mental safety and spiritual comfort. It was Christians against the "world," and I was content with that. Though there were times when I was overcome with sorrow for the lost sheep of the world—those without Jesus—I was generally happy to suppress, ignore, or fail to recognize thoughts that were inconsistent with my faith. If my beliefs did not correspond to those which I knew to be true, it was only the devil tempting me to think doubtful thoughts.

I had a couple of periods of what I would call rebellion—nothing a fundamentalist would consider horrific, like smoking, taking drugs, or, of course, having sex. Rather, I would swear at school. I would write hate letters that I never mailed, and I would viciously tease a guy in my class who didn't fit into my eighth-grade construct of coolness. Rededicating my life to Jesus—reaffirming his invitation into my heart—was a somewhat frequent event in my life, occurring after a period of sinful behaviour. I can remember rededicating my life in grade two, just in case Jesus hadn't heard me ask Him into my heart a couple of years earlier. I would go through this process frequently after Sunday school between bites of stale cookies and sips of watered-down apple juice. And of course youth rallies and youth retreats were excellent venues for revisiting my desire to be born again.

My third-year wedding anniversary is approaching, and in many ways I credit my partner with precipitating a change in me. To this day my beliefs continue to evolve. When I first met Jacob he was an anomaly to me. He came from a Pentecostal family, yet he didn't speak in tongues or raise his hands during the worship time. His dad had been a pastor, yet Jacob questioned the "absoluteness" of God. Jacob played on the worship team, but he seemed disillusioned with the church and its leaders. I remember my silence on our first date as he told me of his skepticism of absolutes. He questioned the purpose of Christianity; he asked me how I would feel if God were to accept Muslims, Hindus, Buddhists, and all others into Heaven along with us Christians. My first response was typical of a fundamentalist—what would be the point of being a Christian if *everyone* got into Heaven? His poignant response shamed me. He asked me softly, "Leia, is that the point? Are you a Christian just so you can get into Heaven?" My exposure to Jacob's thoughts and ideas was the first nail in the coffin, so to speak, of my fundamentalist beliefs.

When Jacob and I met it seemed we could not talk enough. But it wasn't idle chit-chat. Our conversations typically focused on the nature of God, the meaning of salvation, and beliefs that our fellow Christians considered fundamental to our faith. All of our talks lasted hours. When we discussed the need to believe the Creation Story, or whether modern worship was necessary, I often felt a deep unease. My mind was like a beast that had grown up chained to a tree. When released, she can't move beyond the circumference allowed by the chain. Those were the mental boundaries that I had grown up with and that had kept me safe and secure. Throughout my adolescence, the boundaries, though pushed, remained steadfast. In my conversations with Jacob, those boundaries were shattered one by one, and it had an interesting effect on me.

So here I was with a deep sense of unease, feeling that I was betraying my family, my faith, and my soul. As if to reinforce my already guilty conscience, my mother commented during this time: "Leia, I'm more concerned for your eternal salvation than your present-day happiness." In other words, she would rather have had me stay alone, confined in my fundamentalist box. Better to be alone and go to Heaven than explore my mental boundaries with Jacob and possibly wind up in Hell. I realize now that her comment wasn't intended to be hurtful; she was only expressing her heartfelt beliefs. For fundamentalists, daring to explore beyond well-established boundaries is a terrifying endeavour. Fear accompanies any major shift in thought. This fear is somewhat logical, given that a person may feel as if she has wasted one month, three years, or five decades living in the mental confines imposed on her, by herself and others within her belief system. To change your mind on pivotal issues, goes the thinking, is to admit that you've been mistaken in the past and may be once again. There is, as well, the fear that accompanies any significant shift in fundamentalist thought: the fear of Hell. The idea that everyone is damned except those who share your doctrine is a powerful motivator to remain true to beliefs that give assurance of Heaven. It now seems clear to me that the strength with which many fundamentalists adhere to their beliefs is based on fear of eternal perdition.

Second, I felt guilt and fear not only about my questions and potential doubts, but also about the effects my changing thoughts were having on my relationships with friends and family. Those effects were profound. In many ways I attributed my faith to my family. Early on, they had instilled notions of a loving God, sin, Heaven and Hell, and Jesus' saving grace. To question any of the fundamentals seemed to my family to be a slap in the face. Or worse—a sentence to Hell for their eldest daughter.

The process of leaving fundamentalism was by far the most painful time in my life. My family, once so close-knit, was torn. Conversations with my parents and siblings led to tears and broken hearts. There were many sleepless nights. It's as if I had come out of the closet in a family of red-blooded heterosexuals. While my family stood together praying for my soul, I stood alone, begging to be understood and accepted for my changing way of thinking. I heard reports of relatives who had awoken in the middle of the night feeling the need to pray for me. Conversations with my family betrayed their hurt and anger toward me, not to mention their mistrust of Jacob for being the catalyst of my change. Friends and family accused Jacob of changing me. I had always been a strong-willed, independent person who valued logic and intelligence. To be accused of being brainwashed was hurtful—an insult hurled at me by friends and family alike. I saw my changing thoughts as part of a positive, personal, faith-filled journey. I can only assume my family viewed it as flirtation with the Devil.

By the time the proverbial crap hit the fan, Jacob and I were engaged. I moved out of my family's home in order to escape the guilt I felt on a daily basis. Harsh words were said, tears were shed, accusations were made, and relationships were severed. I credit Jacob and a few close friends—and my general stubbornness—for my strength to continue my journey of leaving fundamentalism. It now seems logical that fellow fundamentalists would immediately respond defensively instead of taking time to ask themselves why my thoughts were changing. After all, by recognizing there are legitimate questions that need to be asked about contemporary Christianity, fundamentalists would have been placing themselves in the same position in which I found myself—guilt-ridden, fearful, and attacked by friends and family.

Third, I became a critical thinker. I feel as if my eyes have been opened to the manipulation that is so pervasive in today's society. Nowadays, when I'm watching a commercial and noticing how the lighting affects the subject to which my eyes are drawn, or when I'm in church listening to the soft music playing while the preacher prays, I'm infinitely more aware of the medium that is presenting the message. I'm more adept at noticing manipulation, so that inconsistencies I used to ignore now glare at me. A recent example: One Sunday in church, the preacher was talking about the importance of the ministry of the mundane. Not everyone is called to be a glamorous worship leader or preacher, he said. Then in the next breath he told us how he had recently given up organizing an outreach-type soccer league enjoyed by seventy-five to eighty people each week because it wasn't allowing him enough time to develop relationships. Often while I'm sitting in church I wonder whether I'm the only one who notices how regularly preachers' statements blatantly contradict themselves.

The fourth major change in my thinking is that I can no longer be sure of my beliefs. It's not that I can't hold strongly to ideas, beliefs, or opinions, or that I can't tell right from wrong, or more appropriate from less appropriate. It's more that I no longer hold to new beliefs with my old tenacity. I've developed a gentler, humbler, "I might be wrong about this" attitude. One of the accusations levelled at me during my escape from fundamentalism was that I was becoming proud. I realize now that the accusation of pride is an insult that fundamentalists level at those who have different beliefs or theological training or who aren't afraid to speak out against hypocrisy. It's a catchphrase of indignation made by those who feel that their personal beliefs are being attacked.

Nowadays, I'm defined less by my beliefs than by the way I see and think about the world. I'm able now to maintain passionate yet loosely held beliefs. The capacity to listen, to truly converse, and to change your beliefs when you find yourself in error does not mean you can't take a stand or believe something passionately. Nor does holding a belief mean that arguments and debates are something of the past. It isn't as if there are only two possible camps: fundamentalist and relativist. There's a middle ground—or perhaps more accurately a higher ground—where you can debate, argue, and deny the legitimacy of some beliefs without holding too tenaciously to any one belief or system of beliefs. For me nowadays, debates about ideas and beliefs remain just that—debates about concepts. They don't turn into character attacks, and I don't shut people out for fear they may question my purity, stare in disbelief, or begin screaming at me. For some beliefs, such as my belief that God exists, I no longer think there is irrefutable proof. No longer do I balk at my atheist or agnostic friends. Instead, I happily admit there is no absolute proof for God's existence, and then add that I choose to believe *because* I believe.

I continue to attend church because its value to me still outweighs the pleasure of sleeping late on Sunday mornings. The sense of community, so lacking in our society, is one of the reasons Jacob and I keep going. Our small congregation, with people of all ages and from all walks of life, gives us the chance to learn and appreciate diversity, as much as it exists in any congregation of thought. The spiritual and theological discussions we have in church with our ex-fundamentalist friends also enable us to attend. And perhaps I would still feel guilty if I quit attending. Sermons can be a source of great frustration for me, especially when the preacher is toeing the fundamentalist line. Having had countless conversations with friends who have studied theology, I tend to look with skepticism on a pastor who has just graduated from Bible college, especially when he or she makes Christian theology, doctrine, and faith sound simple. Pat answers no longer satisfy me, which makes for interesting conversations with people like the woman at the hotel. When I think about it, I also consider how her response is typical of the ones I've heard countless times from fundamentalists whom I've challenged to think differently. The retort usually goes something like this: "You're wrong, but don't worry, I'll pray for you. I have to go. Bye!" Or their objections are accompanied by an expression of sympathy and veiled spiritual superiority. Followed, of course, by the reluctance or even outright refusal to discuss it further.

I'm left with an awareness of the inconsistencies in fundamentalist thought and, in general, of life's paradoxes. I'm left with the recognition that though Truth may be absolute (whatever that means), we can never be utterly certain what that Truth is. I'm left with core beliefs that nevertheless may change in the future. Perhaps more important, and quite sadly, I have been left with several damaged relationships that will never be what they once were, though I hope they will become strong again.

Most of all, I'm left with a feeling of awe and wonder at the world around me as well as the spiritual realm. I know now that my mind is finite—that I will never understand everything—yet somehow this knowledge consoles and comforts me. I have come to understand that throughout my time as a fundamentalist, God was capable of doing only those things I deemed good. Now I understand this being we call "God" as unlimited. Not limited to our human conceptions of good or evil, but far surpassing what we might hope to understand.

As I continue on my journey from fundamentalism, hope grows. I meet brothers and sisters whose fundamentalist roots are slowly withering. No longer do we simply repeat the answers we were fed as children; our conversations are alive, sometimes with cogent thoughts and well-articulated ideas, other times with half-formed ideas and the beginnings of heretical musings. I am fully aware that a mind not exercised is one that will inevitably spew pat answers. A commitment to leave fundamentalism is a commitment to read, to maintain humility, and to engage fellow passengers on the journey we call life. All of this regardless of background or beliefs, fundamentalist or not.

ANONYMOUS

The Naked Empress, Queen
of Fundamentalism

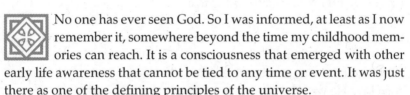 No one has ever seen God. So I was informed, at least as I now remember it, somewhere beyond the time my childhood memories can reach. It is a consciousness that emerged with other early life awareness that cannot be tied to any time or event. It was just there as one of the defining principles of the universe.

It was not a problematic awareness. After all, no one would ever want to see God, because anyone who saw or touched God would die. Yet the descriptions of God were clear and vivid: a being, huge and powerful, all knowing, all controlling, all bullying, all frightening. Every move I made, every thought in my head, every emotion in my body, God saw and knew it all. If it wasn't pleasing to God, it was dangerous, potentially destructive, potentially setting in motion a cascading flood of evil thoughts and actions that would flush a person directly into Hell to burn forever. But never really burn up and be gone. Like the blazing bush that tried to ignite some passion in Moses for the cause of the specially chosen people-of-God-who-had-fallen-on-hard-times, people in Hell would endure the agony of burning and would never be able even to die to get away from the fire.

Who, I thought, would want to burn like that?

The floors were creaky, the air always too hot or too cold in the small room in the back of a frame building with shingle siding that served as a church. One day I would see that unsound and unhealthy environment as a metaphor, but at the time I was just one of the half-dozen children seated at a table in the centre of the room struggling to focus on the things the pastor was saying. And struggling to comprehend Truths that were admittedly incomprehensible.

Comprehensible or not, it was clearly essential that the Pearls of Truth dispensed at those weekly church education sessions be firmly seized, known, and believed. Yet I struggled with knowing and believing things that were incomprehensible. Deliberately incomprehensible at that! Indeed, the Pearls of Truth were wrapped in a shroud of haze because it was *intended* for some people not to understand. Could that be why I was having a hard time comprehending?! The Truth was only for the Elect. Indeed, if you questioned or doubted, if you betrayed the least skepticism, it could well be a sign that you were not part of the Elect. If I entertained the thought that there were inconsistencies or contradictions in the things we were told, that was only a sign of the hardness of my heart and my obstinate efforts to challenge God's plan. A questioning of God's wisdom. Dangerous at the least! How could anyone question a God who is loving and forgiving, a God who wants to save me so much that he slaughtered his only Son? If I challenged and resisted God, if I thought there were contradictions in what he was saying, then despite such love He would make me burn forever in the fire of Hell.

What a terrifying love that was.

I learned quickly that certain kinds of questions were not to be asked out loud. They were to remain locked deep in a secret place within, but even that entailed danger. I knew that God knew about them anyway, which caused me anxiety. It was an anxiety that could not be expressed because it would betray the forbidden thoughts. How were the Pearls of Truth processed in the minds of the others? Of course I could not know. If they had any doubts they wouldn't dare tell me theirs any more than I would dare tell them mine.

The conspiracy of silence created in the back room of the church produced a company of children who could recite word for word the answers to the prescribed and legitimate questions, children who not only knew the answers but believed with all their heart that these things were true. That, anyway, was the face we were given to see, and that was the face I wore. The mysteries of the faith, after all, were the holy secrets of the club, preserved in the hearts and minds of the Elect. It was like the Ark of the Covenant hidden away in the Temple, where, except for the privileged few, none ever saw it and surely none ever touched it. The Pearls of Truth were hidden away inside, not seen, not scrutinized for flaw or error. Instead they were passed from generation to generation of the saved: the wealth of the Chosen that they were to preserve for posterity and eternity.

That was the sole purpose of my life.

I never had to wrestle with questions about the meaning of my life. The church provided the answers. I should know the Truth, defend it, preserve it, pass it on, and be ready always to respond to the beck and call of God in any place and in any way it came. I'd better not be sleeping when it came. The needling questions that sometimes pried their way into my confused and vulnerable mind were banished according to expectation (maybe God would forgive me if I at least tried hard to push away the questions), but they left behind a nagging sense that I was different. Surely the others did not have the thoughts, the questions, the doubts that I had. They all seemed so content in their faith. I was different, but that was my secret. No one would ever know. I could hide my doubts and discomforts and anxieties deep inside, the same way the Pearls of Truth were hidden deep within the church and its members for safekeeping.

And I did!

I think it was in my second year of school that I discovered that disclosure of even a childlike curiosity regarding the mysteries of the faith would get back to the authorities. My teacher in the private Christian school I attended called me out of the classroom one day and forced me to sit on the floor. She towered over me and confronted me: "Why did you say 'pooh pooh' while I was praying?"

"I didn't say 'pooh pooh' while you were praying."

Her hand struck my face hard, stinging. "Don't lie to me. You were heard saying 'pooh pooh' in the prayer before lunch today."

I remembered! Fearful about not keeping my hands folded during the prayer, I had, resourcefully I thought, blown from my arm the fly that I could not swat.

"I was just blowing a fly from my arm. I wasn't saying 'pooh.'"

"And are you going to tell me you didn't tell someone on the playground that you think there are mistakes in the Bible? Was that just blowing a fly away, too?" Her hand struck my cheek once more.

Again I remembered the specific offence. I had discovered with a classmate that our two Bibles were not exactly the same, and we mused how that could be possible if there were no mistakes in the Bible. There was no privacy in my world when it came to any thought or action that might be interpreted as suggesting that maybe my name was not included in the census of the Elect. Now it was clear to me: my naive and heretical conclusion drawn from the comparison of different versions of the Scriptures had been reported back to teacher, seemingly causing *her* to wonder whether I really was one of God's children. Possibly I was one of those wolves in sheep's clothing. She was on alert! She was concerned, and I had better be too. She was not slapping me to hurt me. She was trying to scare, maybe knock, the Devil out of me!

Why were my school friends tattling on me like this? From the distance of decades I see they weren't really tattling. They were afraid for themselves and for me. There was a possibility, frightening beyond imagination, that I was impure and would bring the devil into their company. One value higher than child-friend loyalties was the need to keep the environment pure and devil free. It was not only accepted but also expected that one would rat on a friend if he or she was suspected of threatening the purity of our faith.

A kid next to me in our classroom saw me watching his futile efforts to close an overly full desk. Never taking his eyes from me, with a mischievous grin he pulled out a book and let it drop to the floor, where he pretended to compress it with foot stomping. When he averted his playfully smiling eyes from me to glance down he noticed that it was a Bible he had been stomping. A look of terror spread across his face, intensifying when he realized that teacher had seen it too. I don't know what happened to him. He was shoved from the room, teacher's hands shaking him so violently that the student's head bobbed back and forth as she drove him out of our presence.

I wanted to speak out. I wanted to say it was just an innocent mistake. He did not know he was stepping on a Bible. But I was silent. Speaking would only make me an accomplice to the crime. I was part of the conspiracy. Besides, how could I know for sure that the devil hadn't entered my friend and compelled his behaviour? Why couldn't it have been just a math book? Then teacher, too, would have seen humour in it. She really was quite nice most of the time. But when she sensed that the devil had become incarnate in one of her students, she transformed into a raging monster. Almost God-like, I thought.

I did not see my friend again for a while. After he returned to school we never talked about it. It was too risky. One did not really know whom one could trust. Distrust and pretension were deeply engrained in the susceptible minds of the children of the Christian school, whose motto was "Truth, Faith, and Love."

Distrust, pretension, and fear were the price paid to protect the Pearls of Truth.

The inscrutable realm of Truth included the church's interpretation of the Good Book. Even if one defended the absolute inerrancy and inspiration of the Scriptures, that did not give licence to toy with the notion that the church's understanding of the Scriptures might be even slightly flawed. The Truth and the church's interpretation of Scripture were one and the same. But only, of course, if one happened to be part of the "True Church," which fortunately I was.

"How do we really know that 'Be ye not unequally yoked with unbe-lievers' means that we are not supposed to play with the kids next door who did not go to our church?"

"What? Are you questioning the teaching of the Scriptures? Don't you understand that it is a sin to challenge God?"

An electric fence of fear protected the teachings of our faithful com-munity. Aversion was so strongly programmed into the minds of those who knew themselves to be part of the faithful that even questions of clarification were largely avoided. One central Pearl stood out from the rest as the ultimate touchstone of faith. The key Truth was that there was only one way to true happiness and salvation. One must be saved by the blood drawn in the murderous death of a completely innocent God-man. Jesus' sole purpose in life had been to get Himself brutally executed so that the Elect could be saved. This Pearl was so extraordinary that a person had only one chance to embrace it. If after accepting this Truth one doubted or disbelieved that Jesus' death was a "substitution-ary atonement," there was no second chance, no room to again change one's mind. Once doubt crept in, lost forever was any possibility of ben-efiting from the Midas-touch blood that would transform a wretched sinner. Having been destined because of the Fall to the agony of an ever-lasting Lake of Fire, the sinner on being redeemed would be transformed into a Heaven-bound saint who could look forward to an eternity of bliss. Those were high stakes, and the whole thing was pretty demand-ing for young minds compelled to absorb the Pearls of Truth without seeking clarification. Seeking might be seen as doubt.

Some questions, however, were legitimate. One had only to learn the difference.

An elderly man entered a flower shop. It was Sunday morning. We spied him on our way to church. This was a man well known to my family. He had helped generously and selflessly in a time of crisis. At significant cost to himself he had rescued us from tragedy. Most would have thought him to be an angel, but that did not fit our perspective on the meaning structure of the universe. Here he was, defying the Divine Law by purchasing flowers on Sunday to celebrate his wife's birthday. I ventured the question:

"Will he go to Hell for shopping on Sunday?"

Questions like this were safe questions. They did not challenge the faith; rather, they evoked confirmation and reinforcement of the absolute and unflinching Truths. The answer was prompt and expected. It betrayed not the least discomfort, or even regret, that the Pearls of Truth must be so brutally applied to life. We children must understand that it was not for shopping on Sunday that one would perish everlastingly in Hell, but for failing to embrace the atoning blood and love of Jesus. It was because of *that* failure that people could callously defy the law of God and shop on Sunday.

"Is it fair that someone who is so nice to us should have to go to Hell?"

This, too, was a safe question because it had a ready answer, an answer that had been recited many times before. The principle of the legitimate question was simple: *If you knew before asking the question what the answer would be, it was a safe question.* Posed this way, these questions were not a challenge to the faith but a rehearsal of the Truth that had been well imprinted. The answer, of course, was that God could, and did, use anyone, even evil people, to serve *His* purposes and to take care of *His* Elect. It was as clear that bad people were incapable of doing good things as it was clear that God was to be spoken of as "He," "Him," and "Father." The metaphor of the scaffold explained this mystery quite handily. Just as a builder erects scaffolding to help better build and beautify the edifice he is creating, once the building is finished he tears down the scaffold and throws it away. Its only purpose was to serve the greater purpose of constructing a beautiful building. So God uses those who are not chosen as a scaffold with which to build the Kingdom of the Elect. Once that building is finished the scaffolding can be thrown away.

Thrown into the Lake of Fire, to be exact.

What does it mean when I shudder hearing this awesome wisdom? Is my discomfort doubt? Or are these feelings what is meant by the fear of the Lord, which is the beginning of wisdom? I'm not doubting, I'm just confused. Did I feel a little anger toward God? No, of course not. It is just sad that some people don't get saved and will have to burn in the Lake of Fire. I am angry with those people, of course. Angry because they don't accept God's love. They don't allow themselves to be saved. They just don't believe the incomprehensible Pearls of Truth, which is all they have to do to be spared from eternal torment. It's their own fault! Yet God doesn't really want everyone to be saved. He wants to burn thousands and millions of people in the Lake of Fire—so maybe it isn't their fault after all! It is so confusing.

It is frightening that I am the only one so confused. Why am I the only one?

The arrogance of the Elect was nurtured and shaped. Arrogance is a perfect sublimation for fear and confusion. After all, God only wanted relatively few people to embrace that ultimate Pearl of Truth and be transformed by the blood of the Lamb. Fortunately God had figured out there are advantages to making this a family kind of thing, so he designed a covenant with some important ancestral winners of the predestination lottery. That meant that getting saved was something like a disease that runs in families: if your parents are members of the Elect, your own chances of being included in that census are greatly enhanced. That meant I was quite fortunate because both my parents were part of the chosen. That gave me pretty good chances. I should forsake my fears as childhood silliness and embrace my privileged status as one of the Elect. At least my mind was convinced. There would certainly be temptations in the form of rational thinking, but as long as my faith ruled my mind, reason could be dismissed as the work of the Devil. Any fear I had could easily be suppressed. I entered adolescence with a well-developed ability to distinguish between the safe and the unsafe questions. A restlessness developed. It found expression in questions that did not challenge the Pearls of Truth but that did challenge the inconsistencies in the behaviour of the Elect.

I discovered a growing urge to push the safe questions to the edge.

Woven through the doctrinal Pearls, force-fed into the heads of the children of the Church, was a moral code that sometimes defied reason. The rules for conduct were craftily extrapolated from the Ten Commandments and sundry other verses in the Scriptures, all shaped by the wisdom of the Church to provide exact and clear answers to any conceivable question of conduct.

Drinking was acceptable in immoderate moderation. After all, the Apostle Paul said that wine is good for the stomach. The Bible, being the ultimate authority on everything, was the ultimate authority on medical matters. Dancing was bad. It had something to do with sexuality, which could lead to sin against the Seventh Commandment. But sexuality was not discussed very much, so the exact connection between sexuality and dancing was never exactly spelled out. Sexuality itself was good and bad; mostly bad, which made it something like guns, which we were never allowed to have, not even toy guns. Guns were okay when they had to be used for good things, like war, which was sometimes necessary to protect our religious rights and freedoms, along with some other interests we might have. But if you were not a cop or a soldier you had no use for a gun. That's the way it was with sex, too. You needed it for special undefined purposes on rare occasions, but otherwise not. Perhaps the purpose of sex was not completely undefined. Everyone knew that the only purpose of sex was to have children, who, prayerfully, would also be bound for the Kingdom. But the exact mechanics of that purpose were left to the imagination and to the resources of the street. This was probably the real reason we were not supposed to play with kids who were not part of our Christian community. Moreover, I figured that the similarity between guns and sex provided some clue to the meaning of shotgun marriage, which was another vague expression one just knew lacked a clear and forthright definition.

My challenge to the moral inconsistencies of the Elect generally did not engage the more contentious points of morality. There was, after all, plenty of material in the less complicated issues. My early, theological nuances began with seemingly innocent curiosities:

- If God forbids us to work on the Sabbath, why do dairy farmers milk their cows on Sunday? Aren't they disbelieving God's ability to keep the cows from producing milk on Sunday?
- If children are supposed to honour their father and mother, does that mean we should not invite neighbourhood kids to come to church with us if we know that their parents wouldn't want them to go to church?
- If the only purpose for sex is to have children who are the Elect, does that mean that if a couple does not have children they are not Elect?
- If it is not okay to date people who are not members of the church, but it is okay to marry a person who is willing to become a member, should not church membership be a prerequisite to a first date?

- If marrying a person who is not a member of the Church is one of the ways God uses to lure the covenantal exceptions into the company of the Elect, shouldn't the church encourage everyone to troll for a marriage partner outside the Church?
- If lying is wrong, why is it okay to smuggle bibles into communist countries?

The answers to these questions, ones that would emerge over the next several years, found their inception one night in the aftermath of a violent storm.

The night was dark, much darker than usual. Tornado winds had left a path of destruction. The electrical current was lost to the homes and streets of the neighbourhood. Pale moonlight eased the blackness of a city that had felt the wrath of God, that had been called to repentance and been challenged to cleanse itself by the shed blood of Christ. That is, if you were Elect. For the rest it was a foreshadowing caution of the wretched helplessness and horror of perdition. For the woman who had lured me into the wasteland, my senior by several years, it was opportunity.

She had status, power, and respect in the church community. Her "vulnerability" in this disconcertingly out-of-the-ordinary scenario was surprising to me, and uncomfortable. It caught me off guard, as intended.

"I'm frightened," she said. "I don't know what to think of all of this."

"Do you disagree with this morning's sermon?" I asked.

The sermon had been unambiguous. Psalm 46 was a clear explanation of the devastation:

> God is our refuge and strength, a very present help in trouble. Therefore will not we fear, though the earth be removed, and though the mountains be carried into the midst of the sea; though the waters thereof roar and be troubled, though the mountains shake with the swelling thereof ... The heathen raged, the kingdoms were moved: he uttered his voice, the earth melted ... Come, behold the works of the LORD, what desolations he hath made in the earth ... Be still, and know that I am God: I will be exalted among the heathen, I will be exalted in the earth.

How then could she speak of being frightened?

"I don't know." She paused, searching for words: "Come close to me, it makes me feel better." Her arms surrounded me and drew me close. "Hold me. I need to be held."

Surely there must be a verse somewhere to tell me what to do. My mind was blank.

"Touch me. It feels good to touch."

Touch? Touch! Touch what? What were we doing? This was more touch than I could remember ever ... Why was I speechless? ... thoughtless? ... helpless?

"Kiss me." Her lips and tongue searched for my mouth, her breasts pressed hard against me, her passion terrified me.

Wrenching myself free of her grasp I stepped away into stunned silence.

She spoke. "Why are you afraid? I'm not hurting you. I just want to feel some love ... to make me feel better in this terrible, terrible mess. Don't you want that too?"

I did not know. I could say neither yes nor no.

A new awareness engulfed me, just like the arms from which I had torn myself. The arms of uncertainty, once embracing, could not so easily be flung aside. A flood of awareness surrounded me and took my breath. It felt like I was drowning at the bottom of a lake of uncertainty. I knew there was no answer to that penetrating question that she had plunged like a sword into my mind and into my soul.

I did not know what I wanted. I did not know what I believed. Moments earlier I had known—but I knew no more. I did not know how to respond. All the faculties of reason that had challenged the inconsistencies of the faith and that had identified an answer to every legitimate question of morality that had come my way were rendered impotent by this suffocating awareness. Why could I not dismiss this as an illegitimate question—as a question that affronted God and that therefore was not permitted to be asked, not permitted even to be entertained in one's mind? Among the fallen trees a lowly Tree of Knowledge stood whose fruit produced the taste of uncertainty, one that aroused within a surging sensation of the ejaculation of all the knowledge that had been building over the years. My black-and-white world expired in the darkness of that night and emerged in many shades of grey, even colour here and there. A strange new world I had not known before.

I found my voice. But all I could say was, "I don't know."

The conversation that followed reinforced my confession: a fumbling exploration of a spectrum of notions from the accuracy of the Bible to the meaning of sexual pleasure. It was a conversation less notable for insight than for taboo violations. The boundaries of legitimate questions were trespassed. The shroud of protective mystery was peeled open and the naked Pearls of Truth were exposed. From what I can now recall, this was the first time I saw that what was profoundly wrong was, simultaneously, powerfully right. She took from me my religious power and my spiritual innocence. She stripped away my religious certainty, she violated the sacred secrets, she forced me to touch and hold and fondle the titillating. All brought a sensuous awareness that the unsafe questions were not unsafe because they offended God. They were unsafe because there were no answers.

The questions were but potholes in the highway of the church's theology that could not be filled.

I was transformed, but no one would have noticed that something had happened. Indeed, no one would be allowed to know. One secret had been exchanged for another. The secret of the Pearls from which I had been barred was exchanged for a secret in which I participated. I was now the secret keeper, strangely empowered by my victimization. A mingled stream of resentment and gratitude flowed from that night of mind rape. But it flowed through a soul that was still trapped in a symbiotic relationship with a religious community. It offered protection from a menacing and evil world, rendered no less menacing and perhaps more by the rending of the garments of the faith system.

The realization the empress was wearing no clothes evoked both pleasure and horror.

I delighted in her nakedness, but at the same time I wished to cover that nakedness from the leering eyes of the evil world. So I continued to defend the indefensible tenets. But privately, I sought (for myself if for no one else) whatever could be salvaged from the massive Sacred Mountain of Truths that over the years had filled my head to bursting. One by one, I turned over the stones, examining them for their value in an effort to determine which might truly be Pearls and which were only cheap imitations. A great mountain of stones to be examined one by one! It was (and is) a process of years, a stream of questions, a battle of heart and mind. The questions in my mind were even more serious:

- Prohibition of lying seems to have some merit, but on that basis is it right to dismiss all drama, which is pretension? And books of fiction, which are untruth?

- It seems that the concept of rest on the Sabbath is a good idea, but should that be stretched to mean that playing a game of Monopoly on a Sunday afternoon is sin?
- Adultery is bad (of course!?), but what exactly is adultery?
- Is dancing nothing more than a poorly disguised effort to incite sexual arousal?
- Is all sexual arousal evil if it is not channelled into redeeming efforts to create more covenant children?
- Are all bars nothing but dens of iniquity that must be strictly avoided because they are a risk to one's eternal destiny?
- Undeniably the Bible speaks of slaves and their duty of submission, but does that imply an endorsement of the institution of slavery?
- Did God really make some people black as retribution for sin, clearly intending them to be culled to populate the institution of slavery?
- Are all humans really predetermined to spend eternity in a State of Bliss (Heaven) or a State of Agony (Hell)? Are there truly some people who are the Chosen Ones, the Elect, the People of the Covenant?
- Indeed, is there such a thing as Heaven and Hell?
- Are women inferior to men?
- Was Mary a virgin when she conceived Jesus?
- And did Jesus' bloody execution really give God such a huge sense of satisfaction that he promptly tore up all one-way tickets to Hell for those who were born again?

The relentless stream of questions fuelled a gradual transition from a project of search and rescue within the mountain of Pearls to abandonment of that supposed mountain. Building materials for a new spiritual edifice would be found elsewhere. Small wonder there had been such a strong taboo against examining the Pearls. The wealth believed to have been inherited through the generations of the Elect was exposed as dismal poverty, and the Truth once disrobed was seen to be a lie.

This all seems so long ago. Now it seems clear to me that those who defend the faith and who seek to protect its Truths have no place in their community for any who question, or challenge, or suggest that the empress has no clothes. Prophet and maverick alike are branded with the "T" of traitor and banished from the circle of the Elect. The price one pays for insight is separation and alienation. Family and friend, trusted comrade and intimate mentor are soon distant. Communication becomes like a crackling telephone line that no technology can fix. The exit from fundamentalism is often like the flight of the refugee, who leaves all behind in the hope that distance from the horror will provide opportunity for a new beginning in a new place, for new wealth in a better, safer environment.

I have experienced neither flight nor banishment.

An ambivalent desire to stem the alienation leads to a new conspiracy of pretension and secrecy. Though I consider myself free from the enslavement of fundamentalism, I am not separated from its people and its institutions. I am an exile in self-perception, not formally banished from the circles of those whose perception of the universe I no longer share. I choose with care what will and what will not be disclosed of the values I have come to own and cherish. For a variety of reasons, selfish, practical, and altruistic, I have not claimed the punishment that could well become a gift, in that banishment would likely entail a significant liberation. The fear that glues the community of the Elect is transformed, I suppose, into freedom for those who come unglued. Nakedness of mind is paradoxically a pleasure enjoyed only by the exiles of the kingdom whose empress wears no clothes. Within the domain of the naked empress, the dress code for the mind is strictly in force. The contours of my mind are concealed; the truth I have gradually claimed as my own is protected by the lie of mind garb, carefully designed to conceal and hide. What is it about truth, real or feigned, that rouses us to hide it?

One day, I think, I will step forward and strip away the covers. If banishment is the price, banishment it shall be.

Perhaps this writing is a small, testing step in that direction. What holds me back is not so much a fear of banishment as a lack of time and energy for the process. I have found that in the life that was denied me as a blind defender of the Pearls of Truth there is much to be explored, discovered, and enjoyed. I choose to flirt with the possibilities of the future rather than untangle the complexities of the past or grapple with the tasks and pains of separation. After all, an appropriate dose of selfishness is one of the pleasures afforded those who wrest themselves free from the grasp of fundamentalism.

G. ELIJAH DANN

Confessions of an Ex-Fundamentalist

Over the past twenty or so years, having left Christian fundamentalism that long ago, I've often mused about what purpose
an experience of this sort could play in my life, at least as seen
in the larger scope of things. I still find myself thinking in terms of a
life's purpose—its end, or, put in theological terms, its *telos*. So I've wondered, "Why did God let me waste so much of my youth caught up in
such a lifestyle of spiritual pain and suffering?"

Recent events over the past few years in North America have got me
feeling that my involvement in Protestant fundamentalism might turn
out to be more than just a personal struggle by a young man who called
himself a Christian. This is something worth considering, given that I was
mired in so much misguided, spiritual futility for so many years, all of
which conspired to send me languishing in the struggle against sinfulness and worldly temptations. Not to mention the enormous amount of
time I wasted reading and studying religious material of questionable
scholarship. Now, two decades after leaving fundamentalism, looking
over the landscape of contemporary culture, I've come to think that in
the grand scheme of things, perhaps I went through what I did to better appreciate the so-called culture wars of Western society. But just as
it goes with other stories, I need to start at the beginning. My beginning,
that is.

I was conceived and then gestated in the womb as a Christian. I know
how this must cut the ears of Protestant fundamentalists, to suggest that
becoming a Christian might be a matter of genealogy; that it is not always

a strictly personal, conscious decision. I don't mean there was something miraculous going on. It wasn't a particularly extraordinary event. It happened because my mother's own spiritual nature was so saturated that it was bound to seep into her offspring.

She might be canonized if Protestants handed out such awards. Especially now that she is in her older years, with the advantage of hindsight I see her life as parallel to that of a mystic or a saint. She spends hours with her Bible, not always reading it, often just holding it. Due to her poor health, she passes many of these hours quietly in bed, thoughtfully praying and meditating, mostly reflecting on my welfare and interceding to God on my behalf. She has done this all my life. Her constant companion, the cat Naomi (as in the Book of Ruth in the Old Testament, appropriately named after my mother, Ruth), spending many hours beside her under the electric blanket, has been my mother's steadfast friend since the death of my father a few years ago. A meditative life and kitties go along together quite nicely.

However my religious views may now differ from those of my mother, I know her prayers have saved my life, have been behind every blessing I've had, and have opened every road of opportunity for me. Her own mother, herself a women of spiritual depth, had "Led her to the Lord" as a young girl. If fundamentalists hadn't influenced my mother as a young woman, undoubtedly she could have been a professor of religion, or forgoing a career, perhaps she might have pursued a life of quiet, meditative solitude—an existence devoted to attaining oneness with the Divine, with God.

It never happened that way. My mother and father grew up with the hard-core fundamentalism of the Canadian prairies, the Bible Belt strapped tightly across the belly of Alberta's heartland. It was a territory ruled from the 1920s to the 1970s by Bible-toting, fire-breathing pastors. This assortment of pulpit-pounding evangelists was a familiar environment for my family. My father's mother, herself a daughter of the Rob Roy clan, had joined the Salvation Army. My mother's father, coming from the southern United States, was the great-grandson, grandson, great-nephew, second and third cousin, cousin, and uncle to a long line of staunch Southern Baptist pastors and seminarians. Sadly, there seemed to be no contradiction between my grandfather's religious heritage and a book I found, as a young boy, in his library: *The Clansmen*, by Thomas Dixon. My eyes popped when I read the book's dedication in the Preface:

TO THE MEMORY OF
A SCOTCH-IRISH LEADER OF THE SOUTH

My Uncle, Colonel Leroy McAfee

GRAND TITAN OF THE INVISIBLE EMPIRE
KU KLUX KLAN

The apple doesn't fall far from the tree, but fortunately in my family's case the fruit of Christian inclinations prevailed, rather than racism. My mother inherited a deep feeling of the religious, and it was also in the genes of her youngest brother, my favourite uncle, who for years was a Presbyterian minister. Uncle Al escaped the lure of the fundamentalists; even so, the environment of his parishes couldn't satisfy his need for greater spiritual expansiveness. After many years of dedicated service as a minister, he quit the pastorate to pursue spiritual and philosophical enlightenment of a non-traditional sort. Good for him. Lucky for him.

With so many relatives, distant and near, involved in theological studies and the ministry, it's no surprise "the religious gene" (if indeed there is such a thing), didn't stop with my forebearers. We know that our DNA will give us either brown eyes or blue eyes, yet we like to think that our personalities and choices lay outside the realm of genetic determinism. Academics will debate the nuances, but it's clear to me that I inherited my religious predilections as much as I did my physical characteristics.

It's interesting how the ability to remember childhood events varies significantly from person to person. Some of my friends are able to recall large chunks of their childhood, while others remember nothing. I have assorted memories, best described as "snapshots." I remember the first time I got up on a two-wheeled bicycle, all on my own, and glided effortlessly down the sidewalk. It was one of those few euphoric moments in life, the sort we can count on one hand. It was magic, as if I had gained a new super-power, like suddenly being able to fly. Further snapshots: One day while I was playing in the kitchen beside my mother, I noticed that she had become visibly shaken while listening to a radio announcement. President Kennedy had been shot in Dallas. The first time I fell in love was in grade three, with the prettiest girl in the class. It was a torrid love affair even though it lasted only a few moments, and it was consummated when she locked eyes with me across the row of desks and smiled. The first time I saw my father cry was after my Aunt Ruth phoned to say that their mother, my grandmother, had died.

There was no time during my childhood when I didn't believe that Jesus was my friend and that God was my ever-present companion. My mother had always taught me so. It was as natural and real as anything could be. Years later in Bible college, the New Testament injunction "to pray without ceasing" perhaps sounded strange, even obsessive, to many of my fellow students, but to me it was quite normal—something as natural as breathing. My mind's internal conversation had always assumed that Jesus and God were sitting there quietly listening, sometimes nodding, all the while acknowledging my stream of consciousness. No doubt certain family rituals were a constant reinforcement, like regular prayers before meals and bed. When my brother Bryan and I were called for mealtime blessing, the standard refrain was:

God is Good
God is Great
Let us thank Him for our food
Amen.

Simple as they may sound, later during my theological studies I learned that those lines touched on deep doctrines of theistic religion: that God is omnibenevolent and omnipotent and also providential— that is, he provides for all our needs. Before going to sleep each night, Mother would listen to Bryan and me while we said the prayer she had taught us:

Now I lay me down to sleep
I pray the Lord my soul to keep.
If I should die before I wake
I pray the Lord my soul will take.

Like the meal prayer, this one had its embedded doctrines: (1) the world was fallen, (2) death was the consequence, and most important, (3) eternal life was the hope. Perhaps this would have caused more sensitive children distress, thinking they might not make it through the night. For whatever reason, it wasn't my worry. It still isn't. For me, all was well on earth and in heaven. My faith, belief, and practices made my world happy, hopeful, and carefree.

Yet this faith was not good enough, at least as proclaimed by Christian fundamentalism. That was the message that had such great influence on my mother. Much of it had been passed down to her through her own extended family. As a young wife and mother, concerned for the spiritual welfare of her two sons, she was strongly dissatisfied with the Social Gospel of the more mainstream Protestant churches. In contrast to the fundamentalists' Gospel, Social Gospel amounted to talk from the pulpit about justice issues such as poverty and women's rights. My mother and father had been taught by their parents that you have to first save men's souls before focusing on their more worldly problems. So my family, having attended Presbyterian and United Churches roughly until my teens, began attending the Christian Missionary Alliance Church.

The Christian Missionary Alliance Church is a popular conservative church in Canada, but it isn't especially well known in the United States. Alliance members would be quite at home in most Baptist congregations, albeit with one key difference: the Alliance Church emphasizes the born-again experience as necessary for everlasting life, but it *also* emphasizes—leaning on the teachings of the church's founder, A.B. Simpson—the consequent "second blessing," a necessary appendage to ensure the real-ization of a "spirit-filled life," that is, "a victorious Christian life." Simp-son, influenced by the Methodists' Holiness Movement, saw the Chris-tian life in extreme terms, more so than most fundamentalists. Being born again is one thing. Being spirit filled is something else—it evidences itself in a life full of enthusiastic talk, with weekly Bible readings, Bible studies in people's homes, church twice on Sundays, and people meet-ing non-Christians to "witness" about Jesus being the Saviour.

This is a ratcheting up of fundamentalism and can even lead to talk of "perfectionism" or "entire sanctification." Sunday sermons in the Alliance church speak of the need to be born again and of the subse-quent second blessing, as in "rededicate your life to Jesus." Communion, the Alliance's equivalent to Eucharist, takes place once a month. True to its Protestant fundamentalist roots, grape juice and crackers substitute for wine and bread. Also, each Communion service is accompanied by an altar call. After the sermon, people are invited to come to the front of the church and gather just below the preacher's pulpit, while the rest of the congregation sings the well-known hymn of repentance, "Just As I Am," three, sometimes four times in a row. Made popular by Billy Gra-ham in his crusades, the words, originally written by Charlotte Elliott in 1834, describe Protestant theology quite fittingly:

> Just as I am, without one plea,
> But that Thy blood was shed for me,

And that Thou bidst me come to Thee,
O Lamb of God, I come, I come.
            Just as I am, and waiting not
To rid my soul of one dark blot,
To Thee whose blood can cleanse each spot,
O Lamb of God, I come, I come.
            Just as I am, though tossed about
With many a conflict, many a doubt,
Fightings and fears within, without,
O Lamb of God, I come, I come.
            Just as I am, poor, wretched, blind;
Sight, riches, healing of the mind,
Yea, all I need in Thee to find,
O Lamb of God, I come, I come.
            Just as I am, Thou wilt receive,
Wilt welcome, pardon, cleanse, relieve;
Because Thy promise I believe,
O Lamb of God, I come, I come.

Once at the altar, the sorrowful meet with a counsellor to recommit their efforts to live a more "Christ-like" life out there in the secular, un-Christian, and therefore hostile world.

So as a child, there I was, under the delusion that Jesus was my best friend, that God loved me, that He was my Protector and my Heavenly Father. It was all mistaken. Instead, the pastor of our church repeatedly preached that we were estranged from God. That my sin, both the sin I was born with as a result of "original sin" (because Adam and Eve are our representative parents), and my own sins created in the daily immoral and debauched thoughts and deeds of a ten-year-old, had formed a great chasm between God and me. Jesus wasn't really my friend because I had never "prayed the prayer of repentance." If I did not repent of my sins before dying, I would go to Hell. If I died unsaved there would be no further chance for forgiveness and redemption. I would spend eternity in the Lake of Fire reserved for Satan, his demons, and all other unbelievers.

I really didn't need much convincing that I was a sinner. Even as a young child, I certainly knew I wasn't perfect. Unlike some children who are taught by their parents to believe they can do no wrong, my mother and father made certain their lives weren't going to be run by a two-year-old despot. Fair enough. But after I heard that message at church, I began for the first time to associate my childhood indiscretions with how God and Jesus would think of me. Not only did I have to be wary of any behaviour that might bring a slap to my backside, but now I also had to consider how that action would add to God's displeasure with me. My sins would soon build up into a heaping punishment in the fires of Hell!

And that's where it all began: fearing God's wrath, His anger, and how I must be making Jesus deeply unhappy.

Granted, it wasn't all doom and gloom. The Alliance church is famous for its summer Bible camps. I happily attended, starting as a young teenager. The major draw wasn't my desire to hear more preaching. Rather, summer camp presented the perfect opportunity to meet girls for a timely summer romance. Once at camp, boys and girls were separated into their respective cabins. The boys' cabins had been converted from old grain bins and outfitted with steel bunks. This was an excellent arrangement for us, despite the chinks in the outside walls that gave entrance to nuclear-powered monster mosquitoes, along with a wide assortment of other bizarre bugs and spiders. No matter. Each day was filled with sports designed specifically for blowing the energy out of kids, from swimming, canoeing, archery, and rifle marksmanship to dodge ball and soccer. And of course, there were the wonderful evening campfires.

Every night we would gather down by the lake around a huge bon-fire. We would sing all the typical Christian youth songs, and yes, that included "Kumbaya." The songs all spoke of how much God loved us, how much we loved God, how much Jesus loved us, and how much we should love one another. Most were intermingled with refrains of redemption, pleas for forgiveness, and contrition for sin. We would then pray and listen to a story by the camp director, who was usually a pas-tor recruited for the duty from a local church. All of these activities, car-ried out with precise rhythm and routine, were for a single purpose: to get us to listen to the Gospel, recognize our sinfulness, repent, ask the Lord into our hearts, and be born again.

Giving one's testimony was part of this procedure. Kids who were already born again would tell how they were once sinners and how Jesus saved them. Unfortunately, this strategy had an unintended con-sequence: if we wanted to be something other than run-of-the-mill Chris-tians, our conversions would have to be dramatic. Simply put, the greater our sins before conversion, the more powerful our testimony would be once we accepted Jesus into our hearts! Which meant that as we sat around the fire at night, the confessed sins became more spectacular, from acts of disobeying parents all the way up to smoking cigarettes (at our age and at the time, these were fairly desperate acts of rebellion and wickedness). We were all, in our own way, mimicking the recipe we had heard countless times before in our churches.

One summer at camp had particular significance. I was fifteen when, in the language of fundamentalism, something took place that could only be described as a "revival," a "moving of the Spirit." On the last night of camp the stage had been prepared. The campfire songs had all been sung with the typical lyrics of acceptance, joy, happiness, and unconditional love. Most of us had indeed been thinking about how happy we were. Our week together had been a welcome emotional change, especially for those who would be returning to broken homes, or, more typically, those returning to homes with unhappy siblings and fighting parents. It was the camp director's last chance to win some souls, so the send-off was going to have to be stirring.

I don't recall how it started, but kids started crying at the end of the pastor's message. First it was just a couple of us, then within a few minutes all thirty of us were out-and-out bawling. Not just a few tears shed in anticipated departure of friends, but the crying of sin sorrow. For those unacquainted with this religious context, it probably sounds strange. For those who have felt the "conviction of the Lord," the sensation is difficult to forget. There is an overwhelming sense of guilt, of sin and grief, for every kind of wrongdoing done in word, thought, and deed.

In a setting far from calm, but certainly not mayhem, the pastor and the camp counsellors walked around to sit with every camper, asking if they were ready to "accept Jesus into their hearts as their own personal Lord and Saviour." All of this took a few hours, starting around nine p.m. and going on till midnight. After about an hour around the bonfire, campers and counsellors started wandering and dispersing, sobbing and crying, talking and praying with one another.

Then it was my turn. The camp director found me sitting on a hill close to the lake. He sat down and asked me if I wanted to be born again. Of course I did, I was ready. The crying began with the confession of every sin I could think of, followed by the prayer of forgiveness. One of the things about this event that stands out for me is the memory of how, throughout it all, mosquitoes incessantly and mercilessly stabbed away at my face, eyes, and ears. Even today, a mosquito is the only creature I can bring myself to kill. Nay, I will not only kill mosquitoes, I will do so, as they say, with "extreme prejudice." I still regard the mosquito as the devil incarnate.

Despite how I perceive this experience thirty years later, the great sense of peace and serenity I felt at that moment, the next day, and the weeks that followed, is without parallel in my spiritual journey. The following day still stands out clearly in my mind. I was up early, out in a canoe on the lake. There was a beautiful clear-blue sky and not a ripple on the water. I felt like my insides had been washed out with a scouring pad. I felt clean, new, and incredibly content. It was peace with God: the religious experience that mystics, priests, prophets, and believers of all faiths have spoken of for millennia. The overpowering feeling of God's love and peacefulness was something I had every expectation of retaining.

Despite the deeply held hope of maintaining the sensation of the conversion experience, and the determination to do so, in the life of every fundamentalist there will be, sooner or later, a disconnect between the religious life one aspires to and the reality of everyday living in the actual world. My life was no exception. The first sense of disconnect happened almost immediately after I left the insulated world of Christian summer camp. Life back in the city was decidedly anticlimatic. Camp had lasted only one week; nonetheless, campers and counsellors had developed deep friendships.

This intense bond had been made possible through a profound emotional experience. Back at our regular lives at home, on our farms, in our towns and cities—the mundane existence that only the end of a lazy summer can bring—we all faced an immediate pining. We were missing the perfect environment that had brought us our peace with God. And if a relationship with God was based on success at avoiding sin, life in a cloistered, controlled environment like a church summer camp had to be preferred over city life with ordinary, unsaved teenagers. Thus I first became aware of how important religious segregation would be if I was to keep my spiritual enthusiasm and passion.

I knew, because of my years in Sunday school and listening to church sermons, that once born again, we were to live "the victorious Christian life." That meant no swearing, drinking, or smoking, no seeing secular movies, and no listening to non-Christian music. We would instead spend our time "fellowshipping" with other like-minded Christians at church-related activities, or in the youth groups created to occupy overly energetic, hormone-ridden teenagers. In short, we were to exemplify the spirit-filled life. Such was the life of the Christian "Overcomer." It was to be exhibited in the perfect family dynamic where mom and dad love each other and are utterly kind and caring and where "dysfunctional" has no meaning; a family where no prescription drugs are necessary for depression, anxiety, sleep, or sex; a family with no dark secrets or scandals. The kids would be well adjusted, school loving, and elder respecting. Basically, a scene straight out of a Rockwell painting, albeit an explicitly Christianized version.

This was "lifestyle" evangelism. Fundamentalists had long since abandoned trying to debate secular culture on an intellectual basis. Instead, the reality of Jesus was to be demonstrated in the lifestyle of the individual, born-again believer. This sort of Christian busies himself at work, doing his daily tasks. Unlike his male colleagues who swear and tell off-colour jokes, and who talk about sports, the new female employee, and their ambitions for career success, the spirit-filled believer seems uninterested by all of it. He is diligent in his office duties and has no interest in going for an after-business drink. As the story goes, his colleagues take notice. Because the lives of his fellow workers are so unhappy, they begin asking him what makes him so different, so content and peaceful. This is his opportunity to share the Gospel, to bring someone to the Lord. After all, without being born again, any person we meet may be bound for Hell. These encounters, far from being random, may very well have been predestined by God for the very purpose of witnessing—that is, leading others to Christ. All the heavenly hosts would be holding their breath, watching to see what we would do. Would we make the effort to pluck a soul from eternal damnation? Or merely watch that lost soul walk away?

For me, a fifteen-year-old kid, all of this was more easily said than done. Though my parents understood what had happened, the city wasn't exactly an environment where anyone else would know, or even care to know, what had happened at camp. It was as if I had begun living an alien existence. I was back at home, and while I'd changed, I realized that nothing around me had. This made the task before me all the more onerous. It was my responsibility to share with others my camp experience, to witness to all my friends, to live the victorious Christian life.

Back home with my unsaved friends, not surprisingly, I began the infamous "backsliding" that every fundamentalist is so often warned about during Sunday morning sermons. And it was the same story every summer after camp. After a few days, or weeks, I was back to old habits. It wasn't exactly a life of crime. By most accounts it was a fairly calm and typical life of a teenager living in the city. I was going to parties with friends, drinking more alcohol than I could handle (with wicked hangovers providing their own corrective), listening to music that was popular with my friends, and always on the lookout for that next girlfriend.

Every year after my born-again experience, I repeated the same cycle: summer camp saw a spiritual renewal, a determination to be a victorious Christian, to stand up for what I had learned at camp and church once I returned home. Back in the city, after a couple of weeks, I was living my double life again—one part of me completely at ease with good friends from high school, the other part completely content with those who were part of my church life. According to what I had long been told by my church, this was a sort of spiritual schizophrenia that had to be corrected. For me it was a constant battle, leaving me feeling that I was a disappointment to God. And Jesus.

After repeated failures to attain that "victorious Christian life," at the age of nineteen I decided that the only way to get my life on track was to attend a Bible college. By going to an institute out on the Saskatchewan prairie, sequestered from the temptations of the world (the nearest city being Moose Jaw), I would be able to immerse myself in theological studies. I would gain the knowledge and instruction to live the life I thought God wanted me to live, the one Jesus would be pleased with. So I spent three years intensely studying Scripture, church history, and Christian doctrine. Between academic years, summers back in the city were somewhat similar to what I had faced after Bible camp, yet the struggle wasn't as severe. During my time at college I was learning the psychological tools necessary for buffering the temptations of worldly pleasures. The first was to spend as little time as possible with unbelievers. Other prescriptions were to attend church faithfully every Sunday, and Bible study during the week, and to stay close to Christian-minded friends on the weekends. I had to segregate myself from potential troublemakers. Jesus had hung out with the biggest sinners of his day, whether tax collectors or prostitutes. But Jesus was Jesus, and I was just me.

My time at college began to pay off. In their own way—but similar to those days after my summertime conversion—my days, months, and years at Bible college were blissful. Having frittered away my time in high school, I was determined to dedicate myself wholly to my studies at college. Every minute would be spent trying to make up for lost time, to prepare myself for whatever God had planned for me. The first week, while my fellow students were in orientation, playing games and getting to know one another, I was in my dorm room memorizing the books of the Bible. This was just the tip of the proverbial iceberg. During my three years there, I redeemed the time I spent lining up for lunch and dinner by reading my pocket New Testament. Each evening, after finishing all my homework, I would read the Old Testament for a calculated forty-five minutes. And before going to sleep I'd spend time on my knees in prayer beside my bed. Sometimes I'd wake up a couple of hours later, still beside my bed, knees bent but legs asleep, so that I was forced to crawl into my bed like a quadriplegic. I felt that I was in a race to make up for so many years lost to youthful idleness. During my time at Bible college the ideas I had been taught throughout my earlier days in the fundamentalist church were constantly repeated and reinforced. The true believer was, and had always been, the "Overcomer"—the "spirit-filled," "born-again" believer.

During my teenage years I'd had mixed success at being the Christian my church had told me I needed to be. My time at Bible college brought better results. By the time I completed my studies I was living up to the Code, listening only to "Christian" music, witnessing constantly with everyone I met, plotting how best to do so, attending church, and keeping company only with Christian friends. In fact, I had succeeded so well that my greatest problem was no longer "secular culture." Instead, it was how to reconcile what was openly taught in sermons and in lectures with the apathy and failings of those around me, whether at Bible college or back in my hometown church.

The apathy among various Christians I met, as it related to their living the life we always talked about, struck me as pure hypocrisy. Simply put, if those around me at college, in church, and in the Christian community couldn't put into practice what was taught each Sunday in church, or in class lectures, then why didn't they move on and do something else with their lives? Why put up airs? We were always being told about those in the "liberal" churches who were living a complacent Christian life, going to church on Sundays but doing little else. I told myself that at least the people in those churches weren't living an inconsistent life. They never claimed to be doing anything more. But we were different. Every Sunday we were singing, praying, and worshipping in a spirit that said there was much more to the Christian life than was practised in mainstream Christianity. Despite all outward appearances, few of us were actually living what we preached, sang, and prayed.

Even at the time, I understood that the most dedicated fundamentalist will have failings. All of us at some point say one thing and do another. But again, a central characteristic of the fundamentalist movement is the demand for something beyond mere humanness—the demand is for "Christ-like" behaviour. In some circles there is the exigency for perfection—a life without sin. A few of us in the church and at college really took seriously what we were being taught. As a fundamentalist who was drinking deep at the well, my greatest frustration was with those around me. During worship, singing, and preaching, all would speak the same platitudes, yet afterwards, many showed themselves incapable of mere common decency. It wasn't about being sinless. It was about displaying, at minimum, a kindness, compassion, and empathy in line with the basic teachings of Christ.

During these years, one of the most disconcerting moments for me was when I met someone without religious belief who showed more kindness and goodness than the leaders of my Christian community. If only we committed fundamentalists could be good with God, how were other people able to show more graciousness than those who constantly preached about sin? Whatever my observations, I didn't see any alternative. I had been taught that either one lives the Christian life according to precepts of my church, or one becomes a "liberal"—a member of the mainstream Christian church. Or, of course, one could drop out altogether and become an atheist.

But my faith was real. And whatever problems most religious devotees have, it would be quite wrong for me to characterize my life as one of misery. There is a deep peacefulness that accompanies an existence concentrated on meditation, prayer, Scripture study, and corporate worship. Only later did I recognize a radical distinction: a deeply religious person need not be a fundamentalist. It was a distinction, during all those years, that had never been pointed out to me. At no time did I suspect that the fundamentalist version of a Christian was a twentieth-century invention. And it was exactly there where the terrible struggle found its impetus. Namely, I wanted to please God, not as I thought I did while I was younger, but as my church taught. These leaders were, after all, put in place by God's authority to teach us regular Christian folk what to believe and how to act. But I was constantly failing to live up to what I heard on Sundays. My conscience was repeatedly condemning me for failing to live a life without sin. Going to a mainstream church where I wouldn't be expected to live up to the precepts of fundamentalism wouldn't help. I had learned in Bible college that according to the Book of Revelation, this was the "lukewarm" church that God would vomit up during the Last Days. I had no choice but to think that the problem somehow lay in my own sinful behaviour and lack of dedication.

My deep internal struggles aside, going to Bible college brought me into an academic setting where, whatever else, we were expected to study hard. I had every intention of completing all academic requirements—an intention quite unlike those I maintained during my grade school education, years I essentially slept through. The unexpected result was that once I began applying myself to my studies, my brain—quite literally—was turned on. During my three years at college, my grades became progressively better and my newfound cerebral cortex gave me a pleasure I had never before experienced. It felt good to learn. In my third year at college I decided that the next step in my Christian education (which I thought would be the key to overcoming my still intense internal struggles), would be to travel two thousand miles to an evangelical graduate school in California.

After my teen years in church listening to hundreds of sermons, followed by three years in Bible college, I had about as locked-up a way of seeing things as anyone could have. What happened next, in the first few weeks of my studies in California, was something I could never have predicted. It has had a lasting effect on my spirituality.

At the beginning of my first year of graduate studies, the dean of the school gave a series of lectures. One topic especially intrigued me: the history of Protestant fundamentalism and the rise of the evangelical movement in the United States. It's a chronology I described in the introduction to this book. It had never been suggested to me during all my time in church, by any of the people I had spoken with or listened to, that the version of Christianity I clung to was an invention borne of historical circumstances and traceable to political and theological quarrels in twentieth-century American culture. My naïveté was profound, considering that I was now twenty-four years old: I still believed that my church's prohibition of alcohol, dancing, and all things "secular" was something that all good Christians had accepted since the time of Christ. It was a shock to hear the dean tell us (without any apparent disapproval) that the esteemed German reformer Martin Luther had once bragged he was the best theologian in Wittenberg because he was able to drink the most from his beer stein—which even had the "Our Father" prayer engraved on the outside of it. I had spent so many years thinking that my fundamentalist world view was monolithic that hearing the contrary from a theologian I respected as a man of God was the mental equivalent of the irresistible force meeting the unmovable object. And the dean's lectures described many more things that helped me understand how Protestant fundamentalism began and how the evangelical movement tried to counter it. Yet I'm still not exactly sure how my change of mind happened. I only recall that after a number of lectures over the course of a few nights, my world view had been gutted.

Those who have devoted themselves wholeheartedly to a political or religious movement, who have dedicated every waking moment to its ideals, views, and beliefs—and who then have somehow fallen away, by their own or another's impetus—will understand how traumatic the experience can be. It was no different for me. I no longer believed that God's love for me was based on my adherence to fundamentalist blue laws. And because my entire notion of what constituted a "sinner" also dissipated, gone as well was the thinking that it was on my shoulders to convert all sinners. But it was a Devil's Bargain: the removal of these beliefs, so intertwined with other beliefs that had become central in my understanding of the world, religion, and God, left me hanging in what seemed like empty space.

Soon after leaving fundamentalism in 1984, I abandoned theological studies for philosophy. Yet even twenty years later I couldn't open the Bible without returning to the old ways of understanding and filtering the passages I read. This was still an obstacle in 1994, when I returned to theological studies in France, where I pursued my doctorate. I was fortunate to be specializing in the philosophy of religion and not biblical studies. It was only a year or so ago, having been asked to teach a course on Christian Ethics and Human Sexuality at the University of Toronto, that I found myself with enough years behind me that I could again read the Bible. That other interpretive grid—the fundamentalist world view—took all that time to lose its force.

Though my fundamentalist years are long over, their effects linger, negatively and positively. I find myself still a Christian, but in a way that would require another chapter to explain. Perhaps in another year or two, in another book, I might be ready to try. Above all else, mine is a faith in progress, complete with doubts and thoughts that religion might all be a ruse.

It now seems clear to me that religious fundamentalism works particularly well, though not for the reasons that religious conservatives think. It's not so much that it works effectively with, as they call it, the spiritually "hard hearted." Quite the opposite. The message of fundamentalism works best with the spiritually sensitive. The most susceptible to the message of guilt preached by the fundamentalists are those who hold preciously to their spirituality. Only by leaving fundamentalism will they regain the integrity and joy of their faith.

Contributors

Beverley Bryant has a lifetime of experience both within and without the evangelical community. A registered nurse by profession, she spent two years doing part-time work toward her master's degree in divinity before completing her master of education at the Ontario Institute for Studies in Education (OISE) of the University of Toronto. She is working on a novel that's still in its early stages and spends time reading, critiquing, and enjoying the work of fellow writers in her writing group. With her partner she lives in Mississauga, Ontario, where she works, practises karate, and enjoys the challenges of raising teenagers.

G. Elijah Dann received the PhD in philosophy from the University of Waterloo, and the *doctorat en théologie* from the Université de Strasbourg, France. He is co-author of *Philosophy: A New Introduction* (Wadsworth Press, 2005), and author of *After Rorty: The Possibilities for Ethics and Religious Belief* (Continuum Press, 2006). He has taught in departments of religion, philosophy, and health sciences for universities in southern Ontario, most recently as lecturer for the Department of Philosophy at the University of Toronto. He is currently Visiting Research Fellow for the Centre for Studies in Religion and Culture at the University of Victoria.

Overwhelmed by a mystical experience at the age of twenty, **Keith Dixon** took it to be a call to the ministry. Theological training gave him skills as a clergyman, but the primal experience remained a mystery. He lasted five years before abandoning his congregation and his ordination.

Doubting basic Christian teachings, he declared himself agnostic. Denial eventually melted into the exploration of psychic phenomena, gurus, shamanism, and meditation. Buddhism's world view most closely matched his experience. He took Refuge but chafed at some of the rigidity in Buddhist practice. The mystery of fifty years ago remains unsolved for him, but the subsequent journey has taught him an openness that permits a new respect for what he cast aside.

James Fieser is a professor of philosophy at the University of Tennessee at Martin. He received his BA from Berea College (1980) and his MA and PhD from Purdue University's department of philosophy (1983, 1986). After teaching briefly at the University of Rio Grand and Christopher Newport University, he arrived at UT Martin in 1993. He is author, co-author, and editor of seven textbooks, including *Moral Philosophy through the Ages* (McGraw-Hill, 2001) and *Philosophical Questions* (Oxford University Press, 2005). He edited the ten-volume *Early Responses to Hume* (Thoemmes Press, 1999–2003) and has published articles on various ethical topics. He is founder and general editor of the Internet Encyclopedia of Philosophy website, at http://www.iep.utm.edu.

Lori-Ann Livingston wanted to be two things when she was eleven: a jockey and a writer. The first was achieved by riding her arthritic pony, the second is still her passion. She currently works as a communications and marketing associate for the City of Kitchener. Previously a journalist in Canada and the UK, she wrote for a national Irish weekly newspaper and British music and religious publications. She is also the executive director of Latitudes Storytelling Festival, a festival of diversity and stories. She lives in Kitchener with her Irish husband, preschooler son, baby daughter, and a dog named Sally.

Leia Minaker grew up in southern Ontario, the second child and eldest of four girls in a family of seven. She recently moved to Edmonton with her husband to pursue her master's degree in health promotion at the University of Alberta. She enjoys her program and hopes to follow her master's with a PhD in health studies. Leia is particularly passionate about social equality, economic and environmental justice, and policies that promote population health. In her limited free time, Leia enjoys camping, running, discussion with friends, reading, and spending time with her husband.

Andrea Lorenzo Molinari is the president of Blessed Edmund Rice School for Pastoral Ministry, a satellite of Barry University, in Miami, Florida. He received his PhD from Marquette University (New Testament and Early Christianity, 1996). He is author of three books: *The Acts of Peter and the Twelve Apostles* (NHC 6.1) (Atlanta: Scholars Press, 2000); *'I never knew the man': The Coptic Act of Peter* (Papyrus Berolinensis 8502.4) (Paris: Éditions Peeters, 2000); and *Climbing the Dragon's Ladder: The Martyrdom of Perpetua and Felicitas* (Eugene, OR: Wipf and Stock, 2006). In addition, he has published numerous articles related to early Christianity.

Julie Rak is an associate professor in the Department of English and Film Studies at the University of Alberta. She is the author of *Negotiated Memory: Doukhobor Autobiographical Discourse* (UBC Press, 2004) and the editor of *Autobiography in Canada: Critical Directions* (Wilfrid Laurier University Press, 2005). With Jeremy Popkin, she edited a collection of essays by Philippe LeJeune, *On Diary* (University of Hawaii Press, 2008), and with Andrew Gow she edited *Mountain Masculinity: The Life and Writing of Nello "Tex" Vernon-Wood, 1911–1938* (University of Athabasca Press, 2008). She is writing a book about popular autobiography in North America.

David L. Rattigan was born in Vancouver, BC, and grew up in Liverpool, England, where he now lives and works as a freelance writer. He has a degree in theology from the University of Manchester and is a qualified teacher of secondary religious education. Dave is passionately involved in local arts and music, and has been an active member of his local Anglican parish since returning to Liverpool in 2003. In 2005 he founded LeavingFundamentalism.org, an online resource "for surviving the journey out of conservative Christianity." Another major interest is film, particularly British horror of the 1950s and '60s, and he enjoys an occasional foray into linguistics.

Jeffrey W. Robbins teaches religion and philosophy at Lebanon Valley College in central Pennsylvania, where he lives with his wife and two children. He received his BA from Baylor University, a M.Div. from Texas Christian University, and a PhD in religion from Syracuse University. He is the author of two books in philosophical theology, *Between Faith and Thought: An Essay on the Ontotheological Condition* (2003) and *In Search of a Non-Dogmatic Theology* (2004). He is the editor of *After the Death of God* (2007) and *The Sleeping Giant Has Awoken* (2008).

Glenn A. Robitaille was raised Roman Catholic and ordained through the Brethren in Christ Church. Early on he abandoned dogmatic theology and moved to a more inclusive, multifaith perspective. He received his master of divinity and doctor of ministry degrees from Ashland Theological Seminary and Vision International University, respectively. He is a pioneer in the field of Internet-based counselling and a successful church planter. Glenn is a contributing author in the book *A Peace Reader* (Evangel Press, 2002), and has published regularly in various magazines and journals. A father of five, he resides in Midland, Ontario, with his wife, Debra.

Jacob J. Shelley was born a fourth-generation Pentecostal into a family of pastors past and present. His father was a pastor, and several of his brothers will likely pursue a life in the ministry. For many years he thought that he too would be a pastor, but instead he entered the world of academia. He has completed a BA in religious studies and a master's in theological studies. Although currently in law school, he aspires to complete a PhD. He currently resides in Edmonton with his wife.

Joseph Simons became an evangelical Christian as an adult, abandoning the Roman Catholic practice of his parents. After a long recovery from a nearly fatal accident, he went to bible college. Upon graduation he did not become a pastor but worked at various jobs—including truck driver and group-home counsellor—before moving into writing fiction. He is the author of the novel *Under a Living Sky*. He works with special-needs children in a Catholic junior high school and attends an Anglican cathedral—the pipe organ being the main draw. He believes in generous-hearted communities, whatever the creed, and values beauty found and goodness lived in a precarious world.

After obtaining a degree in English from the University of Waterloo, **Margaret Steel Farrell** began her career in corporate writing, where she focused primarily on employee communications and marketing in the financial services industry. She is a freelance writer in addition to her 9-to-5, belongs to a local writing group, and recently edited her aunt's memoir of life in southwestern Ontario in the 1930s. With her son, Margaret lives in Kitchener, Ontario, where, in addition to writing, she enjoys creative pursuits such as dance and voice-over work for local radio commercials.

LIFE WRITING SERIES

In the **Life Writing Series**, Wilfrid Laurier University Press publishes life writing and new life-writing criticism in order to promote autobiographical accounts, diaries, letters, and testimonials written and/or told by women and men whose political, literary, or philosophical purposes are central to their lives. **Life Writing** features the accounts of ordinary people, written in English, or translated into English from French or the languages of the First Nations or from any of the languages of immigration to Canada. **Life Writing** will also publish original theoretical investigations about life writing, as long as they are not limited to one author or text.

Priority is given to manuscripts that provide access to those voices that have not traditionally had access to the publication process.

Manuscripts of social, cultural, and historical interest that are considered for the series, but are not published, are maintained in the **Life Writing Archive** of Wilfrid Laurier University Library.

Series Editor
Marlene Kadar
Humanities Division, York University

Manuscripts to be sent to
Lisa Quinn, Acquisitions Editor
Wilfrid Laurier University Press
75 University Avenue West
Waterloo, Ontario, Canada N2L 3C5

Books in the Life Writing Series
Published by Wilfrid Laurier University Press

The Life Writings of Mary Baker McQuesten: Victorian Matriarch edited by Mary J. Anderson • 2004 / xxii + 338 pp. / ISBN 0-88920-437-3

Seven Eggs Today: The Diaries of Mary Armstrong, 1859 and 1869 edited by Jackson W. Armstrong • 2004 / xvi + 228 pp. / ISBN 0-88920-440-3

Love and War in London: A Woman's Diary 1939–1942 by Olivia Cockett; edited by Robert W. Malcolmson • 2005 / xvi + 208 pp. / ISBN 0-88920-458-6

Incorrigible by Velma Demerson • 2004 / vi + 178 pp. / ISBN 0-88920-444-6

Auto/biography in Canada: Critical Directions edited by Julie Rak • 2005 / viii + 264 pp. / ISBN 0-88920-478-0

Tracing the Autobiographical edited by Marlene Kadar, Linda Warley, Jeanne Perreault, and Susanna Egan • 2005 / viii + 280 pp. / ISBN 0-88920-476-4

Must Write: Edna Staebler's Diaries edited by Christl Verduyn • 2005 / viii + 304 pp. / ISBN 0-88920-481-0

Food That Really Schmecks by Edna Staebler • 2007 / xxiv + 334 pp. / ISBN 978-0-88920-521-5

163256: A Memoir of Resistance by Michael Englishman • 2007 / xvi + 112 pp. (14 b&w photos) / ISBN 978-1-55458-009-5

The Wartime Letters of Leslie and Cecil Frost, 1915–1919 edited by R.B. Fleming • 2007 / xxxvi + 384 pp. (49 b&w photos, 5 maps) / ISBN 978-1-55458-000-2

Johanna Krause Twice Persecuted: Surviving in Nazi Germany and Communist East Germany by Carolyn Gammon and Christiane Hemker • 2007 / x + 170 pp. (58 b&w photos, 2 maps) / ISBN 978-1-55458-006-4

Watermelon Syrup: A Novel by Annie Jacobsen with Jane Finlay-Young and Di Brandt • 2007 / x + 268 pp. / ISBN 978-1-55458-005-7

Broad Is the Way: Stories from Mayerthorpe by Margaret Norquay • 2008 / x + 106 pp. (6 b&w photos) / ISBN 978-1-55458-020-0

Becoming My Mother's Daughter: A Story of Survival and Renewal by Erika Gottlieb • 2008 / x + 176 pp. (36 b&w illus., 17 colour) / ISBN 978-1-55458-030-9

Leaving Fundamentalism: Personal Stories edited by G. Elijah Dann • 2008 / xii + 234 pp. / ISBN 978-1-55458-026-2